Social Cohesion and ˥
Europe and North An.

Concerns about immigration and the rising visibility of minorities have triggered a lively scholarly debate on the consequences of ethnic diversity for trust, cooperation, and other aspects of social cohesion. In this accessibly written volume, leading scholars explore where, when, and why ethnic diversity affects social cohesion by way of analyses covering the major European immigration countries, as well as the United States and Canada. They explore the merits of competing theoretical accounts and give rare insights into the underlying mechanisms through which diversity affects social cohesion. The volume offers a nuanced picture of the topic by explicitly exploring the conditions under which ethnic diversity affects the "glue" that holds societies together. With its interdisciplinary perspective and contributions by sociologists, political scientists, social psychologists, as well as economists, the book offers the most comprehensive analysis of the link between ethnic diversity and social cohesion that is currently available.

Ruud Koopmans is Professor of Sociology at Humboldt University and Director of the Research Unit Migration, Integration, Transnationalization at the Berlin Social Science Center, Germany.

Bram Lancee is Assistant Professor at the Department of Sociology at Utrecht University, the Netherlands.

Merlin Schaeffer is Senior Research Fellow in the Research Unit Migration, Integration, Transnationalization at the Berlin Social Science Center, Germany.

Routledge Advances in Sociology

Social Cohesion and Immigration in Europe and North America

Mechanisms, conditions, and causality

Edited by Ruud Koopmans, Bram Lancee, and Merlin Schaeffer

LONDON AND NEW YORK

First published 2015
by Routledge
2 Park Square, Milton Park, Abingdon, Oxfordshire OX14 4RN

and by Routledge
711 Third Avenue, New York, NY 10017

First issued in paperback 2016

Routledge is an imprint of the Taylor & Francis Group, an informa business

British Library Cataloguing in Publication data
A catalogue record for this book is available from the British Library

Library of Congress Cataloguing in Publication data
  Social cohesion and immigration in Europe and North America : mechanisms,
  conditions, and causality / edited by Ruud Koopmans, Bram Lancee, Merlin
  Schaeffer.
     pages   cm. – (Routledge advances in sociology)
  1. Assimilation (Sociology)–Europe.   2. Assimilation (Sociology)–
  North America.   3. Immigrants–Europe.   4. Immigrants–North
  America.   5. Cultural pluralism–Europe.   6. Cultural pluralism–North
  America.   I. Koopmans, Ruud.   II. Lancee, Bram.   III. Schaeffer, Merlin.
  HM843.S63 2015
  303.48′2094–dc23
  2014019032

ISBN 13: 978-1-138-23600-4 (pbk)
ISBN 13: 978-1-138-02409-0 (hbk)

Typeset in Baskerville
by Out of House Publishing

Contents

Figures

Tables

Contributors

Ananthi Al Ramiah is an Assistant Professor at Yale-NUS College, Singapore.

Matthew R. Bennett is University Lecturer at the School of Social Policy at the University of Birmingham, UK.

Abigail Fisher Williamson is an Assistant Professor of Political Science and Public Policy at Trinity College in Hartford, Connecticut, USA.

Christina Floe is a Doctoral Candidate at the Department of Experimental Psychology, University of Oxford, UK.

Allison Harell is an Associate Professor of Political Science and Co-Director of the Political Communication and Public Opinion Laboratory at the University of Quebec in Montreal, Canada.

Camille Hémet is a Postdoctoral Research Fellow at the Institute of Economics of Barcelona, Spain.

Miles Hewstone is Professor of Social Psychology and Fellow of New College, University of Oxford, UK.

Frank Kalter is Professor of Sociology at the University of Mannheim and currently Director of the Mannheim Centre for European Social Research (MZES), Germany.

Ruud Koopmans in Professor of Sociology at Humboldt University and Director of the Research Unit Migration, Integration, Transnationalization at the Berlin Social Science Center, Germany.

Hanno Kruse is a Research Assistant at the Mannheim Centre for European Social Research (MZES) at the University of Mannheim, Germany.

Bram Lancee is Assistant Professor at the Department of Sociology at Utrecht University, the Netherlands.

Simon Lolliot is a Postdoctoral Research Fellow at the Department of Experimental Psychology, University of Oxford, UK.

Meenakshi Parameshwaran is an independent researcher in the UK.

Merlin Schaeffer is a Senior Research Fellow in the Research Unit Migration, Integration, Transnationalization at the Berlin Social Science Center, Germany.

Katharina Schmid is a Senior Researcher at the Department of Experimental Psychology, University of Oxford, UK.

Esther Son is a Research Assistant at the Department of Experimental Psychology, University of Oxford, UK.

Dietlind Stolle is Associate Professor of Political Science at McGill University and Director of the Inter-university Centre for the Study of Democratic Citizenship in Montreal, Canada.

Eric M. Uslaner is Professor of Government and Politics at the University of Maryland—College Park, USA; Senior Research Fellow at the Center for American Politics and Law, Southwest University of Political Science and Law, Chongqing, China; and Honorary Professor of Political Science, Aarhus University, Denmark.

Susanne Veit is a Research Fellow in the Research Unit Migration, Integration, Transnationalization at the Berlin Social Science Center, Germany.

Dingeman Wiertz is a Doctoral Candidate at the Department of Sociology and Nuffield College at the University of Oxford, UK.

Ralf Wölfer is a Postdoctoral Research Fellow at the Department of Experimental Psychology, University of Oxford, UK.

1 Ethnic diversity in diverse societies

An introduction

Ruud Koopmans, Bram Lancee, and Merlin Schaeffer

Concerns about immigration and the rising visibility of ethnic and racial minorities have triggered a lively scholarly debate on the consequences of ethnic diversity for social cohesion. Economists suggest that ethnic diversity is one of the reasons for stagnation and corruption in the developing world (Easterly and Levine, 1997), and explains why the USA does not have a European-style welfare state (Alesina *et al.*, 2001). In political science and sociology, Putnam's (2007) "hunkering down thesis" is a central focus of debate: in neighborhoods, cities, or regions that are more ethnically diverse, citizens withdraw from public social life and reciprocity and trust go down.

While the debate originates in the USA, it has been receiving growing attention from European scholars, who fear that the high levels of trust, civic engagement, and redistribution that characterize European countries might be threatened by increasing levels of ethnic diversity. In Sweden, higher levels of ethnic diversity have been shown to be associated with declining levels of support for welfare state spending (Eger, 2010), and in Germany with declining support for unemployment benefits (Stichnoth, 2012). In many other European countries, ethnic diversity is related to a decline in social trust and civic engagement (Delhey and Newton, 2005; Dinesen, 2011; Laurence, 2011).

However, the ethnic diversity hypothesis is also disputed. Critics argue that the role of socio-economic deprivation has been overlooked (e.g., Letki, 2008; Twigg *et al.*, 2010) and that findings that are particular to one national context, especially the US, are generalized to other countries (e.g., Harell and Stolle, 2010; Holtug and Mason, 2010). Moreover, heterogeneous networks often lead to positive outcomes, such as more productive job searches (Granovetter, 1973), more creativity (Burt, 2000), and greater problem-solving capacities (Gurin *et al.*, 2004).

Whatever their disagreements, both sides of the debate agree that under some circumstances ethnic diversity can lead to declines of social cohesion, but also that, in the long run, immigration is beneficial to innovation and economic prosperity (cf. Alesina *et al.*, 1999; Page, 2008; Putnam, 2007). Yet, if ethnic diversification is associated with short and medium-term declines in social cohesion and public goods production, we need to understand *why* and *under which conditions* this is the case. However, until now, most research has focused on the question whether a negative relation between ethnic diversity and social cohesion exists at all. Moreover, almost all evidence in the one or the other direction has been correlational. The causal effect of ethnic diversity therefore remains an issue of further study. Incomplete knowledge about causality and underlying mechanisms makes it hard to propose policy solutions and to bring the research field further.

Ethnic diversity can be a consequence both of indigenous ethnic heterogeneity, and of recent immigration. While many of the arguments discussed in this volume also apply to examples of "native" heterogeneity such as in the cases of Basks, Catalans, and Castilians in Spain or relations between whites, blacks, and Native Americans in the United States, in this volume we focus exclusively on ethnic diversity that derives from recent immigration waves. It is the connection between ethnic diversity and immigration that has been at the heart of recent controversies over alleged declines in social cohesion in Europe and North America.

Social cohesion can include a broad array of phenomena. In this volume, we reserve it in the first place for a community's capacity for collective action in pursuit of public goods, and the attitudes and expectations of trust that undergird this capacity. In a wider sense, the absence of prejudices and hostility among groups, the density and quality of intergroup social contacts, shared norms, values, and identities, and the ability to communicate through a common language are often also counted as aspects of social cohesion. We will argue, however, that the latter are better seen as mechanisms and conditions through which social cohesion—in the sense of cooperative capacity and trust—may be negatively affected by ethnic diversity.

In order to better understand how and why ethnic diversity affects social cohesion in Europe and North America, we move beyond the omnipresent research that analyzes whether or not there is a relationship between diversity and social cohesion. Instead, the chapters in this volume engage explicitly with three core issues that we believe to be most pressing in the current debate: 1) the causal status of ethnic diversity effects; 2) competing explanations and mechanisms; and 3) conditional effects. While the chapters differ in many respects, such as the countries of analysis and the measures of social cohesion that are investigated, the explicit discussion of explanations and mechanisms, conditions and causality, is what unites the chapters into a coherent volume. An additional innovative feature of this volume is that, in addition to the more traditional focus on the diversity of spatial areas such as neighborhoods, the contributions in Part III expand the focus to the analysis of diversity effects in a key functional context: schools. Within the school setting, chapters focus on causality, mechanisms, and conditional effects.

Spurious correlation or causal effect?

The first contribution of this book is to better establish whether the relation between ethnic diversity and social cohesion is causal. The question of causality is very salient in the debate on the consequences of ethnic diversity. Is the observed effect of ethnic diversity spurious, due to unobserved contextual heterogeneity? For example, some scholars argue that studies do not fully take into account socio-economic deprivation (Letki, 2008). In this view, the effect of ethnic diversity is significant only because of its correlation with the socio-economic status of neighborhoods or cities. Similarly, because of data limitations or because the amount of variables that can be included on the contextual level is limited, it could be that previous work suffers from further sources of unobserved heterogeneity. Any such omitted variable bias would render observed ethnic diversity effects at least partly spurious, implying that correlational studies overestimate the effect of ethnic diversity.

Another important issue in establishing a causal relationship between diversity and social cohesion is individual's self-selection. The interpretation of correlations between diversity and social cohesion is complicated by the potential influence of self-selection, for instance if better-situated, high-trusting people move to other areas when the ethnic composition changes (e.g., Alesina and La Ferrara, 2002; Crowder *et al.*, 2011), leaving behind the deprived, low-trusting, and disengaged. In this case, self-selection would also cause an overestimation of negative diversity effects. Alternatively, it may also be the case that more trustful people are more comfortable with diversity and stay in, or move to diverse areas, whereas low trusters avoid or move away from diversity. In this scenario, self-selection would lead to an underestimation of negative diversity effects. Either way, as most previous studies do not control for selection, existing findings may provide biased estimates of the negative effects of diversity.

Experimental and longitudinal designs are the best options to investigate causality issues, and this volume contains several examples of such designs. In order to address the bias arising from endogenous residential sorting, Camille Hémet presents in Chapter 2 a quasi-experimental study on individuals living in the French public housing sector, in which housing is allocated independent of households' ethnic origins or their preferences for diversity. The absence of choice in this section of the housing market eliminates the problem of self-selection. Nevertheless, Hémet finds that ethnic diversity is associated with increases of various indicators of degradation (e.g., vandalism, graffitti, trash lying around) in common areas of housing blocks. In addition, Hémet finds negative effects of ethnic diversity on individuals' chances of finding employment, suggesting that communication barriers and ethnically clustered networks limit the circulation of information in diverse areas. These effects are strongest when analyzed on the level of small neighborhoods rather than larger geographical areas.

In Chapter 3, Bram Lancee and Merlin Schaeffer employ a longitudinal panel design to analyze causal effects of ethnic diversity in Germany. There is hardly any empirical research on diversity effects that relies on longitudinal data. This is problematic because as Hopkins (2010: 160) states: "To understand how diversity influences public good provision, we should look to those towns that are diversifying, not those towns that are diverse." Put differently, the guiding question in the debate is how *changes* in ethnic diversity affect *changes* in trust and social cohesion. Applying a difference-in-difference design, Lancee and Schaeffer investigate how the event of moving to a more diverse neighborhood affects people's opinions about immigration. They show that moving to diversity indeed results in more concerns about immigration. Moreover, the effect lasts over time: even three years after moving, people who moved to a more diverse neighborhood remain significantly more xenophobic.

Another way of dealing with selection problems is to make use of natural experiments. When diversity arrives as an exogenous shock, one can observe potential changes in social capital among a "treatment group" experiencing an increase of diversity it did not choose, compared to a similar "control group" whose level of diversity has not changed. In Chapter 4, Abigail Fisher Williamson reviews the benefits and challenges of using natural experiments, drawing on the example of Lewiston, Maine, which experienced an unanticipated arrival of Somali refugees. With qualitative interviews and survey data she investigates changes in local social capital in Lewiston after the Somalis' arrival and carefully compares these changes to developments in otherwise similar localities. The findings are mixed. On the one hand, on the county and municipal levels of analysis there is no evidence that organizational involvement, trust, and interracial accord have disporportionately declined in Lewiston. However, on the neighborhood level she does find marked declines for various indicators of social cohesion comparing the neighborhoods where diversity had increased most strongly to otherwise similar neighborhoods that had not experienced strong increases in diversity. For instance, agreement to the statement that neighbors are likely to cooperate declined by as much as 41 percent in the neighborhoods that experienced the greatest increases in diversity.

Causality problems are not completely avoided in field-experimental studies, because ethnic diversity is used as an explanatory contextual variable, but is not itself subject to experimental control (see also Falk and Zehnder, 2013; Koopmans and Veit, 2014). Designs that fully randomize experimental and control conditions can establish causal claims with greater confidence. However, existing laboratory experiments that have taken into account ethnicity were usually conducted with interethnic pairs of participants instead of ethnically diverse groups, leading to mixed findings reflecting trust, cooperation, and discrimination among specific ethnic groups rather than general effects of ethnic diversity (e.g., Chuah *et al.*, 2013; Fershtman and Gneezy, 2001). Two exceptions are the studies of Alexander and Christia (2011) and Koopmans and Rebers (2009), which both use public goods games to study cooperation in culturally homogeneous and diverse groups with random assignment and find lower cooperation levels in the latter. While these studies provide a stronger basis for causality claims, they raise—as laboratory experiments generally do—the question of external validity.

In Chapter 9, Susanne Veit presents the results of two survey-experimental studies among neighborhood residents across Germany and parents at primary schools in Berlin. In both experiments, respondents were randomly allocated to experimental primes that heightened the salience of ethnic diversity in their neighborhoods, respectively schools, without, however, suggesting any negative or positive evaluation of such diversity. As control conditions, other respondents were randomly primed either with another form of neighborhood or school diversity or with no particular form of diversity at all. The results show that people who are cognitively exposed to ethnic diversity primes are significantly more pessimistic about the trustworthiness of neighbors and parental cooperation at school than those who are exposed to age or income diversity primes, or to no particular form of diversity at all. The findings for the treatment in which people's attention was directed to income differences are particularly interesting. This study is, as far as we are aware, the first that experimentally tests ethnic diversity and socioeconomic inequality explanations for declines in trust against each other. The results show that raising the cognitive salience of ethnic diversity does reduce trust in neighbors, whereas pointing towards economic inequalities does not.

By eliminating potential biases due to self-selection and unobserved heterogeneity, these four studies provide strong evidence of the causal nature of negative diversity effect. In addition, they provide further evidence for the recurrent research finding (see the literature reviews of Schaeffer, 2014 and Van der Meer and Tolsma, 2014) that negative diversity effects are strongest when investigated on low levels of spatial aggregation. This remarkably consistent pattern in the literature seems to suggest that the negative impacts of diversity are highly spatially (and presumably also socially) concentrated, whereas positive impacts are more dispersed or may even accrue most to those who find themselves at some social and geographical distance from the epicenters of diversity.

A further important finding is that two of the four studies investigate the causality of ethnic diversity effects separately for people of native and immigrant origin. Lancee and Schaeffer find in Chapter 3 that both groups become more concerned about immigration when they move to more diverse areas, and Veit shows in Chapter 9 that both groups become more distrustful of their neighbors and more pessimistic about parental cooperation at school when their cognitive attention is focused on the ethnic diversity of neighborhoods and schools. The evidence for the United Kingdom presented by Dingeman Wiertz, Matthew R. Bennett, and Meenakshi Parameshwaran in Chapter 7 points in the same direction. These results clearly show that negative ethnic diversity effects should not be confused with one-sided xenophobia and racism among majority populations.

Competing explanations and mechanisms

If negative effects of ethnic diversity are real, and affect majority and minority populations very much alike, the question becomes: what explains them? The literature on the consequences of ethnic diversity is multidisciplinary and it is thus not surprising that competing theoretical explanations coexist. There is, however, little systematic comparison of these different explanations. Few, if any, studies test the different theories against one another. Moreover, there is little agreement on suitable methods to carry out convincing tests. We discuss three types of theoretical mechanisms—referring respectively to psychological biases, cultural differences, and social networks—by which ethnic diversity might negatively affect social cohesion. The majority of studies, and especially those undertaken from a social-psychological angle, refer to *in-group favoritism and out-group biases*. Economists have often referred to collective choice theories that suggest that lower levels of public goods provision might be due to *coordination problems* that arise because of cultural differences related to the lack of a shared language, diverging cultural norms, and different values regarding preferred public goods. Finally, more sociological perspectives stress a lack of *social control* in ethnically diverse areas as a result of network clustering along ethnic lines.

In-group favoritism and out-group biases

Explanations for ethnic diversity effects that are based on negative attitudes towards out-groups come in two variants: social identity and group threat theories. Most authors view ethnicity primarily as a social identity, which Tajfel (1978: 63) defines as "that part of an individual's self-concept which derives from his knowledge of his membership of a social group (or groups), together with the value and emotional significance attached to that membership." Social identity theory emphasizes the motivation to have a positive self-conception and since social identities are part of one's self-conception, actors are likely to evaluate their social identities, and the other people belonging to them, in a positive manner relative to out-group members (Tajfel and Turner, 1986). Many studies refer to this theory in order to explain negative diversity effects. The basic argument is that since people favor others who are like themselves, they see out-group members as less trustworthy and are less likely to invest in public goods if out-group members will profit as well (e.g., Alesina *et al.*, 1999).

Out-group biases are also central to group threat theory, which states that people perceive or experience conflicts with other ethnic groups over economic resources and symbolic representations (e.g., Blalock, 1967). These conflicts cause people to see members of other ethnic groups as economic and cultural threats and have been put forward as possible explanations of diversity effects (e.g., Hou and Wu, 2009). In support of both social identity and group threat approaches, some studies have found the negative effect of ethnic diversity to be stronger for people who oppose racial mixing (Alesina and La Ferrara, 2000), or who hold anti-immigration attitudes (Marschall and Stolle, 2004).

If biases against out-groups are a mechanism linking ethnic diversity to social cohesion, it should be the case that prejudices against out-groups are stronger among those living in ethnically diverse areas. However, the evidence here is mixed. Lancee and Schaeffer's longitudinal findings in Chapter 3 demonstrate that people who moved to more diverse areas became more concerned about immigration. However, this effect occurs both for people of native and of immigrant origin. While the finding for natives can be easily interpreted in terms of out-group biases, this is less straightforward for the case of immigrants because, in the German context, diverse areas are those where more other immigrants but also more co-ethnics live. This may imply that the relevant in-group versus out-group distinction is, for immigrants, not so much the one between themselves and natives, but rather the one between their own ethnic group and other immigrant groups. Because of the strong focus in the literature on majority rejection of minorities, tensions between minority groups have thus far hardly been considered as a potential source of negative diversity effects.

Katharina Schmid, Miles Hewstone, and Ananthi Al Ramiah find in Chapter 8 for the United Kingdom no significant effect of diversity on out-group attitudes for minorities, while whites living in diverse neighborhoods hold even significantly more positive attitudes towards minorities than whites living in homogenous neighborhoods. Likewise, Miles Hewstone and colleagues find in Chapter 11 that pupils of racially mixed schools tend to have more positive attitudes towards out-groups than their peers in racially homogeneous schools. A recent field-experimental study in Germany by Koopmans and Veit (2014) casts further doubt on out-group biases as a major mechanism linking ethnic diversity to social cohesion. In neighborhoods across Berlin, they dropped letters addressed to German, Turkish, Christian, and Islamic cultural voluntary associations and investigated, as an indicator of cooperative behavior, whether passersby picked these apparently lost letters up and dropped them in a mailbox. Letters dropped in ethnically diverse neighborhoods were much less likely to be returned, but the rates of return did not differ by type of voluntary association. People in ethnically homogeneous neighborhoods dominated by white Germans were not more likely to return letters addressed to German and Christian associations, nor were the inhabitants of diverse neighborhoods (dominated by immigrants) more likely to return letters addressed to Turkish and Islamic associations. Overall, these results suggest that other factors than in-group favoritism and out-group biases may be responsible for the lower levels of cooperation in diverse neighborhoods.

The reason why there is no consistent relationship between diversity and out-group biases may be that, while the presence of other ethnic groups may provoke in-group favoritism and feelings of threat, diversity is also likely to lead to positive forms of intergroup contact, which according to the famous contact hypothesis (Allport, 1954) may work in the opposite direction by reducing anxiety about out-groups. To the extent that out-group members become friends, schoolmates, or even family members, interethnic contacts may blur the boundary between in-group and out-group altogether. We will discuss these counterbalancing effects of intergroup contacts further below in the section on conditional effects.

Cultural differences and coordination problems

For now, we turn to an alternative mechanism that may explain negative diversity effects on social cohesion. An obvious condition for collective action in pursuit of public goods is that there exists a shared goal in the first place. Accordingly, some scholars have argued that diversity in the goods that people value leads to under-provision of public goods in ethnically diverse communities (e.g., Kimenyi, 2006). In addition, Page (2008: 239) has argued from a social choice perspective that asymmetrically distributed preferences may erode trust because they are a "potential for disagreement [that] may create incentives to misrepresent how we feel. We may try to manipulate process and agenda, creating distrust and dislike." In support of preference diversity as a mechanism, Ruttan (2006) finds more disagreement about collective resource management in culturally heterogeneous communities. By contrast, Habyarimana *et al.* (2007) found no significant differences regarding preferences for various collective goods across individuals of different ethnic backgrounds in Kenya. Baldwin and Huber (2010: 644) advance a preference diversity interpretation for the negative effect of group-based economic inequality on collective goods provision, arguing that "Group-based economic differences can lead to different group needs with respect to public goods, feelings of alienation or discrimination by some groups, different attitudes toward redistribution across groups, and different 'class' identities by different groups." This argument is similarly made in the literature on economic inequality and social cohesion (see, for example, Wilkinson and Pickett, 2009): inequality depresses social cohesion because conditions for social interaction are not met: people belong to different status groups and therefore have fewer opportunities to share common goals. Along this line of argument, increasing differences between people (be they ethnic or economic) result in coordination problems with detrimental consequences for social cohesion.

Others have emphasized the importance of a common cultural "toolkit" (Swidler, 1986). A shared language, as well as commonly understood practices and interpretive schemata are in this view necessary to communicate the existence of shared preferences and to successfully coordinate the production of common goods (Habyarimana *et al.*, 2007, 2009). This is also underlined by experimental studies, which consistently show how groups that are allowed to communicate solve social dilemmas at much higher rates (e.g., Jeffreys, 2008). Yet, the evidence in support of this explanation of diversity effects is mixed. Kooij-de Bode *et al.* (2008) show that ethnically homogenous groups distribute information more efficiently. Some studies have found linguistic diversity to have superior predictive power compared to ethnic diversity (Anderson and Paskeviciute, 2006; Desmet *et al.*, 2012), but this result is not confirmed in Baldwin and Huber's (2010) cross-national study. More confuting findings come from Lancee and Dronkers (2011) and Schaeffer (2013), who found no effects of host-country language proficiency of immigrants.

On the level of actual diversity, it is—at least in the context of immigration-related diversity—often impossible to test cultural explanations of diversity effects directly. Theoretically, this mechanism implies that culturally more proximate forms of ethnic diversity—e.g., Austrians in Germany—should have less of an impact on social cohesion than more culturally distant ones—e.g., Turks in Germany. However, as Schaeffer (2013) has demonstrated, the population distributions of most geographical areas in most Western immigration countries are so skewed towards the majority group that attempts to create separate "culturally weighted" diversity measures are futile because they produce measures that are statistically indistinguishable from the standard ethnic fractionalization index. On the level of perceptions, however, Koopmans and Schaeffer (2014) were able to show that perceived linguistic and preference diversity exert independent effects on various indicators of social cohesion, controlling for actual statistical diversity as well as for other measures of perceived diversity such as the estimated percentage of immigrants or the extent of perceived intergroup conflict (see also Semyonov *et al.*, 2008).

Social networks and social control

Few studies recognize ethnic network clustering as a key factor in explaining diversity effects (e.g., Habyarimana *et al.*, 2007; Miguel and Gugerty, 2005), even though network density is at the heart of Coleman's (1988) explanation of trust and has been known to enable cooperation since Axelrod's (1984) work on the evolution of cooperation. The mechanism underlying the importance of network density is that contacts enable the exercise of social control via sanctioning and defamation. Coleman (1990) called this mechanism of increased social control via network density "closure." Some scholars refer to these network mechanisms and claim that negative ethnic diversity effects are due to ethnically clustered networks that inhibit sanctioning and information diffusion across ethnic boundaries (e.g., Habyarimana *et al.*, 2007; Miguel and Gugerty, 2005). Unfortunately, there are few empirical tests of this mechanism, since it is hardly recognized in the debate. Support comes from Habyarimana *et al.* (2007), who show that the participants of their Uganda-based experiment tend to favor co-ethnics only if their own ethnicity is public, but not when their own identity is anonymous. Against all cognitive biases that would lead one to expect a general tendency to discriminate against out-groups, this result suggests that people fear sanctioning from co-ethnics who could ostracize them later on if they do not display normatively prescribed cooperative behavior. Habyarimana *et al.* (2007) also showed that people who were asked to find random persons in their city are quicker to find co-ethnics than those of other backgrounds. This implies low mobilization rates and knowledge diffusion between ethnic network clusters. Karlan (2007) comes to similar conclusions in his investigation of banking groups in Peru. He shows that, in ethnically homogeneous groups, members know more about collaborators who fail their credit schedule or even dropout altogether. In their public goods game, Alexander and Christia (2011) likewise found that members of ethnically diverse groups refrain from sanctioning free-riders, because they do not believe in its effectiveness. Ruttan (2006) on the other hand only provides partial evidence for reduced levels of sanctioning in his investigation of fisheries and irrigation systems in various countries.

In this volume, Frank Kalter and Hanno Kruse's study reported in Chapter 10 is unique in that it investigates social network mechanisms head-on in a context of immigration-derived ethnic diversity. Their study across school classes in Germany, the United Kingdom, the Netherlands, and Sweden reveals strong tendencies towards ethnic homophily. Friendship networks in school classes cluster strongly along lines of ethnicity: in diverse classrooms, interethnic friendships are far less likely than they would be if kids chose their friends randomly without regard for ethnicity. Hewstone and colleagues provide in Chapter 11 a striking illustration of this phenomenon in their analysis of seating patterns in school canteens, which reveal a strong clustering of pupils along racial lines: in a school in which 59 percent of pupils were white and 35 percent were Asian, they found that only

5 percent of the lunch units they identified in the school cafeteria were racially mixed. They refer to this pattern as "resegregation" because it occurs within the context of schools that are themselves diverse and provide ample opportunities for interethnic contact. In Chapter 4, Fisher Williamson provides evidence of similar patterns in her study of the impacts of Somali immigration in Lewiston. Although overall interethnic contacts increased as a result of the influx of Somali immigrants, the rate of increase was far below what one would expect in the absence of a tendency towards ethnic "homophily," and in the neighborhoods that saw the greatest influx of immigrants the rate of interethnic contact even decreased.

Surprisingly, however, in spite of the strong tendencies towards ethnic clustering, Kalter and Kruse find in Chapter 10 that, with the partial exception of Germany, there is no significant negative relationship between the ethnic diversity of classrooms and two measures of overall network cohesion: density and reachability. In other words, there is no evidence in their study that friendship networks in ethnically diverse classrooms are less dense or that the ethnic clustering that occurs is a significant barrier to the circulation of information, and thus, by extension also for social sanctioning. In view of the fact that the Kalter and Kruse study is, to our knowledge, the first to investigate the role of social networks as a mechanism in detail, it is much too early to discard social network explanations of diversity effects altogether. For instance, it remains to be seen whether the results generalize beyond classrooms, which are perhaps too small in size and too dense in friendship contacts for ethnic diversity to be able to create significant network barriers.

Figure 1.1 visualizes how in-group favoritism and out-group biases, cultural differences, and associated coordination problems, as well as ethnically clustered networks and attendant reduced social control, may mediate between ethnic diversity and reduced social cohesion. We label these factors as "primary mechanisms" because they are the ones that have been put forward in the literature as possible explanations for negative diversity effects. We have visualized them as overlapping spheres because they are obviously interdependent: out-group biases may lead to ethnically clustered networks and inflated perceptions of cultural differences, but vice versa ethnic network clustering and experiences of communication problems and divergent norms and practices may also sustain out-group biases.

Conditional effects

The mixed results of previous studies suggest that the effects of ethnic diversity via the primary mechanisms that we identify may be conditional on other factors. Therefore, research on diversity effects has increasingly begun to investigate moderating factors that may counterbalance or, for some people and some contexts, even fully neutralize the negative effects of diversity. We distinguish two types of such moderators (see Figure 1.1). The first type refers to personal diversity experiences that we label as "moderating mechanisms" to acknowledge that they moderate the mechanisms via which ethnic diversity negatively affects social cohesion, but are also themselves a product of contextual diversity. The chapters in this volume address two such moderating mechanisms: positive interethnic

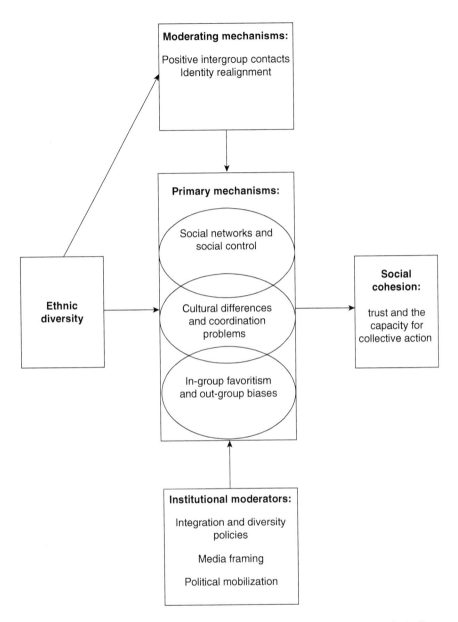

Figure 1.1 Theoretical framework for the analysis of the relationship between ethnic diversity and social cohesion.

contacts and identity realignment. While—as the above-mentioned findings on "resegregation" demonstrate—intergroup contacts do not necessarily and automatically emerge in diverse contexts, diversity at least creates the opportunity structure in which people can develop positive ties, such as friendships, to members of other ethnic groups. Moreover, experiences of diversity may broaden people's cultural horizons and relativize the norms and practices of their own group—a process that Schmid, Hewstone, and Al Ramiah in Chapter 8 label as "deprovincialization."

Positive intergroup ties and inclusive identities may counteract network segregation, decrease the salience of cultural differences, mitigate coordination problems, and reduce negative attitudes towards out-groups. Thus, intergroup ties can temper or cancel out negative effects of diversity on social cohesion.

The second type of moderator that is visualized in Figure 1.1 we label "institutional moderators." The extent to which diversity affects social cohesion may be determined by the way diversity and immigration are framed in integration and diversity policies, mobilized by political parties, or covered by the media. Policies and public discourses on immigration can highlight or downplay cultural differences and, if they highlight them, they can do so in positive or negative ways. Furthermore, policies can influence public norms against discrimination, emphasize cultural assimilation, provide incentives for host-country language acquisition, or actively combat ethnic segregation. We know very little about the nature and direction of such institutional effects.

Interethnic contacts

In line with the idea that interethnic contact acts as an antidote against negative diversity effects, Eric M. Uslaner argues in Chapter 5 that not diversity per se, but segregation and social isolation are the real culprits. At first, this seems to contradict the argument since segregation implies homogeneous neighborhoods, which should not face any diversity obstacles. However, high levels of segregation may be combined with high levels of diversity at higher levels of spatial aggregation, as is the case particularly in many US American cities that tend to have highly diverse populations, which live, however, largely in racially segregated neighborhoods. This leads to a situation in which immediate interethnic contact experiences are very limited while ethnic diversity remains highly present and salient in the wider environment. Against this backdrop, Uslaner posits that segregation makes out-groups seem larger and even more threatening. Hence living next to, rather than in, neighborhoods with many out-group members causes threat. Uslaner concludes that diversity does not harm social cohesion if people live in integrated neighborhoods and particularly not if they also use the opportunity to make friends of other backgrounds.

In line with this argument, Dietlind Stolle and Allison Harell review in Chapter 6 several studies that have posited that negative effects of diversity on trust may be mitigated by the potential for personal interethnic contacts that diverse contexts provide. As Allport (1954; see also Pettigrew and Tropp, 2006) already hypothesized, whether interethnic contact promotes or reduces ethnic biases is likely to depend on its quality. Consequently, Stolle and Harell postulate that researchers need to consider positive personal contact experiences in addition to contextual-level diversity. The conditions for positive intergroup contact that Allport mentions (e.g., equal status or common goals) are best met by interethnic friendships. In this view, out-group biases are the result of fears and negative perceptions of out-groups that arise only if there is a lack of intergroup contact. Stolle and Harell therefore argue that while diversity itself (without contact) may push interpersonal trust downwards, personal positive "contacts work as vaccines—people with interethnic contacts seem to become immune against adverse diversity effects."

In Chapter 8, Schmid *et al.* provide empirical support for these claims. The chapter particularly builds on the extensive social-psychological literature on interethnic contact and group threat, and reports the results of an analysis of white British majority and ethnic minority respondents living in more than 200 British neighborhoods. Schmid and colleagues are able to show how living in diverse neighborhoods is indirectly associated with greater out-group, in-group, and neighborhood trust via positive neighborhood contact for both majority and minority members. Hewstone *et al.* further cross-validate these insights in Chapter 11. Their chapter documents various findings of their extensive research program on ethnic diversity in schools. They thus directly respond to Stolle and Harell's call for more non-neighborhood-based research on ethnic diversity effects. Among others, they discuss evidence that ethnic diversity leads to positive interethnic contact experiences, which in turn reduce negative attitudes towards out-groups in British schools.

However, Hewstone *et al.* also report that ethnic diversity simultaneously increases the probability to make negative interethnic contact experiences, which result in negative diversity effects on attitudes towards out-groups. It is important to recognize the possibility of negative interethnic contact because the few studies that have compared different types of interethnic contact suggest that negative contacts may be more important for understanding out-group categorization and rejection than positive contacts. One explanation for this finding is that the sources of negative experiences tend to be viewed as typical for the ethnic group at large, whereas the sources of positive experiences are more likely to be perceived as (exceptional) individuals (Paolini *et al.*, 2010). Hewstone *et al.*'s arguments in Chapter 11 are a crucial reminder that once we begin to consider personal contact experiences we should not exclude the possibility that some forms of intergroup contact may actually reinforce feelings of group threat and sustain interethnic prejudices. For instance, if minorities and the majority group experience discrimination, unfair treatment, or even harassment and abuse in their encounters with one another. This raises the possibility that interethnic contact in diverse contexts may sometimes be a cause of, rather than an antidote against distrust and prejudice. As Hewstone *et al.* note, this insight "adds an important note of realism to our work, and to the field."

That diversity creates opportunities for both positive and negative contact experiences might also explain why previous diversity experiences as such do not necessarily mitigate negative diversity effects, as two other contributions to this volume show. Veit shows in Chapter 9 that trust levels of people living in neighborhoods with higher levels of actual diversity were less negatively affected by experimental priming that highlighted diversity. Everyday interethnic contact experiences seem to have made people living in high diversity neighborhoods less susceptible to such framing. Yet, Veit conducted a similar experiment in schools. Parents whose children go to diverse schools showed particularly strong reductions in trust when they were primed with ethnic diversity. Presumably, negative contact experiences among parents have dominated their previous experiences. Lancee and Schaeffer's analyses of moves between neighborhoods in Chapter 3 show that the level of diversity in the neighborhood from which people move does not make a difference in how they react to their new neighborhood's diversity. Overall then, ethnic diversity creates the opportunity for both positive and negative personal contact experiences and these experiences may explain why some people are "vaccinated" against negative diversity effects while others become particularly receptive to them.

If diversity results in increased opportunities for both positive and negative contact, it also results in increased opportunities for more superficial forms of interethnic contact that neither unequivocally meet Allport's positive quality criteria, nor per se constitute negative experiences. Several chapters in this volume investigate such forms of contact. Stolle and Harell show in Chapter 6 that those who talk to their neighbors are less affected by negative ethnic diversity effects. Yet, such contacts still assume a minimum level of acquaintance between neighbors to mitigate negative diversity effects (Schaeffer, 2014: ch. 7). Koopmans and Veit (2014) go one step further and show that superficial interethnic neighborhood encounters between strangers, for instance in parks, playgrounds, and restaurants, do not do the job; they actually result in mistrust.

Hewstone and colleagues (Chapter 11) cross-validate some of these insights for the school context. They discuss evidence according to which indirect, so-called "extended," contact also reduces negative out-group attitudes. To put it differently: the more interethnic friends a child's direct co-ethnic friends have, the more positive are a child's own attitudes towards ethnic out-groups. Importantly, this association holds irrespectively of the amount of a child's own interethnic contact experiences. Taken together, these results provide strong evidence that diverse school contexts—at least to the extent that tendencies of resegregation within schools can be counteracted—rather than provoking feelings of threat can lead to improved intergroup attitudes. To what extent this also leads to more social cohesion in schools in the form of overall levels of trust and cooperativeness remains a question for further investigation. While positive intergroup attitudes are obviously important in their own right, there is, as we have seen above, reason to doubt that out-group biases are the main reason for lower levels of trust and cooperation in diverse contexts.

Inclusive identities

Negative diversity effects may also be moderated through the formation of inclusive identities that encompass both minorities and the majority group. If people who live in diverse contexts are more likely to develop such identities, in-group versus out-group distinctions will become blurred, cultural differences will be perceived as less conflictive, and social network ties may be formed based on such shared identities. On the other hand, the mechanism of in-group favoritism and group threat implies the opposite: in diverse contexts, particularistic group identities are strengthened while inclusive identities are weakened. In Chapter 7, Wiertz *et al.* show that, in the British context, minorities do not identify more strongly with their ethnic group if they live in diverse neighborhoods. However, in line with group threat and in-group favoritism perspectives, white British do identify more strongly with their own racial group when they live in diverse neighborhoods. For identification with the overarching British identity, they find no relationship with neighborhood diversity for whites, but minorities tend to see themselves less as British when they live in more diverse neighborhoods. Overall, then, there is some support for the idea that diversity undermines (for minorities) overarching identities, and strengthens (for whites) particularistic identities, and no evidence that points towards the opposite view of diversity as a promoter of inclusive identities. The chapter also shows that identification patterns have some impact on social cohesion. For minorities, identification has no impact on trust, but their weaker British identity in diverse neighborhoods leads to a significant reduction of their civic participation. Whites' stronger racial identity in diverse contexts also leads to a significant reduction in civic engagement, as well as, to a lesser extent, lower trust in neighbors. Overall, however, identification patterns explain only a small part of diversity effects for both groups.

In Chapter 8, Schmid *et al.* present a slightly different argument on the role of identities, which emphasizes what they label "social identity complexity." When people see their various social identities as only loosely coupled rather than as tightly overlapping, it becomes easier for them to see commonalities with members of other ethnic groups. For instance, someone who views being British as largely synonymous to being white and Christian, excludes minorities from his social identity, in contrast to someone who acknowledges that being British is not necessarily tied to a particular faith or race. Putting this idea to an empirical test in separate studies in the United Kingdom and Germany, the authors find that majority members living in diverse areas tend to have more complex social identities and that such social identity complexity in turn is associated with more positive attitudes towards out-groups.

Institutional effects

The final and least researched type of moderators are institutional effects. Since here lies the most direct angle for potential interventions, the question of the potential relevance of the political context to mitigate or even reverse negative effects of ethnic diversity on social cohesion is of utmost importance. For instance, do multicultural policies that were designed to accommodate diverse populations attenuate the negative effects of ethnic divisions? Research on developing countries suggests they might not. Comparing Kenya and Tanzania, Miguel (2004) argues against the accommodation of diversity via multiculturalism or federalism and emphasizes instead the attenuating effects of policies that emphasize a common national identity. While Tanzania has a policy tradition that weakens ethnic cleavages, Kenya's polity is strongly organized along the lines of ethnic groups. Ahlerup and Hansson (2011) make essentially the same argument in their cross-national analysis of developing countries. Their evidence shows that nationalism mitigates the negative effects of ethnic diversity on good government.

However, such results for native ethnic diversity in developing countries that are still in the process of state formation do not necessarily generalize to developed countries where diversity results from immigration and where established national cultures and identities are already in place. The few studies that are available for Western immigration countries do not suggest that multicultural policies are harmful to social cohesion, but do not point towards positive effects, either (see Koopmans, 2013 for an overview). For instance, in a cross-national analysis, Banting *et al.* (2006: 79) find evidence of a negative effect of immigration on levels of social spending, but multicultural policies have no significant impact. Kesler and Bloemraad (2010) find no effect of increases in immigration on generalized trust, regardless of whether countries have multicultural policies or not. Hooghe *et al.* (2007), show in a cross-European comparison that, although there is no effect of multicultural policies, other types of inclusive policies, in their case voting rights for foreigners, do have a positive effect on generalized trust. In Chapter 6, Stolle and Harell refer to a few other studies that point towards positive effects of inclusive policies. In addition, they point towards evidence that shows that party-political mobilization and negative framing of immigration in the media may have harmful impacts on social cohesion. While research on institutional effects is already scarce for the national level of analysis, whether local diversity effects can also be related to variation across localities in policies, political mobilization, and media framing is even more an open question. The only study that we are aware of refers to the local German level and provides no empirical support for effects of local policies and political mobilization. Koopmans *et al.* (2011) analyze municipal integration policies in Germany, indicated by naturalization rates, minority councils, and the salience of migration issues in the election platform of the ruling mayor. Their results suggest that these local policy measures have no impact on the direction or strength of the negative relationship between ethnic diversity and social cohesion across German municipalities.

While much remains to be done to entangle the complex relationship between diversity and social cohesion, we believe that the right way forward is to focus on issues of causality, to tease out the mediating mechanisms and test them against each other, and to investigate moderating factors, both psychological and institutional. The contributions in this book provide ample evidence of the fruitfulness of such an approach.

References

Ahlerup, P. and Hansson, G. (2011) Nationalism and government effectiveness. *Journal of Comparative Economics*, 39: 431–451.
Alesina, A. and La Ferrara, E. (2000) Participation in heterogeneous communities. *Quarterly Journal of Economics*, 115(3): 847–904.

—— (2002) Who trusts others? *Journal of Public Economics*, 85(2): 207–234.

Alesina, A., Baqir, R., and Easterly, W. (1999) Public goods and ethnic divisions. *Quarterly Journal of Economics*, 114(4): 1243–1284.

Alesina, A., Glaeser, E., and Sacerdote, B. (2001) Why doesn't the United States have a European-style welfare state? *Brookings Papers on Economic Activity*, 2001(2): 187–254.

Alexander, M. and Christia, F. (2011) Context modularity of human altruism. *Science*, 334(6061): 1392–1394.

Allport, G. W. (1954) *The Nature of Prejudice*. Cambridge, MA: Addison-Wesley.

Anderson, C. J. and Paskeviciute, A. (2006) How ethnic and linguistic heterogeneity influence the prospects for civil society: a comparative study of citizenship behavior. *The Journal of Politics*, 68(4): 783–802.

Axelrod, R. M. (1984) *The Evolution of Cooperation*. New York: Basic Books.

Baldwin, K and Huber, D. J. (2010) Economic versus cultural differences: forms of ethnic diversity and public goods provision. *American Political Science Review*, 104(4): 644–662.

Banting, K., Johnston, R., Kymlicka, W., and Soroka, S. (2006) Do multicultural policies erode the welfare state? An empirical analysis. In K. Banting and W. Kymlicka (eds) *Multiculturalism and the Welfare State: Recognition and Redistribution in Contemporary Democracies*. Oxford: Oxford University Press, pp. 49–91.

Blalock, H. M. (1967) *Toward a Theory of Minority-Group Relations*. New York: Wiley.

Burt, R. (2000) Structural holes versus network closure as social capital. In N. Lin, C. S. Cook, and R. S. Burt (eds) *Social Capital: Theory and Research*. New York: Aldine de Gruyter, pp. 31–79.

Chuah, S. H., Fahoum, R., and Hoffmann, R. (2013) Fractionalization and trust in India: a field-experiment. *Economics Letters*, 119(2): 191–194.

Coleman, J. S. (1988) Social capital in the creation of human capital. *American Journal of Sociology*, 94: 95–120.

—— (1990) *Foundations of Social Theory*. Cambridge, MA: Harvard University Press.

Crowder, K., Hall, M., and Tolnay, S. E. (2011) Neighborhood immigration and native out-migration. *American Sociological Review*, 76(1): 25–47.

Delhey, J. and Newton, K. (2005) Predicting cross-national levels of social trust: global pattern or Nordic exceptionalism? *European Sociological Review*, 21(4): 311–327.

Desmet, K., Ortuño-Ortín, I., and Wacziarg, R. (2012) The political economy of linguistic cleavages. *Journal of Development Economics*, 97(2): 322–338.

Dinesen, P. T. (2011) Me and Jasmina down by the schoolyard: an analysis of the impact of ethnic diversity in school on the trust of schoolchildren. *Social Science Research*, 40(2): 572–585.

Easterly, W. and Levine, R. (1997) Africa's growth tragedy: policies and ethnic divisions. *Quarterly Journal of Economics*, 112(4): 1203–1250.

Eger, M. A. (2010) Even in Sweden: the effect of immigration on support for welfare state spending. *European Sociological Review*, 26(2): 203–217.

Falk, A. and Zehnder, C. (2013). A city-wide experiment on trust discrimination. *Journal of Public Economics*, 100(1): 15–27.

Fershtman, C. and Gneezy, U. (2001) Discrimination in a segmented society: an experimental approach. *Quarterly Journal of Economics*, 116(1): 351–377.

Granovetter, M. (1973) The strength of weak ties. *American Journal of Sociology*, 78: 1360–1380.

Gurin, P., Nagda, B., and Lopez, G. (2004) The benefits of diversity in education for democratic citizenship. *Journal of Social Issues*, 60: 17–34.

Habyarimana, J. P., Humphreys, M., Posner, D. N., and Weinstein, J. M. (2007) Why does ethnic diversity undermine public goods provision? *American Political Science Review*, 101(4): 709–725.

—— (2009) *Coethnicity: Diversity and the Dilemmas of Collective Action*. New York: Russell Sage Foundation.

Harell, A. and Stolle, D. (2010) Diversity and democratic politics: an introduction. *Canadian Journal of Political Science/Revue Canadienne de Science Politique*, 43(2): 235–256.

Holtug, N. and Mason, A. (2010) Introduction: immigration, diversity and social cohesion. *Ethnicities*, 10(4): 407–414.

Hooghe, M., Reeskens, T., and Stolle, D. (2007) Diversity, multiculturalism and social cohesion: Trust and ethnocentrism in European societies. In K. Banting, T. Courchene, and L. Seidle (eds) *Belonging? Diversity, Recognition and Shared Citizenship in Canada*, Vol. III. Montreal: Institute for Research on Public Policy, pp. 387–410).

Hopkins, D. J. (2010) Politicized places: explaining where and when immigrants provoke local opposition. *American Political Science Review*, 104(1): 40–60.

Hou, F. and Wu, Z. (2009) Racial diversity, minority concentration, and trust in Canadian urban neighborhoods. *Social Science Research*, 38(3): 693–716.

Jeffreys, M. (2008) How can "cheap talk" yield coordination, given a conflict? *Mind & Society*, 7(1): 95–108.

Karlan, D. S. (2007). Social connections and group banking. *The Economic Journal*, 117(517): F52–F84.

Kesler, C. and Bloemraad, I. (2010). Does immigration erode social capital? The conditional effects of immigration-generated diversity on trust, membership, and participation across 19 countries, 1981–2000. *Canadian Journal of Political Science/Revue Canadienne de Science Politique*, 43(2): 319–347.

Kimenyi, M. S. (2006). Ethnicity, governance and the provision of public goods. *Journal of African Economics*, 15(1), 62–99.

Kooij-de Bode, H. J. M., van Knippenberg, D., and van Ginkel, W. P. (2008) Ethnic diversity and distributed information in group decision making: The importance of information elaboration. *Group Dynamics: Theory, Research, and Practice*, 12(4): 307–320.

Koopmans, R. (2013) Multiculturalism and immigration: a contested field in cross-national comparison. *Annual Review of Sociology*, 39: 147–169.

Koopmans, R. and Rebers, S. (2009) Collective action in culturally similar and dissimilar groups: An experiment on parochialism, conditional cooperation, and their linkages. *Evolution and Human Behavior*, 30(3): 201–211.

Koopmans, R., and Schaeffer, M. (2014). Perceptions of Ethno-Cultural Diversity and Neighborhood Cohesion in three European Countries. WZB Discussion Paper, SP VI 2014–103. Berlin: WZB.

Koopmans, R. and Veit, S. (2014) Cooperation in ethnically diverse neighborhoods: a lost-letter experiment. *Political Psychology*, 35(3): 379–400.

Koopmans, R., Dunkel, A., Schaeffer, M., and Veit, S. (2011) Ethnische Diversität, soziales Vertrauen und Zivilengagement: Projektbericht. *WZB Discussion Paper* SP IV 2011–703. Berlin: WZB.

Lancee, B. and Dronkers, J. (2011). Ethnic, religious, and economic diversity in Dutch neighbourhoods: explaining quality of contact with neighbours, trust in the neighbourhood and inter-ethnic trust. *Journal of Ethnic and Migration Studies*, 37(4): 597–618.

Laurence, J. (2011) The effect of ethnic diversity and community disadvantage on social cohesion: a multi-level analysis of social capital and interethnic relations in UK communities. *European Sociological Review*, 27(1): 70–89.

Letki, N. (2008) Does diversity erode social cohesion? Social capital and race in British neighbourhoods. *Political Studies*, 56(1): 99–126.

Marschall, M. J. and Stolle, D. (2004) Race and the city: neighborhood context and the development of generalized trust. *Political Behavior*, 26(2): 125–153.

Miguel, E. (2004) Tribe or nation? Nation building and public goods in Kenya versus Tanzania. *World Politics*, 56(3): 327–362.

Miguel, E. and Gugerty, M. K. (2005) Ethnic diversity, social sanctions, and public goods in Kenya. *Journal of Public Economics*, 89(11–12): 2325–2368.

Page, S. E. (2008) *The Difference: How the Power of Diversity Creates Better Groups, Firms, Schools, and Societies*. Princeton: Princeton University Press.

Paolini, S., Harwood, J., and Rubin, M. (2010) Negative intergroup contact makes group memberships salient: explaining why intergroup conflict endures. *Personality and Social Psychology Bulletin*, 36(12): 1723–1738.

Pettigrew, T. F. and Tropp, L. R. (2006) A meta-analytic test of intergroup contact theory. *Journal of Personality and Social Psychology*, 90(5): 751–783.

Putnam, R. D. (2007) *E pluribus unum*: diversity and community in the twenty-first century. *Scandinavian Political Studies*, 30(2): 137–174.

Ruttan, L. M. (2006) Sociocultural heterogeneity and the commons. *Current Anthropology*, 47(5): 843–853.

Schaeffer, M. (2013) Can competing diversity indices inform us about why ethnic diversity erodes social cohesion? A test of five diversity indices in Germany. *Social Science Research*, 42(3): 755–774

—— (2014) *Ethnic Diversity and Social Cohesion: Immigration, Ethnic Fractionalization and Potentials Civic Action*. Aldershot: Ashgate.

Semyonov, M., Raijman, R., and Gorodzeisky, A. (2008) Foreigners' impact on European societies: public views and perceptions in a cross-national comparative perspective. *International Journal of Comparative Sociology*, 49(1): 5–29.

Stichnoth, H. (2012) Does immigration weaken natives' support for the unemployed? Evidence from Germany. *Public Choice*, 151(3): 631–654.

Swidler, A. (1986) Culture in action: symbols and strategies. *American Sociological Review*, 51(2): 273–286.

Tajfel, H. (1978) Social categorization, social identity and social comparison. In H. Tajfel (ed.) *Differentiation Between Social Groups*. London: Academic Press, pp. 61–76.

Tajfel, H. and Turner, J. C. (1986) The social identity theory of intergroup behavior. In S. Worchel and W. G. Austin (eds) *Psychology of Intergroup Relations*. Chicago: Nelson-Hall Publishers, pp. 7–24.

Twigg, L., Taylor, J., and Mohan, J. (2010) Diversity or disadvantage? Putnam, Goodhart, ethnic heterogeneity, and collective efficacy. *Environment and Planning A*, 42(6): 1421–1438.

Van der Meer, T. and Tolsma, J. (2014) Ethnic diversity and its supposed detrimental effects on social cohesion. *Annual Review of Sociology*, 40(1).

Veit, S. and Koopmans, R. (2014) Ethnic diversity, trust, and the mediating role of positive and negative interethnic contact: a priming experiment. *Social Science Research*.

Wilkinson, R. G. and Pickett, K. E. (2009) *The Spirit Level: Why More Equal Societies Almost Always Do Better*. London: Allen Lane.

Part I

The causal nature of diversity effects

2 Diversity and well-being

Local effects and causal approaches

Camille Hémet

Introduction

As was pointed out in the first chapter of this book, bringing together people from different origins and cultural backgrounds may affect individual behavior and collective decisions, which in turn affect individuals' well-being. In this context, this chapter asks the following question: do individuals living in more diverse neighborhoods fare better or worse than those living in more homogeneous areas? More specifically, the research presented in this chapter focuses on the effect of diversity on outcomes related to individuals' well-being, measured by their living conditions and their employment prospects. To give a preview of the results, my research leads to the following conclusions: local diversity is found to lower the quality of housing conditions (intentional degradations such as graffiti, and poor quality of the basic housing facilities such as the heating system) in a given area and to reduce employment prospects for its residents. However, diversity does not have any significant impact on public safety.

In order to arrive at these conclusions, I handle the endogeneity issue associated with the study of diversity. A dependent variable, say ethnic diversity, is endogenous if it is correlated to the error term. This can happen for various reasons that will be detailed later in the particular context of ethnic diversity. When the assumption of orthogonality between the regressor and the residuals is violated, any linear estimate of this regressor is biased. Concretely, and as will be made explicit in the next section, endogeneity implies that the estimated effects of diversity are over- or underestimated. In this chapter, I present alternative empirical methodologies that enable me to correct potential biases in the estimates of diversity, and to establish a causal relationship between diversity and the considered outcome, from the former to the latter. The first methodology, developed by Algan *et al.* (2013), is a natural experiment based on the absence of residential sorting in the French public housing sector. The second approach, developed by Bayer *et al.* (2008), takes advantage of the exceptionally small geographical size of the survey unit, assuming that no selection takes place in very small geographic units. Both strategies are very useful when it comes to tackling the problem of endogeneity of diversity, and the second one is particularly relevant when studying diversity in very local contexts, such as neighborhoods. More importantly perhaps, the methods can be easily extended to other countries. Finally, given the results obtained, these strategies highlight the importance of correcting for the endogeneity biases.

An additional, yet smaller contribution of this chapter is to provide a better understanding of the mechanisms driving the relationship between diversity and the various outcomes considered. Because I am using very detailed data collected by the French Statistical Institute (INSEE) in quite small geographic units (e.g., the neighborhood), I am indeed able to dig deeper into the channels through which diversity may affect the outcomes considered. In particular, some of the data I use allow me to look more closely at the existence and the quality of social relationships. The proposed mechanisms are rather tentative, based on a careful interpretation of the results, and backed up by some tests. The general finding is that in the French context, diversity seems to generate anomie, i.e., the absence of common rules and social norms, which can in turn explain the various findings (see Chapter 1 for an overview of the mechanisms revealed in the literature).

The remainder of this chapter is organized as follows. The following section is devoted to the endogeneity issue. The objective is not only to explain how it may arise and what kind of estimation problem it may generate, but also to review briefly the solutions that have been proposed in the economic literature on diversity. I also propose two approaches to tackle this issue. Subsequently, I focus on the empirical analysis, describe the data used and present the main results. Finally, I address the question of the mechanisms explaining the uncovered relationships.

The issue of endogeneity

Where does endogeneity come from? What problems does it raise?

The issue of endogeneity is perhaps the most important challenge in dealing with the question of the impact of diversity on various social or economic outcomes. As mentioned earlier, ethnic diversity is endogenous if it is correlated to the error term, biasing any linear estimate of this dependent variable. This issue can arise for several reasons that I am now describing in more detail, in the specific context of the study of ethnic diversity. Problems of endogeneity occur mostly due to residential sorting, i.e., to the fact that people do not choose their living area at random, but according to certain characteristics that may be correlated to the outcome considered. One important concern is that individuals may have a preference for living close to their ethnic peers and thus tend to form neighborhoods with fairly consistent ethnic backgrounds. A further confounding factor arises from the fact that individuals who are less constrained with respect to their housing choices, i.e., the wealthiest, may be able to self-segregate. Because immigrants tend to be poorer than the natives, this implies that the most homogeneous areas systematically correspond to wealthy places, while diverse areas end up being the most deprived. Hence, any estimates on the social or economic implications of diversity will be biased. They may in particular overestimate negative effects of diversity, given that those living in more diverse areas would be not only poorer, but also less satisfied to live in their neighborhood than those living in less diverse areas. In this specific example, it might also be difficult to disentangle the direction in which the causality runs. Does diversity imply poorer neighborhood and worse living conditions? Or is it rather that more deteriorated neighborhoods attract poorer households, which are more likely to be immigrants, hence generating diversity? Endogeneity may also work in the opposite direction if diverse areas attract unprejudiced or more trusting individuals. In this case, any estimated effect of diversity on outcomes related to, for instance, social capital might be biased. In the most extreme scenario, if diverse areas are only inhabited by trusting people who actually chose to live there, then any positive impact of diversity would be overstated. A different, yet related issue could arise if immigrants purposefully decide to settle in more economically affluent areas. If the question at stake is to assess the impact of diversity on economic conditions, this particular setting would lead to a problem of reverse causality. In this case, favorable economic conditions would affect the level of diversity by attracting more immigrants, rather than the other way around.

How can the endogeneity issue be tackled?

In order to estimate unbiased causal effects, diversity must not be driven by any factor that also affects the outcome considered. If this condition is not satisfied, the researcher has to develop or use methods and tools to disentangle the two effects. Only recently has the economic literature begun to tackle this issue. A widely used approach, instrumental variable estimation, consists in finding variables explaining diversity but being unrelated to the outcome considered, except through its impact on diversity. Most of the papers on ethnic diversity that seek to establish causality rely, for example, on past settlement of immigrants or analogous historical data as instruments (see for instance Miguel and Gugerty, 2005; Ottaviano and Peri, 2006; Glennerster *et al.*, 2013). In the same vein, the results of Alesina *et al.* (2013) are obtained by specifying a gravity model to predict the diversity of immigration based on exogenous bilateral variables. An alternative way to identify the effect of diversity is to study individuals who are assigned to their place of residence exogenously, that is, without consideration of ethnic characteristics, preferences, or any (unobservable) characteristic that may be related to the considered outcome. Part of the literature therefore relies on natural or randomized experiments, whereby diversity is necessarily exogenous as its variation comes from a random or unanticipated shock. A famous example of a randomized experiment is the Moving to Opportunity program that randomly allocated housing vouchers to deprived US households so that they could relocate into richer neighborhoods. Several papers take advantage of this setting to examine the effect of social diversity. For instance, Ludwig *et al.* (2013) established that living in a wealthier neighborhood improved the physical and mental health of members of households previously living in poorer areas. Chapter 9 in this book also provides an example of a controlled (or randomized) experiment: the authors implement an experiment in which respondents are randomly allocated to experimental primes that heightened the salience of ethnic diversity in their neighborhoods or schools in order to study the effect of ethnic diversity on trust and cooperation. Alternatively, the next chapter of this book relies on a natural experiment, namely the unexpected arrival of Somali refugees in Lewiston, Maine, to measure the effect of ethnic diversity on social capital. In the remainder of this section, I present two identification strategies to study the causal effect of diversity at the neighborhood level.

The absence of sorting in the (French) public housing sector

The first strategy that I am using was recently developed by Algan *et al.* (2013). It builds on the absence of sorting of households across neighborhoods within the French public housing sector (HLM, *Habitations à Loyer Modéré*, French for low-rent housing). This setting implies that diversity can be considered as exogenous within this specific segment of the housing market. The general argument supporting this identifying assumption is that the public housing sector is very tight and highly regulated, so that tenants in this particular sector have very limited control over the time when they will be assigned a vacant dwelling and over the precise location where they will live.

Let me now briefly explain why this is the case. First of all, there are very few restrictions on public housing eligibility, so that the number of eligible families is about three times larger than the available number of public housing units (see Jacquot, 2007). The only conditions are to be living in France legally and for household income to amount to less than a—relatively high—specified threshold. In consequence, several priority criteria are specified by national law to ensure that vacant dwellings are allocated to households confronted with clear economic or social hardship. In addition, the attribution process takes place at a fairly aggregate geographic level called *département*, and the commission is not only composed of local housing representatives, but also of *département* representatives, who ensure that local considerations (e.g., the ethnic composition of the neighborhood) do not play a role in allocation. Given the French constitution, it goes without saying that taking the ethnicity of applicants into account is impermissible. Finally, public housing rents are considerably lower than those in the private housing market, so that the turnover is very low. More specifically, the mobility rate in the public housing sector is even lower than for recent owners (see Debrand and Taffin, 2005). In addition to these arguments that outline the limited capacity of the public housing market, more formal statistical tests of the exogeneity of diversity show that the allocation of households across public housing blocks does not take the ethnicity or preference for diversity of assignees into account. In particular, the distribution of the shares of French and Maghrebian households across public housing blocks is not significantly different from a randomly simulated distribution (Algan *et al.*, 2013: 8–13).

All in all, this identification assumption implies that restricting the data to a sub-sample of public housing tenants enables the researcher to identify unbiased causal effects. This strategy could also be used in other countries, provided it has a similar type of government-planned social housing. It could also be extended to slightly different settings, such as boarding schools or military barracks, where people do not get to choose with whom or where they live.

The absence of selection in very small geographic units

The second approach that I adopt builds on the exceptionally small geographical size of the survey unit and is therefore particularly relevant when the geographic unit at which the research is conducted is very small. It follows Bayer *et al.* (2008) who study the extent to which one's neighbors' place of work determines one's own workplace. The general idea behind their approach is that although households are able to select a given neighborhood in which they want to live, they are, due to the limited availability of vacant housing at any given point in time, usually unable to select a precise location, e.g., a specific street or housing block, within this given area. This assumption means that, even if households are able to choose a given residential area, there will not be any correlation in unobserved factors affecting the considered outcome among individuals living in the same small cluster within the larger selected area.

Several arguments support this assumption. First, because supply on the housing market is often highly restricted, it is reasonable to think that a household targeting a given area is very unlikely to have a choice regarding the precise micro-area, e.g., block, where it will take up residence. This would indeed require that at least one housing unit satisfying the other decision criteria of the household (e.g., the size of the dwelling) be vacant in each micro-area within the larger area at the time when the household is looking for a new place. A second consideration is that it is difficult for households to identify the characteristics of neighbors and other contextual characteristics for each micro-area, prior to moving into a neighborhood. To put it differently, although the household may have a realistic *ex ante* view on the characteristics of the neighborhood they target, it is less likely that the household is actually able to identify differences in these characteristics specific to any one particular street or housing block within it. Finally, an interesting feature of the French micro-areas which will be taken advantage of in the next section when looking at employment, is that they do not follow any kind of administrative zoning. They are very small areas of about 20–30 adjacent households and are distinct from police districts, as well as from school zones determining to which school children must go. The micro-areas considered here correspond to the labor force survey primary units called *aires* and are only designed for statistical purposes, meaning in effect most people are not aware this delineation exists or which *aire* they are part of. For those reasons, it is practically impossible that households purposely decide to live in a given *aire* rather than in a contiguous one.

All these arguments support the validity of the assumption that there should be no correlation in unobserved factors affecting well-being among neighbors living in the same micro-area within a larger selected neighborhood. As a consequence, once we control for the characteristics of the larger area selected by the individual, the remaining spatial variance of diversity across micro-areas within this larger geographical zone is supposed to be exogenous. This is done through the inclusion of fixed effects of larger areas than the micro-areas under study. Yet, the researcher generally cannot know with complete certainty which is the larger area initially selected by an individual prior to moving to a new home. For this reason, I run several regressions controlling for fixed effects for successively smaller areas. Comparing the various results brings some insight about the level at which selection takes place.

Empirical analysis

This section presents the main results of this chapter, showing how neighborhood diversity affects individuals' well-being. I first focus on living conditions, which encompass housing quality and public safety in the neighborhood. These results are the object of the companion paper by Algan *et al.* (2013). I then look at individuals' probability to be employed.

Diversity and living conditions: data description

The data used in this section come from the 2002 wave of the French housing survey (*Enquête sur le logement*, INSEE), which provides very detailed information about housing conditions in a broad sense, localized at a very low geographic level: the block (*îlot*) level. More precisely, each surveyed individual is asked to report the existence and frequency of various types of degradation, to assess the quality of the basic housing facilities, and to account for neighborhood relationships.

Living conditions are assessed based on three sets of factors. The first set pertains to vandalism and intentional degradations in the common areas of the apartment buildings, for which the tenants can be held responsible. This includes graffiti on the walls, broken mailboxes, broken doors, trash on the floor, and so on. The second set pertains to the general quality of basic housing facilities, such as the heating system, the insulation, the functioning of the toilets or of the elevator. These are typical facilities the maintenance of which falls under the responsibility of the public housing offices (the landlords). Finally, a number of factors relating to public safety in the neighborhood are considered as well: burglaries, assaults, and robberies.[1]

In addition, the survey contains the relevant social and demographic characteristics of the household, including the national origin of the household head, along with most of the building's characteristics, from construction date to number of inhabitants. Most importantly, it also provides a very detailed classification in 27 categories of the socio-economic environment of each neighborhood, which characterizes each area according to the socio-professional category and the occupation of all the men in that area. This index was built using the 1999 census data by Tabard (2002).

In this subsection on housing conditions, I rely on the first identifying assumption presented above, i.e., on the absence of sorting in the public housing sector.

Given this assumption, the empirical strategy consists in restricting the sample to public housing tenants, which amount to 15.8 percent of all households living in France, and 39.8 percent of all the tenants. In total, the public housing subsample contains slightly more than 5,000 households.

Diversity and living conditions: measuring diversity

The measure of diversity used is a standard fractionalization index, which indicates the probability that two randomly drawn individuals in a given area belong to different groups (see for example Alesina *et al.*, 2003). More precisely, we focus here on diversity based on individuals' nationality at birth, computed at the block level (*îlot*). Because we work at such a low geographic level, we observe too few individuals in each block to compute a representative measure of diversity at the block level. Instead, we rely on the 1999 French population census, which is representative at this level and can be matched to the housing survey data. In the housing survey sample, the average level of block diversity is of 0.16, while it is 0.25 when this sample is restricted to individuals living in the public housing sector. In terms of median block diversity, the gap is even more notable, with a median of 0.12 in the complete housing survey sample and of 0.23 in the public housing sub-sample. Given that immigrants and second generation French are more likely to be eligible for public housing dwellings on income criteria than native French, this does not come as a surprise.

Diversity and living conditions: results

The basic estimated equation writes as follows:

$$Y_{jkl} = \alpha + \beta DIV_l + \gamma X_j + \delta Z_k + \theta W_l + \varepsilon_{jkl} \tag{2.1}$$

Where Y_{jkl} denotes the housing outcome we are interested in, as stated by household j in building k and block l, and the main variable of interest is DIV_l, the level of diversity in block l described above. X_j is a vector of household characteristics, including a quadratic function of age, gender, level of education, labor market status and nationality of the household head, as well as household size, and total household income per capita. Z_k is a vector of building characteristics: the (log) number of apartments in the housing project, and its date of construction. The size and the number of occupants might affect the ability of the households to coordinate for improving the commons or to enforce norms, while the age of the building might explain part of the degradations observed and tenant satisfaction. W_l is a vector of socio-economic characteristics of the block, including its unemployment rate, and the Tabard index mentioned above. We also control for *département* fixed effects since the spatial allocation of households across public housings is decided at the *département* level. All results are derived from OLS estimates, with robust standard errors clustered at the block level.

Table 2.1 The impact of diversity on housing conditions.

| | Voluntary degradation | | Housing quality | | Public safety | |
	Graffiti	Garbage on the floor	Breakdown of the elevator	Toilet malfunction	Assaults	Burglaries
	(1)	(2)	(3)	(4)	(5)	(6)
Diversity	0.313***	0.298***	0.106**	0.133**	−0.024	−0.001
	(0.063)	(0.060)	(0.051)	(0.051)	(0.038)	(0.027)
Unemployment rate	0.351***	0.415***	0.074	0.084	0.200***	0.042
	(0.068)	(0.072)	(0.057)	(0.060)	(0.051)	(0.031)
# dwellings (log)	0.068***	0.055***	0.069***	−0.007	0.004	−0.002
	(0.006)	(0.005)	(0.005)	(0.005)	(0.004)	(0.003)
R-squared	0.157	0.091	0.151	0.040	0.024	0.002
N	4,379	4,379	4,379	4,379	4,379	4,379

Note: Each column presents the estimates from a different regression, corresponding to the various dependent variables, as specified in the first line. Robust standard errors clustered at the block level are reported in parentheses. In each regression, the following controls are included, in addition to those reported in the table: household head characteristics (gender, age, education, log income, employment status, and nationality), household size, date of construction of the building, Tabard index and *départements* fixed effects. Significance levels: *** p<0.01, ** p<0.05, * p<0.1, two-tailed test.

The main results are displayed in Table 2.1.[2] Each column corresponds to a separate regression, with a different outcome variable. For the sake of interpreting the results, note that the worse the associated circumstance is evaluated, the higher the value of the outcome variable is. The estimated effects of diversity are reported in the first line. A first glance at these results reveals that diversity increases the extent of voluntary degradations in the common areas of the building, and reduces the quality of basic housing facilities. However, it has no significant impact on public safety outcomes. To give an idea about the order of magnitude of the results, I interpret the results in terms of standard deviations. Regarding vandalism, we observe, for example, that a one standard deviation increase in ethnic diversity is associated with a rise of 5.6 percentage points in the probability of observing graffiti (column 1), which represents 12.8 percent of the total standard deviation of this outcome. Turning to housing quality, we find that when diversity increases by one standard deviation, the probability that the elevator was out of order during at least 24 hours over the last three months rises by 1.9 percentage points (column 3). This corresponds to 5.2 percent of the standard deviation of this outcome.

It is important to note that there are further factors with a strong explanatory power with respect to living conditions. First, the local unemployment rate is always positive and strongly significant in explaining vandalism outcomes, revealing that poor economic environment explains part of the observed degradations. More importantly, while diversity does not affect assaults, the local unemployment rate does. Then, it is interesting to note that vandalism and degradations are to a large extent explained by the number of tenants living in the building (measured as the log of the number of dwellings), while general housing quality is largely explained by the date of construction of the building.

Diversity and employment: data description

In order to study the impact of neighborhood diversity on individuals' employment status, I use the 2007 to 2011 waves of the French labor force survey, which is conducted quarterly. It contains the following relevant information about individuals' labor market situation: employment status, wage, type of contract, tenure, job search methods, and socio-economic category. It also provides individuals' characteristics such as age, gender, education, and marital status. Individuals' ethnic background can be inferred from their country of birth, their nationality, and their parents' origin. For the purpose studied in this section, I restrict the sample to working-age individuals (16 to 65 years of age), and I exclude students, so that my final sample consists of about 160,000 observations.

The sampling strategy of the quarterly labor force survey is unique: instead of randomly sampling individuals in France, the sampling unit is a small delineated residential area called *aire*, consisting of 20 to 30 adjacent households, within which all households are surveyed comprehensively. This sampling strategy has two important implications. First, the comprehensive survey of each area implies that they can be perfectly characterized in terms of the population's social and economic characteristics. In particular, it means that it is possible to compute a representative measure of diversity at this level. Second, with the sampling unit being a geographic area as small as 20 to 30 adjacent households, I am able to use the second identifying assumption presented above, i.e., the absence of selection in very small geographical units.

Diversity and employment: measuring diversity

As mentioned above, the particular sampling strategy of the French labor force surveys enables me to compute a representative measure of diversity at the micro-area level. I measure diversity using the same fractionalization index as in the case study on housing conditions, at the *aire* level, and based on various definitions of individuals' origin. More specifically, I use two different measures of origin: nationality and parents' origin. I argue that measuring diversity based on these two definitions of origin encompass different dimensions of diversity. Parents' origin diversity is a better proxy for ethnic diversity as it encompasses second-generation immigrants and is more likely to reflect color of skin, while diversity based on nationality reflects cultural rather than ethnic diversity, as it considers naturalization. Indeed, regarding parents' origins, it is reasonable to think that a person whose parents are Senegalese is very likely black, even though s/he is French and born in France. On the other hand, regarding diversity based on nationality, one may consider that two individuals sharing the same nationality are more likely to speak a common language and to share other cultural traits, even if they have different origins.

I compute two indices of diversity based on measures of nationality and parents' origins distinguishing the following six categories: France, southern Europe, other European countries, Maghreb, other African countries, and rest of the world. Obviously, these categories are rather aggregate. However, computing the level of diversity based on more detailed categories of origins does not affect the results because of the very small number of observations in these more detailed categories. The average level of neighborhood diversity is 0.09 when origin groups correspond to nationalities and 0.28 when parents' origins are taken into account. The corresponding median levels of neighborhood diversity are of 0.03 and 0.25 respectively.

Diversity and employment: results

The basic estimated equation writes as follows:

$$EMP_i = \alpha + \beta DIV_{j(i)} + \gamma X_i + \delta U_{j(i)} + FE_t + FE_g + \varepsilon_{ij} \qquad (2.2)$$

The dependent variable EMP_i is a simple dummy variable equal to one if individual i is employed and zero if s/he is unemployed or inactive. The main explanatory variable is the level of diversity in neighborhood j described above, $DIV_{j(i)}$. I also control for a set of individual characteristics, X_i, which includes the standard social and demographic variables: age (quadratic form), gender, ethnic origin, education, socio-economic category, and potential labor market experience (quadratic function), i.e., the number of years since the highest degree was obtained. The origin variable has six values: France, south Europe, rest of Europe, Maghreb, rest of Africa, and rest of the world. Specifically, I alternatively include nationality, country of birth and parents-based origin indicators when diversity is measured based on nationality, country of birth, and parents' origins respectively. $U_{j(i)}$ then represents the unemployment rate in neighborhood j. I also include quarter dummies FE_t and geographic fixed effects FE_g, specified below. The equation is estimated as a linear probability model, using simple ordinary least squares estimations (see Wooldridge, 2010: ch. 15.2), for the sake of an easier interpretation of the results, with robust standard errors clustered at the *aire* level.

In this subsection, I rely on the second identifying assumption presented above, i.e., on the absence of selection at very small geographical units, taking advantage of the very small spatial unit studied here. The empirical strategy then consists in including fixed effects of the larger area in which households self-select. Yet, one cannot know for sure which is the larger area initially selected by an individual prior to moving in a new home. I therefore run several regressions where I successively control for the fixed effects of increasingly smaller areas, as is described below.

Table 2.2 The impact of diversity on employment probability.

	Employment zone fixed effects	Municipality fixed effects	Sector fixed effects
	(1)	(2)	(3)
Diversity by nationality	−0.109***	−0.140***	−0.110***
	(0.010)	(0.013)	(0.017)
Diversity by parents' origin	−0.054***	−0.075***	−0.060***
	(0.007)	(0.009)	(0.012)

Note: The dependent variable indicates the employment status of an individual, equal to 1 if the individual is employed, and 0 otherwise (unemployed or inactive). The measure of diversity is based on the six-categories origin variables (nationality and parents' origins respectively). Each regression controls for the full set of individual characteristics, annual quarter fixed effects, and local neighborhood unemployment rate. In addition, different geographic fixed effects are included alternatively in each column, as specified in the first line. Standard errors clustered at the neighborhood level are reported in parentheses. Significance levels: *** p<0.01, ** p<0.05, * p<0.1, two-tailed test.

The results are summarized in Table 2.2. The first set of results corresponds to regressions focusing on diversity by nationality, and the second set on those focusing on diversity by parents' origins. I simply report the coefficients for diversity and for individuals' origins, but the estimates for the other covariates, which all have the expected sign, are available upon request. Each column corresponds to a separate regression, with a different geographic fixed effect. At first glance, the estimated coefficient of diversity is always negative and strongly statistically significant, suggesting that larger micro-area diversity is associated with lower employment prospects.

As a first step, I control for the characteristics of the *département*, which is a large administrative area (there are 96 such areas in mainland France) (the estimates are not reported in the table but are available upon request). As *départements* are quite large areas, it is reasonable to think that households are able to select the exact *département* that they want to move to, but it is also very likely that they can target a more precise location within the chosen *département*. Hence, I control for employment zone fixed effects, which corresponds to a local labor market (there are around 300 employment zones in mainland France). The corresponding estimates are reported in column 1, and are slightly more negative than in the *département* fixed effects specification. This indicates that the previous estimates of the negative effects of micro-area diversity were underestimated. Employment zones still being rather large areas, I go one step further and include municipalities (i.e., cities) fixed effects in column 2. In particular, the *arrondissements* of Paris, Lyon and Marseille are separate municipalities (there are about 36,000 municipalities in mainland France). The estimated effects of micro-area diversity are even lower than in the previous set of regressions, as we control for the characteristics of a more precise area in which individuals are more likely to self-select. All in all, these results underline the usefulness of such an identification technique, and confirm

that there is indeed self-selection into larger geographical units, which biases estimates of diversity effects. The fact that negative diversity effects become stronger
when we control for selection into larger geographical areas suggests that people
who are already more trusting tend to be more likely to move into diverse communities or that immigrants are attracted by favorable economic opportunities.
At any rate, these findings run against the idea that negative diversity effects are a
spurious effect of more trusting people moving disproportionately out of diverse
communities, because this mechanism should have resulted in less rather than
more negative effects of micro-area diversity once we control for the characteristics
of larger communities. I finally control for the characteristics of the sector where
the individual lives, which is the smallest identifiable area after the micro area, the
aire. More precisely, a sector is an area delimited by topographical elements such
as streets, roads, railways and rivers, containing between 120 and 240 homes and
hence between six and eleven *aires*, out of which six are randomly selected to be
included in the labor force survey sample. The last column reports the estimates of
diversity when sector fixed effects are included. The estimates are still significantly
negative, but are not lower than with the municipalities fixed effects.

One can see that the estimated effect of diversity on employment status is larger
for diversity by nationality than for diversity based on parents' origins, suggesting a larger role of cultural over ethnic diversity. To be more precise and give an
idea of the order of magnitude of the estimated effects, I interpret the results in
column 2 (the specification with municipality fixed effects) in terms of standard
deviations. A one-standard deviation increase in the level of local diversity by
nationality implies a reduction in the probability of being employed that amounts
to 4 percent of the standard deviation of this outcome. A one standard deviation
increase in the level of local diversity by parents' origins reduces this outcome by
3.3 percent of its standard deviation.

Understanding the mechanisms

So far, the presented evidence suggests that increased diversity in terms of origins
generates more voluntary degradations, a lower quality of local public goods, and
reduced employment prospects, but has no implication regarding public safety. I now
propose a tentative interpretation of the mechanisms behind these various findings.

As far as living conditions are concerned, being able to separate the outcomes
into different categories allows for the drawing of some conclusions about the
driving mechanisms, in particular regarding voluntary degradations and basic
housing facilities. Indeed, as mentioned earlier, the former can mostly be imputed
to tenants' deviant behavior, while the latter is mostly under the responsibility
of the public housing offices. From that, one can infer two mechanisms through
which diversity affects housing conditions. First, regarding vandalism, it is possible that diversity prevents the creation of social norms to punish defectors, so
that deviant behavior cannot be deterred. Indeed, the threat of social sanctions
is not credible in less cohesive societies and in particular across ethnic groups
(see for instance Miguel and Gugerty, 2005; Coleman, 1988). As a test of this

assumption, it is possible to look at neighborhood relationships using the housing survey, which reveals that people living in more diverse areas tend to report having fewer relationships with their neighbors and, when they have any relationship, they report bad relationships more often than good relationships. Second, regarding basic housing conditions, our interpretation is that more diverse communities are not only less able to coordinate (e.g., due to language barriers), but also less able to undertake efficient collective action to pressure the public housing offices into improving the quality of housing facilities. This interpretation simply derives from the two different types of outcomes considered here (voluntary degradations versus poor housing quality), which are problems that could be avoided or solved through different channels: social norms and peer pressure for the former, versus coordination and collective action for the latter. Some support for this explanation can be found looking at the causes of the heating issues. As we have seen above, households living in more diverse neighborhoods report more often that they are cold in their apartment, but they are also more likely to report that this is due to the poor quality of the heating equipment, and not due to the fact that they do not turn on the heating purposely in order to save money. To put it differently, the more frequent heating failures observed in more diverse areas can be imputed to the public housing office, which is in charge of the maintenance of the heating system. Finally, regarding the absence of effect of diversity on public safety, it can be interpreted as an expression of social indifference related to the absence of any relationship between neighbors in more diverse communities.

Turning to the impact of diversity on employment prospects, this effect is likely to be due mostly to limitations in communication: if communication is hindered in more diverse communities, for instance due to cultural or language barriers, then job information transmission might be prevented, and hence employment prospects reduced. There is indeed considerable evidence that information transmission plays a key role in the labor market. Many empirical studies conducted over various time periods and on diverse countries agree that relying on friends and family is a very popular job search method and that, on average, half of all jobs are found through social networks (see for instance Corcoran *et al.*, 1980; Granovetter, 1995; Holzer, 1988). In particular, several papers focus on the role of ethnic and immigrant networks. A recent paper by Battu *et al.* (2011) shows that ethnic minorities in the UK rely extensively on personal networks when searching for a job, although this does not necessarily lead to better employment prospects. Lancee (2012) shows that this is dominantly the case for contacts with natives only. Sociological literature also emphasizes the importance of ethnic networks in business relations and entrepreneurship, as it increases the capacity to cooperate due to common language and values (Light and Rosenstein, 1995; Light, 2005). Because communication across ethnic groups may be hindered either by a tendency to self-segregate, or due to different religious beliefs and culture, or because of differences in the languages spoken, diversity may prevent network formation and information transmission, thus having a negative impact on individuals' labor market performances. Most importantly in regard to this chapter, this effect is likely to be even more salient at the neighborhood level, as networks tend to be very local (see for instance Wellman, 1996). A few recent studies have shown in particular that local social interactions within neighborhoods do affect employment and wage outcomes. For instance, Weinberg *et al.* (2004) show that a one-standard deviation increase in neighborhood employment is associated with a 6.1 percent increase in annual hours worked for adult males on average. Bayer *et al.* (2008) estimate that living in a particular block increases by more than 33 percent the probability to work at the same location as other residents of that block. In a paper dealing explicitly with ethnic networks, Patacchini and Zenou (2012) show that the individual probability of finding a job increases with the number of ties, but that the magnitude of the effect decreases with distance. To summarize, if individuals are unable to create social ties within their neighborhood because they live in a diverse environment, this might hinder their ability to search and find jobs through the network. Three facts tend to support this assumption. First, as shown in the previous section, diversity in terms of nationality matters more than diversity in terms of parents' origins, suggesting an important role of having a common culture and language. Second, using the housing survey data, I observe that people living in more diverse neighborhoods are more likely to report having bad relationships with their neighbors, which is in line with the idea of a lack of communication. A third strain of evidence comes from the fact that individuals benefit a lot from living close to people from the same origin: the larger the share of neighbors from one's own origin, the more likely one is to be employed.

To summarize, the broad conclusion that can be drawn from these results is that diversity generates anomie, i.e., the absence of common rules and social norms, which is characterized by lower coordination and communication, hence negatively affecting the production of collective goods related to the quality of the housing environment, as well as, due to diversity's association with lower-quality social networks, individual opportunities to find employment.

Notes

1 For more details on the precise questions asked in the survey, refer to Algan *et al.* (2013)
2 The coefficients that are not displayed are available upon request, or can be found in Algan *et al.* (2013).

References

Alesina, A., Devleeschauwer, A., Easterly, W., Kurlat, S., and Wacziarg, R. (2003) Fractionalization. *Journal of Economic Growth*, 8(2): 155–194.

Alesina, A., Harnoss, J., and Rapoport, H. (2013) Birthplace diversity and economic prosperity. *NBER Working Papers, 18699*.

Algan, Y., Hémet, C., and Laitin, D. (2013) The social effects of ethnic diversity at the local level: a natural experiment with exogenous residential allocation. *AMSE Working Papers, 2013–2038*.

Battu, H., Seaman, P., and Zenou, Y. (2011) Job contact networks and the ethnic minorities. *Labour Economics*, 18(1): 48–56.

Bayer, P., Ross, S. L., and Topa, G. (2008) Place of work and place of residence: informal hiring networks and labor market outcomes. *Journal of Political Economy*, 116(6): 1150–1196.

Coleman, J. S. (1988) Social capital in the creation of human capital. *American Journal of Sociology*, 94: S95–S120.

Corcoran, M., Datcher, L., and Duncan, G. (1980) Information and influence networks in labor markets. *Five Thousand American Families: Patterns of Economic Progress*, 7: 1–37.

Debrand, T. and Taffin, C. (2005) Les facteurs structurels et conjoncturels et depuis 20 ans. *Économie et Statistique*, 381(1): 125–146.

Glennerster, R., Miguel, E., and Rothenberg, A. D. (2013) Collective action in diverse Sierra Leone communities. *The Economic Journal*, 123(568): 285–316.

Granovetter, M. S. (1995) *Getting a Job: A Study of Contacts and Careers* (2nd edition). Cambridge, MA: Harvard University Press.

Holzer, H. J. (1988) Search method use by unemployed youth. *Journal of Labor Economics*, 6(1): 1–20.

Jacquot, A. (2007) L'occupation du parc HLM: Eclairage à partir des enquêtes logement de l'INSEE. *Direction des Statistiques Démographiques et Sociales, Document de Travail*, F0708.

Lancee, B. (2012) *Immigrant Performance in the Labour Market: Bonding and Bridging Social Capital*. Amsterdam: Amsterdam University Press.

Light, I. (2005) The ethnic economy. In N. J. Smelser and R. Swedberg (eds) *The Handbook of Economic Sociology* (2nd edition). Princeton: Princeton University Press, pp. 650–677.

Light, I. and Rosenstein, C. (1995) *Race, Ethnicity, and Entrepreneurship in Urban America*. New York: Aldine deGruyter.

Ludwig, J., Duncan, G. J., Gennetian, L. A., Katz, L. F., Kessler, R. C., Kling, J. R., and Sanbonmatsu, L. (2013) Long-term neighborhood effects on low-income families: evidence from moving to opportunity. *American Economic Review*, 103(3): 226–231.

Miguel, E. and Gugerty, M. K. (2005) Ethnic diversity, social sanctions, and public goods in Kenya. *Journal of Public Economics*, 89(11–12): 2325–2368.

Ottaviano, G. I. and Peri, G. (2006) The economic value of cultural diversity: evidence from US cities. *Journal of Economic Geography*, 6(1): 9–44.

Patacchini, E. and Zenou, Y. (2012) Ethnic networks and employment outcomes. *Regional Science and Urban Economics*, 42(6): 938–949.

Tabard, N. (2002) Inégalités et disparités entre les quartiers en 1999. *Données sociales, La société française*, INSEE.

Weinberg, B. A., Reagan, P. B., and Yankow, J. J. (2004) Do neighbourhoods affect hours worked? Evidence from longitudinal data. *Journal of Labor Economics*, 22(4): 891–924.

Wellman, B. (1996) Are personal communities local? A Dumptarian reconsideration. *Social Networks*, 18: 347–354.

Wooldrige, J. M. (2010) *Econometric Analysis of Cross Section and Panel Data* (2nd edition). Cambridge, MA: MIT Press.

3 Moving to diversity

Residential mobility, changes in ethnic diversity, and concerns about immigration

Bram Lancee and Merlin Schaeffer

Introduction

While the amount of studies that analyze the relation between ethnic diversity and social cohesion is burgeoning (see Chapter 1), there is virtually no empirical research that relies on longitudinal data. Moreover, the few longitudinal studies that are available do not analyze individuals over time but rely on repeated cross-sections of countries (Meuleman *et al.*, 2009), municipalities (Dinesen and Sønderskov, 2012) or panels of municipalities (Hopkins, 2009). The scarcity of dynamic studies is problematic for several reasons, since the questions underlying the relation between diversity and trust are often more fruitfully put in a longitudinal perspective. For some, longitudinal analysis allows for concerns about causality to be better dealt with. As Chapters 2, 4, and 9 of this volume demonstrate impressively, such concerns can also be tackled using other methods. In this chapter, we demonstrate that a longitudinal perspective also provides substantial insights. As Hopkins (2009: 160) states: "To understand how diversity influences public good provision, we should look to those towns that are diversifying, not those towns that are diverse." Or, put differently, the guiding question in the debate is how *changes* in ethnic diversity affect *changes* in trust and social cohesion.

Yet, such a question can hardly be solved satisfactorily with cross-sectional data (Jackson and Mare, 2007). Improving upon purely cross-sectional work, some studies show relations between changes in diversity or recent increases therein and (cross-sectional) levels of xenophobia (Hopkins, 2010) or social cohesion (Schaeffer, 2014). Still, these studies face the problem of cross-sectional analysis that it is very difficult to empirically separate cause and effect, because there is only one time point measured. In this chapter, we use longitudinal data to analyze residential mobility across neighborhoods with different levels of ethnic diversity. By modeling moving house transitions, we analyze how changes in ethnic diversity affect changes in people's attitudes towards immigrants. Such attitudes are not orthodox indicators of social cohesion, such as social trust or civic engagement. Yet, sentiments towards ethnic minorities, also referred to as xenophobia, are an important obstacle to cohesion in any immigration country. Along the same line of reasoning, Uslaner (Chapter 5) argues that positive intergroup attitudes are an important pre-condition for more general levels of social trust. Irrespective of the particular indicator of social cohesion, one should keep in mind that a change in diversity because of moving is not the same as a changing neighborhood composition. For example, if the diversity of one's neighborhood increases twofold within a year, this is probably a more extreme experience than moving to a neighborhood that is twice as diverse.

Besides its potential for causal analysis, another great advantage of using longitudinal data is that it allows for answering different questions. For example, one can model transitions and thus differentiate between origin and destination. Larger shares of the immigrant population have been argued and found to be both positively (via intergroup contact) and negatively (via group threat) correlated with anti-immigrant attitudes simultaneously (Dixon, 2006; Schlueter and Scheepers, 2010; Schlueter and Wagner, 2008). Such opposite findings could potentially be explained by the nature of where someone came from, i.e., the origin category. It is likely that how a change in diversity matters depends on previous experiences with diversity. It could be that increasing diversity is threatening for those who previously lived in homogeneity, because little intergroup contact is made in homogenous areas. On the other hand, individuals moving from diversity to very high diversity are more accustomed to diversity and might see the increase in diversity as an opportunity for further intergroup contact (Martinovic *et al.*, 2009). However, there is virtually no research that differentiates origin categories.

Also with regard to the destination of one's move one can expect different effects on xenophobia. In that case, different destinations imply different effects. For example, Schneider (2008) and Schaeffer (2013) find a non-linear relationship between out-group size and perceived ethnic threat, which suggests that threat effects level off. Yet, there is no previous research that analyzes whether moving to a neighborhood with a very high level of diversity has different effects than moving to a moderately diverse neighborhood.

A methodological advantage of longitudinal analysis is that one can better deal with the problem of potential bias due to selection. When the ethnic composition of a neighborhood changes, better-situated people tend to move to other areas, leaving behind the deprived, low-trusting, and prejudiced inhabitants (Clark, 1992; Crowder, 2000; Crowder *et al.*, 2011; Harris, 2001). Conversely, prejudice determines the choice for a more homogenous destination neighborhood (Bobo and Zubrinsky, 1996; Eric Oliver and Wong, 2003), which would imply that, over time, homogenous neighborhoods not only become more homogenous, but their inhabitants also more prejudiced. As Gundelach and Freitag (2013: 16) put it: "Affluent and high-trusting residents chose to live in homogeneous neighborhoods. Regarding the choices of residents with fewer financial resources, self-selection could mean that minority members predominantly self-select into neighborhoods where the least-trusting residents live."

The contribution of this chapter is fourfold. First, by analyzing changes in ethnic diversity and attitudes toward immigrants, we better test the causal path that is assumed in the theory. Second, by defining specific transitions, we take both origin and destination into account. Third, we estimate the effect of moving to diversity over time and see whether the reaction to diversity wears off and how long it takes to do so. Fourth, our empirical method allows us to better deal with potential bias due to unobserved heterogeneity and selection.

We make use of the German Socio-Economic Panel Survey (SOEP) and detailed neighborhood data. Applying a difference-in-difference (DID) design, we use moving as a "treatment" of changing diversity and calculate changes in people's attitudes to immigration over multiple years after they have moved. The DID design controls for all unobserved heterogeneity between individuals, which enables us to isolate the effect of moving from possible confounding factors. Furthermore, in our DID design we model the causal ordering as we assume it in the theory. This is a big improvement over, for example, regular fixed-effects models.

Ethnic diversity and attitudes towards immigrants— longitudinal evidence

As outlined in the introductory chapter, there is a substantial body of (cross-sectional) work that examines the relation between diversity and attitudes towards immigrants. Yet, longitudinal evidence is rare. One of the few longitudinal studies analyzing out-group size is the work of Meuleman *et al.* (2009). They relate changes in migration flows on the country level to changes in attitudes towards immigrants and find that higher inflow is related to more negative attitudes. Lancee and Pardos-Prado (2013) use individual-level longitudinal data in Germany to explain attitudes towards immigrants. They find that the proportion of foreigners predicts attitudes towards immigrants. However, this effect is no longer significant when using fixed-effects estimation, suggesting that the effect is explained by unobserved variables or only occurs after a longer period of time. Dinesen and Sønderskov (2012) use longitudinal data (in the form of repeated cross-sections) to predict the effect of ethnic diversity (operationalized as out-group size) on generalized trust in municipalities in Denmark. While trust is not the same as attitudes towards immigration, Dinesen and Sønderskov show, using fixed-effects estimation, that diversity negatively predicts generalized trust, suggesting a group threat mechanism. As we will outline below, our aim in this chapter is to go a step beyond merely testing the relation between diversity and cohesion longitudinally.

Moving to diversity: theoretical expectations

Studies that analyze residential mobility show that moving is selective. For example, supporting the "white flight hypothesis," in the US the likelihood of leaving the neighborhood increases significantly with the size of and the increase in the minority population (Crowder, 2000; Crowder *et al.*, 2011). Bobo and Zubrinsky (1996) conclude that pre-move levels of prejudice determine the preference and choice for a more homogenous destination neighborhood. Yet, while there is much research that analyzes why and which people move, studies that analyze the effect of moving itself are scarce.

What then, can we expect of the effect of moving? In general, residential mobility is an "interrupting" event, i.e., it pulls people out of their networks and everyday life. As such, it is associated with lower well-being (Stokols and Shumaker, 1982). More specifically, residential mobility is said to have both psychological and attitudinal consequences (Lin *et al.*, 2011; Oishi, 2010). Moving is associated with the "personal" over the "collective self" and with duty-free friendships and group memberships, rather than duty-based friendships (Oishi, 2010). In line with this, it is also found that residential mobility decreases (behavioral) social capital (De Souza Briggs, 1998; Nisic and Petermann, 2013; Pettit and McLanahan, 2003). Furthermore, residential *stability* is related to more pro-social community and helping behavior (Oishi *et al.*, 2007). It is also often reported that longer duration of residence is associated with more neighbor-interaction, close-knit networks of local ties, and local social capital (Kang and Kwak, 2003; Sampson, 1988). As moving interrupts people's lives, it might very well make one particularly prone to perceptions of threat, including out-group threat.

The question is, however, whether *particular* moves affect people's intergroup attitudes differently. When moving implies changing diversity, it is likely that intergroup conflict and contact mechanisms operate. The question is which mechanism dominates. That is, *ceteris paribus*, does a change in ethnic diversity result in positive, negative, or no changes in attitudes towards immigrants? Although not studying individual-level changes, previous work that analyzed changes in diversity dominantly supports the group-threat mechanism explaining attitudes towards immigrants (Lancee and Pardos-Prado, 2013; Meuleman *et al.*, 2009) and social trust (Dinesen and Sønderskov, 2012). As diversity increases, people experience (or perceive) the larger out-group size as a threat to their interests, identity, and community. It seems likely that a move to increasing diversity results in more anti-immigrant sentiment.

We should also acknowledge that moving is surely a disruptive, but not an accidental event. People plan to move and thus know where they will live in the future. In other words, because people imagine how their future life will be, there could be anticipation effects. Insofar as group threat is one of the mechanisms explaining negative diversity effects, it could be that we observe increasing concerns about immigration already before people move. In other words, once people know that they are going to move to a more diverse neighborhood, the outlook of increased competition over resources and conflicting ways of life might start to threaten them, resulting in increasing concerns prior to the event of moving itself.

A related question is how threat develops after the actual move. Both increasing and decreasing effects are theoretically plausible. Because of familiarization (Schneider, 2008) threat could decline over time. To the extent that threat is reflected in real competition over scare resources (Olzak, 1992), threat could also stabilize or even increase. As a general hypothesis, we therefore expect that moving to a more diverse neighborhood causes negative attitudes towards immigrants after the event, but also shortly before. It is an open question how this effect develops after people have moved.

However, this does not necessarily imply that when diversity *decreases*, people become less xenophobic, too. Certainly, increases in out-group size or diversity trigger perceptions of threat, due to fear of job-loss and increasing housing prices. One could argue that decreases in out-group size result in more relaxed views on competition over scarce resources on the labor market or housing market. However, we do not know whether people who have experienced diversity and have become concerned about immigration as a consequence, "forget" their concerns once they move to homogeneity. Put differently, to the extent that people move to more homogenous neighborhoods *because* they hold prejudiced attitudes (Bobo and Zubrinsky, 1996), it is the question whether such individuals change their mind about this contentious political issue, once they have less intergroup contact on an everyday basis. We thus refrain from formulating a general hypothesis on the consequences of moving to homogeneity and treat this aspect of the analysis as exploratory.

Origin and destination

It is plausible that previous experiences with diversity matter for the effect of moving to diversity on attitudes towards immigrants. In other words, there could be an origin effect. Schlueter and colleagues (Schlueter and Scheepers, 2010; Schlueter and Wagner, 2008) conclude that perceived out-group size increases perceived group threat, which in turn is related to anti-immigrant attitudes. Semyonov *et al.* (2004) find that, in Germany, higher perceived, but not actual, group size is related to anti-immigrant attitudes. If the perception of out-group size matters for people's feelings of threat, it is likely that these perceptions differ for people with and without experience of diversity. However, there are no studies that differentiate previous from current experience with diversity. We propose that while perceived group threat increases after moving to diversity, this increase is stronger for people without "experience" with diversity, i.e., those who lived in homogenous neighborhoods before moving. In contrast, people who move from a diverse to a highly diverse neighborhood have experience with diversity and are therefore less likely to "over-perceive" the out-group sizes; consequently, out-group threat is lower. We therefore hypothesize that the effect of moving from diversity is different from that of moving from homogeneity.

Similarly, the destination might matter: Moving to high diversity may be different from moving to diversity. As Semyonov, Raijman, and Gorodzeisky (2006: 430) put it: "Because hostility, prejudice, and discriminatory views are constrained by a certain threshold (a ceiling effect), we expect negative views toward outsiders to increase at a faster rate early on, but then to stabilize." Yet, Semyonov *et al.* do not find a curvilinear effect. Schneider (2008) does find (across countries) a non-linear relationship between out-group size and perceived ethnic threat. Schneider labels this the "familiarization hypothesis": because of more experience with immigration and integration there is a "getting used to effect": at some point, a higher percentage of immigrants does not increase anti-immigrant attitudes anymore. Also Schaeffer (2013) finds that, in Germany, the odds of using ethnic categories to describe neighborhood problems rises with larger out-group size. However, at very high levels of foreign nationals in the neighborhood, this effect levels off and the odds even decrease. Aside from familiarization, an explanation for non-linear effects of diversity could be that at high levels of diversity opportunities for contact are pervasive and cancel out ethnic threat. It has repeatedly been found that intergroup contact (such as interethnic friendships, and intermarriages) increases with the percentage of ethnic minorities, because the opportunities for contact rise (Martinovic *et al.*, 2009). Yet, the non-linear effect reported by Schneider (2008) controls for having immigrant friends and colleagues, suggesting that familiarization with immigrants in the form of weak intergroup neighborhood acquaintances or encounters explain differential effects of ethnic diversity (Veit and Koopmans, 2014).

Overall, it seems that medium levels of diversity do not necessarily translate into medium increases of concerns about immigration. Instead, they could result in effects that are of similar size as moving to high levels of diversity. Having said that, we should again consider the timing of cause and effect. During the anticipation period neither familiarization nor intergroup contact can level off threat effects, because both these moderators function via experiences that are only made once a person has moved. For this reason we expect initially (particularly during the anticipation period) stronger effects of moving to high diversity rather than to medium level diversity, but also expect these stronger effects to wear off over time.

Data and measurement

We test our hypotheses using the German Socio-Economic Panel Survey (SOEP), a panel survey with a yearly questionnaire since 1984 (Wagner *et al.*, 2007). Under strict privacy conditions, the SOEP data can be connected with detailed neighborhood-level data that is provided by MICROM (Goebel *et al.*, 2007; Lersch, 2014: 88–89). The MICROM data contains spatial data on the "block" level, resulting in a unique dataset containing geographical cells of as little as on average 460 households. The small size is an advantage, since the micro-neighborhood is found to be especially relevant for diversity effects (Dinesen and Sønderskov, 2012). The blocks were originally defined by MICROM for geo-marketing purposes. Because of the availability of the MICROM data, we restrict our analysis to the years 2008–2011. Overall, our sample contains 27,890 individuals and 78,311 person-year observations.

Dependent variable

Each survey year, respondents are asked what their main concerns are. The question is: "What is your attitude towards the following issues—are you concerned about them?" One of the issues is "immigration to Germany" with the response categories "very concerned" (32 percent), "somewhat concerned" (44 percent), "not concerned at all" (24 percent). We recoded the variable into "very concerned" (1) versus "somewhat concerned"/"not concerned at all" (0).

Items capturing concern, or being worried about immigration are valid indicators to capture a negative attitude or feeling *vis-à-vis* immigration that is salient for the respondent (Fournier *et al.*, 2003; McGhee and Neiman, 2010). Accordingly, being concerned about immigration predicts center right-wing party identification (Pardos-Prado *et al.*, 2013). Wlezien (2005) shows that survey items measuring a public concern have two indistinguishable attributes: the salience of an issue and the degree to which it is seen as a problem. It is therefore plausible that respondents express both a salient and a negative attitude when they state to be very concerned about immigration.

Independent variable

Each year, respondents are asked whether they changed residence in the last year (yes/no). We combine this variable with the neighborhood information that we have for each respondent. Based on name analysis, MICROM provides the percentage of ethnic groups per block. The following groups are included: Germans, Turks, Spain/Portugal/Latin America, Italy, Greece, former Soviet Union, Eastern Europe, Balkan, sub-Saharan Africa, South/East/Southeast Asia, other non-European Islamic countries, other. Based on these 12 groups, we calculated a Hirschman-Herfindahl Index (HHI) (Hirschman, 1964). The advantage of a name analysis is that it includes both nationals and non-nationals (such as naturalized citizens, or second- and third-generation immigrants), herewith describing the diversity of the neighborhood much better. Another advantage is its level of detail: it allows including multiple ethnic groups.

The disadvantage of the measure is that MICROM—for commercial reasons—does not provide much background information on how exactly the name analysis is carried out. We therefore correlated the percentage of persons of immigrant origin in the MICROM with the percentage of non-nationals from the (publicly available and official) Destatis data on the "Kreise" level. Although Kreise are much larger than the MICROM units, this is the smallest geographical unit for which harmonized data is publicly available in Germany (Friedrichs and Triemer, 2008). We hence collapsed our MICROM data to the Kreise level. The correlation is 0.87 (p<0.00), which suggests that MICROM is reliable.

We combine the moving information with the MICROM data on neighborhood diversity in the following way. First, we define the 15 percent most diverse MICROM blocks in Germany as high-diversity neighborhoods. Conversely, we define all blocks with levels of diversity that lie below the median (50 percent) as homogeneous neighborhoods.[1] All other blocks are medium-level diversity neighborhoods (above the median, but below the top 15 percent). We define a change in diversity as a jump from one of these categories to another. This coding scheme allows us to look at both origin and destination effects. To make sure that people who experience only very small changes in HHI do not move categories, we additionally define a move to a different level of ethnic diversity as a change of at least half the interquartile range (IQR)[2] in the HHI compared to the origin neighborhood. We also considered other coding schemes to define changes in ethnic diversity, but this did not make a substantial difference. The coding scheme results in 270 moves from homogeneity to medium level diversity, 139 moves from homogeneity to high diversity, and 266 moves from medium-level diversity to high diversity. For moves to homogeneity, we only consider the second rule, that is, a move to homogeneity is a move that is followed by a reduction in the HHI of at least half the IQR (930 moves). The reason is that here we have no expectations regarding origin and destination effects. All other moves are treated as moves to equal levels of diversity (2,415 moves).

Control variables

On the individual level, we control for household type, labor market status, homeownership, and the number of previous moves. To control for potential selectivity in moving that is not captured by the DID-design (see below), we control with dummy variables for 13 reasons of moving (measured post-move). Reasons can be work-related, family-related, a notice given by the landlord, financial, or that the respondent bought a new place. On the block level, we control for the average purchasing power, population density, and residential stability (all are measured by MICROM on a scale from one to nine).

Empirical strategy

To estimate the effect of moving, we make use of a difference-in-difference design (DID). The DID design is often used to measure the causal effect induced by a particular event (the treatment) (Brüderl, 2005). By constructing a counterfactual (the control group) that is as similar as possible to the treatment group, one can estimate the effect of an event (Legewie, 2012). Veit (Chapter 9), Hémet (Chapter 2), and Fisher Williamson (Chapter 4) all use different, innovative designs to identify comparable treatment and control groups. In this chapter we propose another strategy, which is particularly suited for panel data.

Yet, people who move are different from those who do not, particularly since people might move because they are upset about diversity. Therefore, the central idea of DID is not to compare movers to non-movers, but to compare the yearly *trends* in xenophobic attitudes of movers and non-movers (cf. Angrist and Pischke, 2009, ch. 5). Movers might indeed hold different attitudes than non-movers. However, in the years that "movers" do not move, the *trend* in xenophobia probably resembles that of non-movers—irrespective of the different average levels of xenophobia that both groups hold. Insofar as the yearly trend of movers and non-movers is similar before the move, any change observed thereafter can be regarded as causal. Thus, one of the great advantages of the DID estimator is that time-constant unobserved heterogeneity is no longer a problem. The DID estimator is unbiased and consistent, even when the assumption that the unit effects are uncorrelated with the explanatory variable is violated. Furthermore, by respecting the causal ordering of events, reverse causality is unlikely. The DID estimator is therefore often used to estimate causal effects (Halaby, 2004).

In this analysis, the event of moving is the treatment. In other words, moving to a different neighborhood implies that individuals are "treated" with a change in diversity. The treatment effect represents the average change in anti-immigrant attitudes before and after the move, corrected for the general trend in attitudes for those individuals who did not move (the control group). The DID estimator is specified as follows:

$$y_{it} = \alpha_i + \lambda_t + \delta_{it} + \varepsilon_{it} \tag{3.1}$$

where y is the outcome of interest of individual i at time t. α is an individual-specific intercept that captures time-constant differences between all individuals. λ is a dummy variable that captures the yearly trends in y, and δ is a dummy variable that identifies person-time observations that have moved in the previous year. As such, δ captures the trend divergence of movers from the general yearly trends in y, i.e., it captures the difference in the yearly differences. ε is the error term.

One of the fundamental assumptions of the DID estimator is the common trends assumption: the over-time (pre-move) trend in anti-immigrant attitudes should be the same for the control group (the non-movers) and the treatment group (the movers). If the (pre-move) trend in the outcome variable is similar for the two groups, this indicates that the groups are comparable. Consequently, differences between the groups that occur after the treatment can be interpreted as "caused" by the treatment. To test the common trends assumption, following Angrist and Pischke (2009) we include yearly pre-treatment dummies for the movers. Statistically significant dummies indicate that the common trends assumption is not met: control and treatment group display different trends in attitudes towards immigrants before the event of moving.

Last, to find out whether the effect of moving persists or "wears off" with time we estimate the effect separately for each year after the move. It is likely that the effect is strongest very close to the time of moving. As discussed in the theory section, it could even be that there is an anticipation effect. That is, it could be that attitudes already change (shortly) before the move (Bobo and Zubrinsky, 1996). We therefore estimate the effect of moving half a year *before* the actual move, half a *year* after the move, and subsequently in yearly intervals. As a result, the DID estimator is specified as follows:

$$y_{it} = \alpha_i + \lambda_t + \delta_{-2}d^{(-2)} + \delta_{-1}d^{-1} + \delta_1 d^{(1)} + \delta_2 d^{(2)} + X_{it}\beta + \varepsilon_{it} \tag{3.2}$$

which we estimate as a two-way fixed-effects equation.

Results

Figure 3.1 visualizes the main findings: On the left-hand side, individuals who moved to diversity, on the right-hand side those who moved to equal diversity or homogeneity. At y=0, the x-axis (black line) represents the trend for the non-movers. More specifically, non-movers are people who did not move in the survey year, will not move in the next two years, and have not moved in any of the previous years. Accordingly, the figure only shows the divergence from the general trend in concerns about immigration (2008–2011). The visualization of Figure 3.1 hence conceals that, overall, concerns about immigration decreased in the observed years. Compared to 2008, non-movers were less concerned about immigration in the following years: In 2009, 4 percent of the sample changed their attitude from being very concerned about immigration to not being concerned at all. In 2011, this number is 2.9 percent. Theoretically, these trends are not very meaningful, but they represent the baseline against which we compare the change in immigration concerns of movers. The x-axis represents the time relative to the event of moving, the vertical dashed line identifies the moving event, and lastly, the grey box acknowledges that moving is not an unanticipated accident but a planned transition, i.e., people know that they will move in the next months and they probably also know where they will move to. Finally, the y-axis is the divergence from the general trend in the probability to be very concerned about immigration.

In principle, the estimates for our control variables (not shown here) are also interesting since they are rare longitudinal evidence from two-way fixed effects models. Note, however, that in such a set-up, contextual neighborhood effects might be too conservative since a neighborhood's average purchasing power, for example, does not change much in one year. With hardly any changes on the contextual level, it comes as no surprise that neither purchasing power (as a measure of neighborhood socio-economic status), nor population density or residential instability are associated with concern about immigration. Our analysis of moving to diversity does not suffer from this problem, because we defined moving to diversity in such a way that movers experienced a substantial increase in diversity (at least half the inter-quartile range). Against this background, we focus on our main research questions and analysis.

Figure 3.1 shows that the pre-treatment dummies are not statistically significant. This means that trends in concern about immigration of people who will move in the next one or two years (the treatment group) are not significantly different from non-movers (the control group). In other words, the common trends assumption is not violated and in principle assures that any significant differences after persons have moved can be interpreted as causal. Apart from looking at significance levels only, the assumption seems best met for people who move to medium-level diversity. The trends of those who move to high levels of diversity look somewhat different, even though these differences are insignificant.

Yet, against the common trends assumption, the pre-treatment dummies also show that six months or less before the move, those individuals who are moving

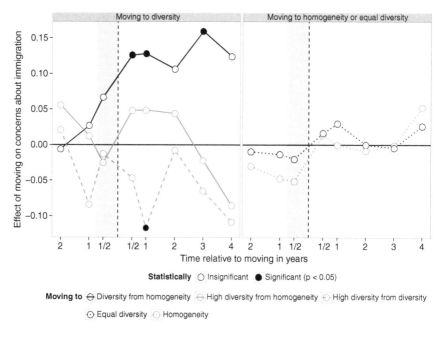

Figure 3.1 The effect of moving on being very concerned about immigration.

to diversity are slightly (but not statistically significantly) more concerned about immigration than non-movers. In other words, shortly before people move to medium-level diversity, the common trends start to diverge. Yet, this expected anticipation effect is not statistically significant, even though the trend continues after the move and eventually becomes significant.

For people who move to medium levels of diversity, we see an increase in concern about immigration. More than 13 percent of movers become concerned about immigration directly after they have moved. That is, when individuals are confronted with increasing diversity, perceived threat increases, resulting in more negative attitudes towards immigration. What is more, this effect does not wear off; we do not see a short time shock with a quick adaptation. In Figure 3.1, it is also visible that the effect of moving to diversity persists over time: for the years after moving, people who moved to diversity are more xenophobic than they were before and compared to non-movers.

For two time points, the coefficient is not statistically significant at the 5 percent level (with p-values of .08 and .09 in a two-tailed test). Yet, the N of movers is relatively low. Furthermore, if one would assume a directed hypothesis, these time points are significant on a 5 percent level. Last, the effect size remains substantial, that is, more than 10 percent (after two years) remain concerned throughout the first four years after moving and none of our results suggest a leveling off after that period. Indeed, if one estimates a model without specifying separate years after moving, the effect of moving to diversity is significant. In conclusion, it seems that, even four years after moving, neither familiarization with diversity, nor interethnic contacts balance threat effects.

Surprisingly, for people who move to high levels of diversity we do not observe changes in their concern about immigration. Theoretically, for people who move to high diversity we expected strong anticipated threat effects, which level off after the move because of familiarization (Schneider, 2008) and opportunities for interethnic contact (Schaeffer, 2013). Instead, we find no anticipation effects, irrespective of whether people come from diversity or from homogeneity. This off-setting finding continues as a trend, that is, feelings of threat do not occur after people move to high diversity, either.

Last, people who move to homogeneity, or to equal levels of diversity do not significantly change their concerns about immigration. It seems that, despite the reduced competition over resources, people stick to their political opinion about immigration when they settle in a more homogeneous neighborhood.

Robustness check: threat-immune movers?

While our analytical strategy is thorough and excludes bias from unobserved heterogeneity, the null-results about moving to high diversity are partly implausible. Perhaps people who move to high levels of diversity are immune to diversity-induced threat, just like men are immune to the contraceptive pill, whether randomly treated in a double-blind experiment or not. Put differently, in a DID design, we estimate the average treatment effect for the treated (ATT) (Morgan and Winship, 2007), but who are the treated? Based on the literature on determinants of xenophobia (Ceobanu and Escandell, 2010), there are five arguments why people might be immune for diversity-induced threat. First, people who move to high diversity could be predominantly immigrants and, for them, co-ethnics or other immigrants are less likely to be a threat. Second, people who move to high diversity might have so many close intergroup friends that they are threat-immune. Third, it could be that such movers are all highly educated full-time workers who do not fear any competition from immigrants. Fourth, people who move to high diversity might be frequent movers who are not affected by their neighborhood because they stay only shortly. Finally, there could be a ceiling effect: movers might hold such negative attitudes that their concerns cannot increase any further. Conversely, one might expect people who move to high diversity to favor cultural richness and to hold such positive attitudes about immigrants that they are threat-immune. Here too we would expect differences in pre-move levels of xenophobia.

To empirically test these explanations, Figure 3.2 shows estimates of a multinomial logistic regression predicting the likelihood to move to high diversity (from homogeneity or diversity respectively) as compared to medium-level diversity as a function of the above-mentioned determinants of xenophobia. This comparison of diversity movers shows that there are indeed significant differences with regard

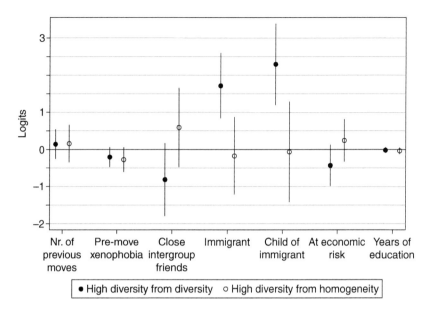

Figure 3.2 Threat-immune individuals? Multinominal regression predicting the likelihood to move to high diversity as compared to medium level diversity.

to having an immigrant origin. Both first- and second-generation immigrants are more likely to move to high diversity from diversity and less likely to move to medium-level diversity or high diversity from homogeneity. In contrast to previous research we do not see any differences in terms of pre-move levels of xenophobia (i.e., xenophobic people are not less likely to move to high diversity than to medium level diversity), nor in terms of education, being subject to labor market competition (unemployed, in education or vocational training as compared to being employed or inactive), the frequency of moving, or having intergroup friends. Does being of immigrant origin explain the null findings of moving to high diversity?

In Figure 3.3, we present estimates from a similar DID set-up, but excluding individuals of migrant origin (both first and second generation). In other words, we exclude the potentially "threat-immune" people from the analysis. As can be seen in Figure 3.3, the overall pattern remains. The reduced sample size implies a loss of statistical power, but the pattern of increased xenophobia after moving to medium-level diversity remains and does not wear off either. Furthermore, the estimates that lose significance still have a p-value below 10 percent. Excluding the potentially threat-immune population does not change the results for moves to high diversity in statistically significant ways, either. Although estimates for moves to medium and high diversity look similar up to two years after the move, the coefficients of the latter have p-values larger than 0.7 and are thus far from

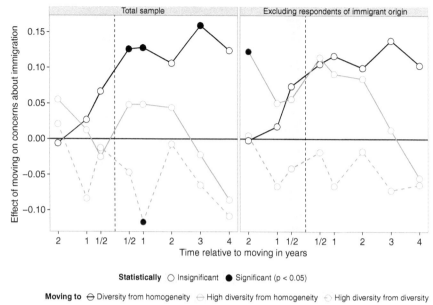

Figure 3.3 Sensitivity analysis for the effect of moving on being very concerned about immigration.

meeting any criteria of statistical significance. Rather, the results question the validity of the common-trends assumption for persons moving to high diversity. All in all, this robustness check questions the orthodox assumption that persons of immigrant origin are a diversity-threat-immune population. If they were, we should see an increase in the negative response to diversity. Instead, the results remain virtually unchanged, suggesting that persons of immigrant origin are also subject to negative diversity effects, just like majority group members. The case numbers are too low for a direct inference-statistical test of this conclusion. But additional results indeed suggest that after a move to medium diversity concerns about immigration increase as much (if not more) for persons of immigrant origin as they do for natives.[3] This interpretation is corroborated by Veit's experimental study (Chapter 9).

In summary, the robustness check supports a causal interpretation of the effect of moving to medium-level diversity. Yet, the robustness check did not solve the puzzle of the null-results for moving to high diversity. Last, the robustness check suggests that also for persons of immigrant origin concerns about immigration increase as they move to more diverse neighborhoods. Indeed, if we restrict the sample to immigrants only, the point estimates for moving to diversity are even larger, but due to the small sample size, none of the coefficients are statistically significant.

Conclusion

In this chapter, we made use of longitudinal data to analyze to what extent people's attitudes toward immigration change when they move to a more diverse neighborhood. Generally, our findings corroborate negative ethnic diversity effects, that is, we show that individuals who move to a more diverse neighborhood are about 13 percent more likely to become very concerned about immigration, suggesting that increasing diversity operates as a trigger for (perceived) ethnic threat, rather than for an increase in contact. Because individuals who move to equal or lower diversity neighborhoods do not change their attitudes, it is not the event of moving as such that makes people more negative towards out-groups, but the change towards a more diverse environment. By applying a difference-in-difference design, we also methodologically improved upon previous work. Our longitudinal set-up not only excludes reverse causality, but also renders unobserved heterogeneity a very unlikely alternative explanation.

Beyond the general finding of a negative effect of diversity, our results offer further insights. First, we are able to show that the negative effect of diversity is not a short-term shock that wears off soon after adapting to the new environment. We observe an increase of concerns over immigration that remains even three years after the move. This implies that adaptation processes that attenuate cognitive biases take quite a long time. Alternatively, it could mean that the mechanisms behind negative diversity effects are more complex, including cooperation problems or incongruent preferences, as laid out in Chapter 1. Such obstacles are of course not overcome by individual adaptation.

This study is the first to investigate whether previous experiences with diversity eliminate any threat effects of moving to a more diverse place. Interestingly, our results lend no consistent support for this hypothesis: while it is only people who come from homogeneous neighborhoods that become more concerned about immigration, those who move from homogeneity to high levels of diversity do not change their views. We also investigated destination effects and expected that moving to high levels of diversity rather than to medium-level diversity should result in initially larger concerns about immigration that wear off once familiarization and interethnic contact experiences set it. Surprisingly, however, we found no statistically significant reactions of people moving to highly diverse neighborhoods whatsoever. We considered whether the null-effect for those moving to the top 15 percent most diverse neighborhoods might be due to "threat-immunity" of such movers. Our sensitivity analyses questions this objection. Instead, it suggests that populations often thought to be immune to threat might respond similar to the majority population. That is, persons of immigrant origin equally react with growing concerns over immigration when they move to more diverse neighborhoods.

One should keep in mind that these findings are specific to the levels of diversity that we observed. Germany's "very high" diversity is fairly moderate compared to other countries. In Germany, the cut-off point for the top 15 percent most diverse neighborhoods is at HHI = 0.21. This is certainly low in terms of the range that is analytically possible. Similarly, it is important to keep in mind that the event of moving to diversity is not the same as changing diversity of the neighborhood. Moving involves a large degree of choice and people that do move represent a certain part of the general population. Homeowners probably react in a more extreme way to a change of their environment that lies beyond their control. When moving to diversity increases concerns about immigration, it is likely that the level of diversity in the neighborhood a person lives in changing has an even stronger effect on people's attitudes. In other words, our test of the diversity hypothesis is a very conservative one. Unfortunately, our data did not allow us to test the effect of a changing neighborhood. In the four years of survey data that we had at our disposal, the diversity of neighborhoods changed very little.

Future analyses could focus on replication of the current results in different contexts, such as, for example, the US. Insofar as future studies continue to find no threat effects for those moving to high levels of diversity, social scientists have another puzzle to solve. Furthermore, future analyses will need to show whether our findings equally hold true for other outcome variables that are relevant in the study of social cohesion, such as trust, cooperative behavior, and collective action.

Notes

1 When we use lower cut-off values to define homogeneity, our results remain similar but because of low case numbers, they drop from significance.
2 The interquartile range, also called the midspread or middle 50, is a measure of statistical dispersion, equal to the difference between the upper and lower quartiles. In case a variable is skewed, the IQR is a better measure of dispersion than, for example, the standard deviation.
3 With regard to moves to high diversity, the common-trends assumption for persons of immigrant origin is strongly violated and thus the results are inconclusive.

References

Angrist, J. D. and Pischke, J.-S. (2009) *Mostly Harmless Econometrics*. Princeton: Princeton University Press.
Bobo, L. and Zubrinsky, C. L. (1996) Attitudes on residential integration: perceived status differences, mere in-group preference, or racial prejudice? *Social Forces*, 74(3): 883–909.
Brüderl, J. (2005) *Panel Data Analysis*. www2.sowi.uni-mannheim.de/lsssm/veranst/Panelanalyse.pdf.
Ceobanu, A. M. and Escandell, X. (2010) Comparative analyses of public attitudes toward immigrants and immigration using multinational survey data: a review of theories and research. *Annual Review of Sociology*, 36(1): 309–328.
Clark, W. V. (1992) Residential preferences and residential choices in a multiethnic context. *Demography*, 29(3): 451–466.
Crowder, K. (2000) The racial context of white mobility: an individual-level assessment of the white flight hypothesis. *Social Science Research*, 29(2): 223–257.
Crowder, K., Hall, M., and Tolnay, S. E. (2011) Neighborhood immigration and native out-migration. *American Sociological Review*, 76(1): 25–47.

De Souza Briggs, X. (1998) Brown kids in white suburbs: housing mobility and the many faces of social capital. *Housing Policy Debate*, 9(1): 177–221.

Dinesen, P. T. and Sønderskov, K. M. (2012) Trust in a time of increasing diversity: on the relationship between ethnic heterogeneity and social trust in Denmark from 1979 until today. *Scandinavian Political Studies*, 35(4): 273–294.

Dixon, J. C. (2006) The ties that bind and those that don't: toward reconciling group threat and contact theories of prejudice. *Social Forces*, 84(4): 2179–2204.

Eric Oliver, J. and Wong, J. (2003) Intergroup prejudice in multiethnic settings. *American Journal of Political Science*, 47(4): 567–582.

Fournier, P., Blais, A., Nadeau, R., Gidengil, E., and Nevitte, N. (2003) Issue importance and performance voting. *Political Behavior*, 25(1): 51–67.

Friedrichs, J. and Triemer, S. (2008) *Gespaltene Städte? Soziale und ethnische Segregation in deutschen Großstädten*. Wiesbaden: VS Verlag für Sozialwissenschaften.

Goebel, J., Spieß, C. K., and Gerstenberg, S. (2007) *Die Verknüpfung des SOEP mit MICROM-Indikatoren: Der MICROM-SOEP Datensatz*. Berlin: DIW.

Gundelach, B. and Freitag, M. (2014) Neighbourhood diversity and social trust: an empirical analysis of interethnic contact and group-specific effects. *Urban Studies*, 51(6): 1236–1256.

Halaby, C. N. (2004) Panel models in sociological research. *Annual Review of Sociology*, 30: 507–544.

Harris, D. R. (2001) Why are whites and blacks averse to black neighbors? *Social Science Research*, 30(1): 100–116.

Hirschman, A. O. (1964) The paternity of an index. *The American Economic Review*, 54(5): 761–762.

Hopkins, D. J. (2009) The diversity discount: when increasing ethnic and racial diversity prevents tax increases. *The Journal of Politics*, 71(1): 160–177.

—— (2010) Politicized places: explaining where and when immigrants provoke local opposition. *American Political Science Review*, 104(1): 40–60.

Jackson, M. I. and Mare, R. D. (2007) Cross-sectional and longitudinal measurements of neighborhood experience and their effects on children. *Social Science Research*, 36(2): 590–610.

Kang, N. and Kwak, N. (2003) A multilevel approach to civic participation: individual length of residence, neighborhood residential stability, and their interactive effects with media use. *Communication Research*, 30(1): 80–106.

Koopmans, R. and Veit, S. (2014) Ethnic diversity, trust, and the mediating role of positive and negative interethnic contact: a priming experiment. *Social Science Research*, 47: 91–107.

Lancee, B. and Pardos-Prado, S. (2013) Group conflict theory in a longitudinal perspective: analyzing the dynamic side of ethnic competition. *International Migration Review*, 47(1): 106–131.

Legewie, J. (2012) Die Schätzung von kausalen Effekten: Überlegungen zu Methoden der Kausalanalyse anhand von Kontexteffekten in der Schule. *KZfSS Kölner Zeitschrift für Soziologie und Sozialpsychologie*, 64(1): 123–153.

Lersch, P. M. (2014) *Residential Relocations and Their Consequences: Life Course Effects in England and Germany*. Berlin: Springer Verlag.

Lin, K.-C., Twisk, J. W. R., and Rong, J.-R. (2011) Longitudinal interrelationships between frequent geographic relocation and personality development: results from the Amsterdam growth and health longitudinal study. *American Journal of Orthopsychiatry*, 81(2): 285–292.

Martinovic, B., van Tubergen, F., and Maas, I. (2009) Dynamics of interethnic contact: a panel study of immigrants in the Netherlands. *European Sociological Review*, 25(3): 303–318.

McGhee, E. M. and Neiman, M. (2010) Concern over immigration and support for public services. *California Journal of Politics and Policy*, 2(1): 1–26.

Meuleman, B., Davidov, E., and Billiet, J. (2009) Changing attitudes toward immigration in Europe, 2002–2007: a dynamic group conflict approach. *Social Science Research*, 38: 352–365.

Morgan, S. L. and Winship, C. (2007) *Counterfactuals and Causal Inference: Methods and Principles for Social Research.* Cambridge: Cambridge University Press.

Nisic, N., and Petermann, S. (2013) New city = new friends? The restructuring of social resources after relocation. *Comparative Population Studies-Zeitschrift für Bevölkerungswissenschaft*, 38(1): 199–226.

Oishi, S. (2010) The psychology of residential mobility: implications for the self, social relationships, and well-being. *Perspectives on Psychological Science*, 5(1): 5–21.

Oishi, S., Rothman, A. J., Snyder, M., Su, J., Zehm, K., Hertel, A. W., and Sherman, G. D. (2007) The socioecological model of procommunity action: the benefits of residential stability. *Journal of Personality and Social Psychology*, 93(5): 831.

Olzak, S. (1992) *The Dynamics of Ethnic Competition and Conflict.* Stanford: Stanford University Press.

Pardos-Prado, S., Lancee, B., and Sagarzazu, I. A. (2013) Immigration and electoral change in mainstream political space. *Political Behavior*, 1–29 (doi: 10.1007/s11109-013-9248-y).

Pettit, B. and McLanahan, S. (2003) Residential mobility and children's social capital: evidence from an experiment. *Social Science Quarterly*, 84(3): 632–649.

Sampson, R. J. (1988) Local friendship ties and community attachment in mass society: a multilevel systemic model. *American Sociological Review*, 53(5): 766–779.

Schaeffer, M. (2013) Which groups are mostly responsible for problems in your neighbourhood? *Ethnic and Racial Studies*, 36(1): 156–178.

—— (2014) *Ethnic Diversity and Social Cohesion: Immigration, Ethnic Fractionalization and Potentials for Civic Action.* Aldershot: Ashgate.

Schlueter, E. and Scheepers, P. (2010) The relationship between outgroup size and anti-outgroup attitudes: a theoretical synthesis and empirical test of group threat and intergroup contact theory. *Social Science Research*, 39(2): 285–295.

Schlueter, E. and Wagner, U. (2008) Regional differences matter: examining the dual influence of the regional size of the immigrant population on derogation of immigrants in Europe. *International Journal of Comparative Sociology*, 49(2–3): 153–173.

Schneider, S. (2008) Anti-immigrant attitudes in Europe: outgroup size and perceived ethnic threat. *European Sociological Review*, 24(1): 53–67.

Semyonov, M., Raijman, R., Tov, A. Y., and Schmidt, P. (2004) Population size, perceived threat, and exclusion: a multiple-indicators analysis of attitudes toward foreigners in Germany. *Social Science Research*, 33(4): 681–701.

Semyonov, M., Raijman, R., and Gorodzeisky, A. (2006) The rise of anti-foreigner sentiment in European societies, 1988–2000. *American Sociological Review*, 71(3): 426–449.

Stokols, D. and Shumaker, S. A. (1982) The psychological context of residential mobility and well-being. *Journal of Social Issues*, 38(3): 149–171.

Wagner, G., Frick, J., and Schupp, J. R. (2007) The German Socio-Economic Panel study (SOEP)-evolution, scope and enhancements. *Schmollers Jahrbuch*, 127(1): 139–169.

Wlezien, C. (2005). On the salience of political issues: the problem with 'most important problem'. *Electoral Studies*, 24(4): 555–579.

4 Declining trust amid diversity?

A natural experiment in Lewiston, Maine*

Abigail Fisher Williamson

Introduction

Between February 2001 and July 2002, more than 1,000 Somali refugees migrated to Lewiston, Maine from other cities across the United States. In the year 2000, Lewiston—Maine's second largest city at 36,000 residents—was 96 percent non-Hispanic white, with a black population of just over 1 percent (US Census, 2000). By 2010, Lewiston was 9 percent black, largely due to continued Somali migration (US Census, 2010). What will increasing ethnic diversity in Lewiston mean for local social capital? As this volume attests, recent scholarly findings suggest that amid diversity, social capital—the human bonds that enable communities to act collectively—may atrophy (e.g., Putnam, 2007). Yet most existing studies have two related limitations. First, examining the effects of local racial composition is complicated by self-selection bias. If people choose where they live based on racial composition, researchers cannot differentiate whether residents' social capital varies because of demographic context or because systematically different people choose to live in more or less diverse places. Second, cross-sectional studies that examine uniform geographic units fail to clarify the mechanisms through which diversity affects social capital over time and space. Indeed, we do not know at which scale diversity affects social capital. Is it through face-to-face contact, or more broadly, perhaps through competition over goods at the municipal or regional level?

The case of Lewiston, Maine, serves as a natural experiment testing the effect of racial diversity on social capital for residents who were not predisposed to live amid diversity. Drawing on repeated cross-section data from the Lewiston area in 2000 and 2006, I test this relationship at multiple geographic scales, allowing

* The author thanks the Center for American Political Studies and the Saguaro Seminar for Civic Engagement in America at Harvard University for funding support. For helpful critiques, the author thanks this volume's editors, Ryan Allen, Sarah Dryden-Peterson, Archon Fung, Daniel J. Hopkins, David Lazer, Helen B. Marrow, Christopher S. Parker, Robert D. Putnam, Tom Sander, Thomas Soehl, Van C. Tran, Mary Waters, and participants in Harvard's Migration and Immigrant Incorporation Workshop, the Harvard-Manchester Summer Workshop, MPSA 2008 Panel 29–2, the Trinity College Connecting to the City Symposium, and the WZB Social Science Research Center Berlin Ethnic Diversity and Social Capital Conference.

consideration of the mechanisms through which diversity operates. In multiple levels of carefully paired comparisons at the municipal, regional, and neighborhood levels, I use a non-longitudinal difference-in-difference (DID) method to examine how a sudden influx of racial diversity to a previously homogeneous white place affects long-term, white residents' levels of inter- and intragroup trust and friendship.

On the municipal and regional level, a marked increase in racial diversity is not associated with declines in social capital, although it is associated with some increase in anti-immigrant sentiment. Taking into account patterns of social capital change elsewhere in the United States, the Lewiston area's only unique social capital change is an increase in interracial friendships. In contrast, on the neighborhood level, living in the census block groups that experienced the greatest increase in diversity is associated with declines in some forms of trust. Most strikingly, while the Lewiston area as a whole experienced substantial differential increases in interracial friendships, the neighborhoods where opportunities for interracial contact were most prevalent experienced differential declines in interracial ties. Recent research suggests that intergroup contact may moderate the negative effect of diversity on social capital (Stolle *et al.*, 2008; Laurence, 2009). The case of Lewiston indicates that those living in closest proximity to rapid increases in racial diversity become less likely to form positive intergroup ties. The findings provide suggestive evidence that, at least in its early stages, the effect of diversity on social capital operates through mechanisms involving face-to-face contact.

Predictions and mechanisms

A review of related literature indicates that Lewiston's experience presents conditions where social capital is especially likely to decline. In a quantitative analysis of 172 studies on the relationship between ethnic diversity and social capital, Schaeffer (2014) argues that a negative relationship is more commonly found when ethnic boundaries are highly salient; for instance, when diversity is measured with respect to linguistic diversity, when contextual units of analysis are smaller than the city-level, and with studies in the United States as opposed to other geographic regions. Taking these conditions into account, the rapid in-migration of linguistically and racially distinct Somalis to previously homogeneous Lewiston, amid the already high relevance of racial boundaries in the United States, presents a "perfect storm" where social capital is highly likely to decline. Moreover, the case of Lewiston allows for examination of geographic scale in the relationship between diversity and social capital, including analysis at the neighborhood level. Thus, I predict that inter- and intragroup trust will decline in Lewiston, perhaps particularly at the neighborhood level.

Whereas the literature presents clear predictions with respect to trust, predictions are less clear with respect to interracial friendships. The phenomenon is crucial to study, however, since intergroup contact may mitigate the effect of diversity on social capital (Stolle *et al.*, 2008; Laurence, 2009). Intergroup friendship is strongly related to opportunity for contact within a geographic area (De

Souza Briggs, 2007; McPherson *et al.*, 2001). Indeed, studies of homophily, or the tendency to associate with those like oneself, distinguish between "baseline homophily," which refers to levels of homophily generated by the opportunities for contact within the "potential tie pool," and "in-breeding homophily," which refers to levels of homophily beyond what opportunities within the tie pool would predict (McPherson *et al.*, 2001: 419; see also Kalter and Kruse, Chapter 10, this volume). Naturally, with an increase in diversity, we would expect to see levels of interracial friendship rise as the pool of potential out-group contacts grows. Indeed, Putnam (2007: 27) notes that at first glance, diversity appears to be positively associated with interracial friendship. Yet higher rates of interracial friendship could merely be the result of increased opportunity for interracial contact in more diverse settings. Controlling for opportunity for contact—that is, the probability that a random draw of contacts from a given area would result in an interracial tie—interracial friendships are in fact more common in less diverse areas. Using the same dataset, De Souza Briggs (2007: 278) confirms this relationship, writing "white residents of Los Angeles are far more likely than their counterparts in Maine to have a friend of another race, but not nearly as much as the racial composition differences between the two places would predict."

With these results in mind, I predict that levels of interracial friendship will increase in Lewiston in response to increased opportunity for contact, but I also consider the degree to which the actual increase corresponds to the increase that would be predicted by a random draw amid greater diversity. If I find increases in interracial friendship in Lewiston, these may be attributable simply to greater opportunity for contact. On the other hand, if interracial friendship rates decrease despite increased opportunity for contact, this finding would suggest that interracial contact was not promoting harmony. In sum, I hypothesize that amid increasing diversity in Lewiston, inter- and intraracial trust will decline, while interracial friendship will increase due to increased opportunity for contact. While these predictions address the directionality of the relationship between diversity and social capital, they do little to identify the mechanisms through which it operates.

Indeed, we do not yet know at what geographic scale a "treatment" of diversity operates (Eric Oliver and Wong, 2003). Does increasing racial diversity affect relations at the neighborhood level through processes associated with face-to-face contact? Does it affect relations at the municipal level, perhaps through competition over locally distributed goods? Or does it affect relations at a broader regional level, perhaps through labor market competition? As outlined in Chapter 1, four primary mechanisms have been proposed to explain the negative relationship between diversity and social capital; namely, coordination problems, threats to social control, out-group biases, and divergent preferences. Mechanisms related to coordination problems and social control are more likely to operate at a geographic scale where face-to-face contact is common, such as the neighborhood level. Mechanisms related to out-group biases and divergent preferences should operate at any geographic scale where competition among groups can emerge, but perhaps especially at the geographic scale where distribution of goods—whether government resources or jobs—takes place. In the case of Lewiston, if out-group biases or divergent preferences mechanisms were operative, the effect of diversity on social capital could appear at any geographic scale at which competition emerged, although perhaps particularly at the municipal level, where public school funding and other government resources are distributed, or at regional labor market level. On the other hand, for the coordination problems and social control mechanisms to operate, average people from different ethnic groups must be encountering one another regularly. Thus, if these mechanisms were operative, I would expect to see the strongest effect of diversity on social capital not on the municipal or regional level, but on the neighborhood level, where repeated face-to-face interaction occurs.

Research design: Lewiston as a natural experiment

While reviews of the literature offer some sense of the conditions under which diversity may result in hunkering down, they also acknowledge that studies of the relationship suffer from methodological weaknesses. As Chapter 1 describes, virtually all studies examining the relationship are cross-sectional, leaving results vulnerable to self-selection bias and complicating claims of causality. Natural experiments, on the other hand, aim to approximate randomized controlled experiments, considered the gold standard in assessing causality. A controlled experiment randomly assigns participants to treatment and control groups, such that they should not differ systematically prior to treatment. Any subsequent differences between groups can be ascribed to the treatment, rather than other factors. A natural experiment, on the other hand, assigns groups to treatment and control conditions "as if at random" (Dunning, 2008). Here, I examine change in social capital from 2000 to 2006 among white Americans who have lived in their communities for more than five years. Those who lived in Lewiston over this period constitute a "treatment group" that experienced a change in diversity exogenous to their preferences, thus allowing me to analyze the effect of diversity on social capital in a setting that minimizes self-selection bias.

Justifying the plausibility of a natural experiment requires demonstrating that the treatment and control group are equivalent on observables prior to treatment and detailing why the assignment to treatment and control can be considered "as if" random (Dunning, 2008). My knowledge of the Somalis' migration to Lewiston stems from five visits to the city between 2003 and 2007, during which I conducted 66 interviews with Lewiston residents and new Somali arrivals. The "treatment" of Somali settlement can be considered "as if random" because Somalis arrived in Lewiston through processes exogenous to the preferences of Lewiston residents. Moreover, the reasons Somalis migrated to Lewiston could equally have applied to many other small US cities. Their ultimate choice of Lewiston was essentially happenstance.

Two complementary quests combined to bring more than 3,000 Somalis to Lewiston, Maine, beginning in February 2001. Since Somalia dissolved into chaos in 1991, more than a million Somalis have fled the country (United Nations High Commission on Refugees, 2013) and 96,960 have been resettled in the United

States (Office of Refugee Resettlement, 2009; US Refugee Admissions Program, 2010–2011). Placed by the federal government in locations such as Atlanta, Georgia, and Columbus, Ohio, some Somalis were disturbed by the prevalence of drugs and gangs and sought a tranquil place where they could raise their children in the Somali, Muslim tradition. At the same time that Somali elders were seeking a new home, Catholic Charities, the refugee resettlement contractor in Maine, sought relief from a serious housing crunch. For years, Portland had welcomed roughly 250 refugees annually. By 2002, Portland's Somali refugee population numbered 356 (Braga, 2003). In 2001, Catholic Charities recognized that Lewiston, 45 minutes north, had a vacant stock of affordable housing particularly suitable for large Somali families. Thus, the first Somalis came to Lewiston through the suggestions of social service providers in Portland. Finding favorable conditions, Somali elders then encouraged friends and family across the nation to follow. As extensive interviews confirm, the Somali migration to Lewiston was driven by the recommendations of Catholic Charities workers outside of Lewiston and the preferences of the Somali elders, rather than by the actions of Lewiston authorities or residents.

In addition, the characteristics that attracted the Somalis to Lewiston—its relative safety and tranquility coupled with abundant vacant housing—were far from unique to Lewiston. Indeed, as I will discuss below, neighboring Auburn, Maine, bore similar characteristics and did not attract many Somalis. Likewise, Keene, in Cheshire County, New Hampshire, had a similar vacant housing stock situated in proximity to Manchester, the state's center of refugee resettlement, but did not attract any noticeable number of Somalis over this period. While Auburn and Keene are far from the only towns sharing these characteristics, their existence demonstrates that the Somalis' choice of Lewiston was a matter of contingency, rather than a purposive selection based on characteristics peculiar to Lewiston.

One might wonder, however, whether the Somali settlement in Lewiston is not solely a treatment of diversity, but also a treatment of poverty or associated social ills, thus obscuring the actual relationship between racial diversity and social capital. Counter to that claim, from 2000 to 2006, poverty and levels of public assistance utilization increased and then returned to levels similar to those prior to the Somalis' arrival (American Community Survey, 2000–2006). Crime rates in Lewiston's Androscoggin County declined throughout the period (Federal Bureau of Investigation Uniform Crime Reports, 2000–2006). Available data strongly suggest that the arrival of a substantial Somali population in Lewiston can be reasonably considered a treatment of diversity, rather than of other socio-economic changes. Even so, it would be problematic to treat this case as a natural experiment testing the effect of diversity on social capital if other unique changes were taking place in Lewiston that could also be shifting social capital. While I cannot rule out this possibility, Lewiston residents consistently identify the Somali settlement as the "biggest change" in the past decade in interviews even many years after the Somalis' initial arrival. Other than the racial demographic change associated with Somali settlement, little else is going on in Lewiston that makes it substantially different from other small New England cities.

In sum, Lewiston exemplifies a natural experiment in that a sudden racial demographic change was assigned to Lewiston residents through exogenous processes that involved a great deal of contingency. That said, Lewiston does not represent an absolutely archetypal natural experiment. Selection of Lewiston as the "treatment group" cannot be considered entirely random since the Somalis did choose to move there. Likewise, the treatment is applied on the group level—throughout a geographic area—rather than on the individual level. As I shall discuss below, however, neither concern proves insurmountable. Indeed, even if Lewiston is not a perfect natural experiment, some methodologists suggest that comparing geographically proximate, intact comparison groups accurately replicates experimental results (Cook *et al.*, 2008).

Methods

The Social Capital Community Survey (SCCS), developed by Robert Putnam and used in his 2007 article, enables analysis of the Lewiston natural experiment. The initial SCCS, conducted in 2000 with a national sample (n = 3,003) and 41 community samples, included a 500-person sample in Lewiston's Androscoggin County (AC). In 2006, a second wave of the SCCS included a national sample (n = 2,741) and repeat samples in 11 of the initial 41 communities, including AC.[1] The 2006 SCCS consists of new representative samples from these areas, rather than recontacting respondents from the 2000 SCCS. In order to capture social capital change among Lewiston residents experiencing a level of diversity they did not choose, my population of interest within the SCCS is non-Hispanic whites who have lived in their communities for more than five years; that is, prior to the in-migration of Somalis. Since my data is non-longitudinal, consisting of separate representative samples of the Lewiston area in 2000 and 2006, my analysis would be vulnerable to self-selection bias if Lewiston had experienced marked exit following the arrival of the Somali population, leaving behind a group that might respond in systematically different ways. Examination of census data, however, suggests that this was not the case. Lewiston did experience a 7 percent decline in its white population from 2000 to 2010; however, this rate of decline actually marked a tapering off of population loss, which began in the 1980s and accelerated in the 1990s. In 1990–2000, prior to the Somalis' arrival in 2001, Lewiston experienced a 13 percent decline in white population. Moreover, as I will discuss later, the census block groups that experienced the most concentrated Somali settlement averaged similar rates of white exit as a comparable group of census block groups that did not experience concentrated Somali settlement. Demographic data suggest that, if anything, white population decline lessened following the Somalis' arrival.

  The natural experiment research design also requires that a comparison group be readily identifiable. An ideal comparison group would not be systematically different in 2000 and would share characteristics such that it approximates the counterfactual; that is, what would have happened to Lewiston's social capital in the absence of the Somali migration? To accomplish this task, comparison groups at each level of geographic scale should possess four main similarities to their respective treatment groups. First, the comparison group should be previously homogeneous white prior to 2001, and maintain similarly low levels of diversity through 2006. Second, the comparison group should be similar to Lewiston in terms of the characteristics that brought the Somalis to the city, namely abundant vacant housing, affordable rents, and a small, safe atmosphere. Third, the comparison group should be as similar as possible to Lewiston in terms of its social capital and other characteristics that contribute to changing social capital over time. As such, it would need to be located in the northeast, and thus subject to similar regional conditions that might affect social capital change; and it would need to share Lewiston's history of recent economic decline and population loss. Finally, the comparison group would need to experience no shocks from 2000 to 2006 that would set it on a social capital trajectory different from Lewiston. Clearly, identifying an ideal comparison group is a tall order. Since we do not know at what scale a "treatment" of racial diversity operates, I conduct multiple levels of carefully paired analyses at the municipal, regional, and neighborhood level.

Comparison groups

To examine changes at the municipal level, neighboring Auburn, just across the Androscoggin River, provides an ideal foil for Lewiston. Table 4.1 compares mean scores on key social capital and well-being measures in Lewiston and Auburn in 2000. In t-tests, I find no significant differences in social capital between the two cities before the arrival of the Somali population. In the year 2000, Auburn was demographically similar to Lewiston, although somewhat smaller and wealthier, as Table 4.2 demonstrates. Like Lewiston, it had a high vacant housing rate and similar rental prices, and was under an hour from the Somali refugee community in Portland. In terms of the reasons Somalis relocated to Lewiston, the towns were not readily differentiable. Interviews strongly suggest that the Somalis' choice of Lewiston over Auburn was not purposive. Moreover, Lewiston and Auburn, known locally as the "Twin Cities," are so closely linked that, apart from the Somali influx, changes over time are likely to be similar across the two towns.

Even so, comparing the cities would be problematic if residents exited Lewiston for Auburn following the Somalis' arrival. While I cannot rule out this possibility, demographic evidence does not speak in its favor. If white Lewiston residents had departed for Auburn, we would expect to see an uptick in Auburn's white population. Instead, we see Auburn's white population continue the decline that began in the 1990s, with a 4 percent decline in the decade following the Somalis' arrival. Demographic data also suggest, however, that we cannot consider Auburn entirely "untreated" by diversity. Between 2000 and 2010, Auburn's black population grew from less than 1 percent to 2 percent (net increase 439). Lewiston's black population grew from 1 percent to 9 percent (net increase 2,756). If anything, the small Somali presence in Auburn would understate the effect of diversity on social capital in Lewiston.

Table 4.1 Mean social capital among treatment and comparison populations at municipal, regional, and neighborhood levels.

	Lewiston	Auburn	Androscoggin County	Nation	Concentrated Blocks	Comparison Blocks
2000						
Generalized social trust	0.56	0.63	0.57	0.55	0.67	0.57
Trust in neighbors	2.27	2.41	*2.38*	*2.47*	2.27	2.21
Cooperation with neighbors	4.13	4.29	4.27	4.38	4.50	4.13
Intraracial trust (whites)	2.29	2.42	*2.36*	*2.26*	2.50	2.50
Anti-immigrant sentiment	2.65	2.75	*2.67*	*2.91*	2.88	2.70
Trust blacks	2.28	2.39	*2.33*	*2.17*	2.47	2.59
Interracial friendship count	0.76	0.67	*0.80*	*1.3*	*1.00*	*0.55*
N =	131	105	363	1373	33	24
2006						
Generalized social trust	*0.44*	*0.55*	0.53	0.53	0.41	0.46
Trust in neighbors	2.34	2.35	2.42	2.49	2.24	1.92
Cooperation with neighbors	4.19	4.32	*4.28*	*4.37*	4.12	4.21
Intraracial trust (whites)	2.36	2.41	*2.42*	*2.31*	2.34	2.38
Anti-immigrant sentiment	*3.33*	*2.89*	3.21	3.24	3.50	3.17
Trust blacks	2.25	2.32	*2.31*	*2.24*	2.13	2.21
Interracial friendship count	1.03	1.22	1.07	1.50	*0.68*	*1.13*
N =	144	102	367	1599	34	24

Note: (Means in bold and italic are those in which the treatment and comparison group are statistically significantly different in two-sided t-tests.) Source: SCCS 2000 and 2006.

Comparing Lewiston and Auburn before and after the Somalis' arrival allows me to consider how an influx of diversity might affect social capital at the municipal level. It remains possible, however, that diversity impacts social capital on a broader geographic scale. Thus, I also look for evidence that the demographic shock in Lewiston affected social capital countywide, by comparing changes in Androscoggin County (AC) to those in other samples in the 2000–2006 SCCS. Unfortunately, finding an ideal comparison group for AC within the SCCS proves impossible.[2] Thus, I evaluate whether AC has experienced unique changes in social capital over this period in a two-step process. First, I compare AC to the national sample, identifying differential changes in social capital. Second, I

Table 4.2 Treatment and comparison group socio-economic and demographic characteristics.

	Lewiston	Auburn	Androscoggin County	Nation	Concentrated Blocks	Comparison Blocks
Median rent 2000	$408	$446	$433	$602	$400	$411
Vacancy rate 2000	0.07	0.08	0.09	0.09	0.11	0.10
Rental rate 2000	0.48	0.38	0.32	0.29	0.67	0.61
Median HH income 2000 (in 00$)	$29,191	$35,652	$35,793	$41,994	$23,092	$24,729
Median HH income 2010 (in 00$)	$28,353	$32,139	$34,316	$40,060	$19,684	$20,422
Percentage change median HH income	−0.03	−0.10	−0.04	−0.05	−0.16	−0.16
Population 2000	35,690	23,203	103,793	281,421,906	11,541	5,560
Population 2010	36,592	23,055	107,702	308,745,538	12,459	5,383
Percentage change population 2000–2010	0.02	−0.01	0.04	0.09	0.07	−0.03
Percent white 2000	0.96	0.97	0.97	0.75	0.94	0.95
Percent white 2010	0.87	0.94	0.93	0.72	0.73	0.93
Average white percentage change 2000–2010	−0.07	−0.04	−0.01	0.06	−0.05	−0.06
Percent black 2000	0.01	0.01	0.01	0.12	0.02	0.01
Percent black 2010	0.09	0.02	0.04	0.13	0.22	0.02
Average black percentage change 2000–2010	7.29	3.16	4.76	0.12	77.62	1.04

Source: US Census 2000, 2010; for 2010 median household income, American Community Survey five-year estimates.

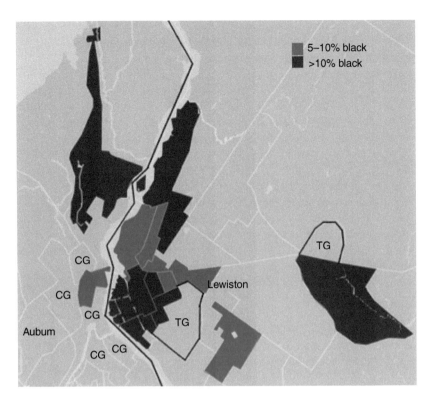

Figure 4.1 Lewiston-Auburn neighborhood treatment and comparison groups.

Note: The treatment group consists of the census block groups with greater than 10 percent black population in 2010 and the additional regions labelled "TG," which were part of these census block groups under the 2000 block group definitions used in the SCCS data. The comparison group consists of the census block groups labelled "CG." Map generated using Social Explorer, drawing on US Census 2010 data.

conduct placebo tests comparing the ten other samples in the 2000 and 2006 survey to the national sample. In so doing, I evaluate whether AC experienced unique changes in social capital with respect to the nation following the Somalis' arrival, or whether other samples experienced similar changes over this period.

Finally, analyses at the municipal and regional level may obscure changes in social capital occurring at a more micro level in Lewiston-Auburn's neighborhoods. Thus, I compare social capital change in neighborhoods that experienced high levels of Somali settlement to those that did not. In order to identify neighborhoods of concentrated Somali settlement, I rely on the proportion of blacks reported in the 2010 US Census data.[3] According to the 2010 Census, nearly three-quarters of Lewiston-Auburn's black population is clustered in seven of the towns' 42 census block groups, which each have a black population of greater than

10 percent.[4] As Figure 4.1 displays, six of these seven block groups are located in Lewiston, to the right of the jagged black line representing the Androscoggin River; one is located in Auburn, just to the northwest of the river's border with Lewiston. I classify these seven block groups as those with concentrated Somali settlement. Drawing on fieldwork and demographic analysis that reveals why the Somalis chose to settle in the concentrated block groups, I identify comparison census block groups that fall within the range of the concentrated block groups along three dimensions: median monthly rent, proportion rental housing, and housing vacancy rate. Comparison block groups must also be less than 5 percent black in 2010, having experienced no notable change in racial diversity from 2000 to 2010.[5]

As Figure 4.1 displays, these characteristics apply to five block groups in Auburn's downtown, identified with "CG" (for comparison group) on the map. As Table 4.2 displays, on average, this comparison group is remarkably similar to the concentrated block groups, save for the latter's marked increase in black population over this time period. As Table 4.1 attests, in t-tests the concentrated block groups had no significant pre-existing differences in social capital, save for a higher level of interracial friendships in the concentrated block groups prior to the Somalis' arrival. Table 4.1 also demonstrates that at the neighborhood level, sample sizes are quite small. Across the two waves of the survey, the sample of long-term white residents in the concentrated block groups is 67, with 48 in the comparison block groups.[6]

Variables and method of analysis

I focus my analysis on three sets of dependent variables; namely, those that measure interracial trust, intraracial trust, and interracial friendship. In terms of interracial trust, I consider anti-immigrant sentiment, using a question on whether respondents agree that "immigrants are getting too demanding in their push for equal rights." Response categories range from "disagree strongly" to "agree strongly." I also employ a question asking the respondent "how much you trust" blacks, with four response categories ranging from trust "a lot" to "not at all." In terms of intraracial trust, I employ one similar question asking how much the respondent trusts whites. In response to ongoing debates about appropriate trust measures (Uslaner, 2010; Sturgis and Smith, 2010; Torpe and Lolle, 2011), I analyze three measures, including trust in neighbors, generalized social trust, and perceived likelihood of community collective action.[7] Finally, in terms of interracial friendship, I examine an index consisting of the number of types of interracial ties the respondent has, ranging from zero (no interracial ties) to three (interracial ties with at least one black, Asian, and Hispanic friend). The count of interracial ties measures "racial exposure (or isolation) in friendships" and not the full extent or intensity of interracial relationships within the respondent's network (De Souza Briggs, 2007: 264).

In all of my analyses, I control for a range of variables that are widely considered to be determinants of social capital and are used in Putnam's (2007) models. At the individual level, I control for gender, age, education, income, homeownership, and length of residence in the community. When comparing the Lewiston area to the national sample, I also control for contextual variables associated with social capital, including the following census tract level variables from the year 2000: population density, percent in same town as five years earlier, percent Bachelor's degree, poverty rate, Herfindahl index of diversity,[8] Gini index of inequality, average commute time, percent renters, and percent citizens.[9] Finally, in comparisons with the national sample and placebo tests, I include a variable corresponding to whether the respondent took the survey after the US public was widely aware of the 2006 immigration rallies. As Hopkins (2010) has demonstrated, the increased salience of immigration over this period contributed to rising anti-immigrant sentiment, particularly in places experiencing immigrant population growth.[10]

To identify differential changes in social capital over this period, I employ a difference-in-difference technique for non-longitudinal data. To identify changes over time, I generated a variable called "wave," which is equal to one when the observation is from 2006. When statistically significant, the coefficient on wave can be interpreted as the change in the dependent variable associated with being a respondent in 2006 as opposed to 2000, controlling for the other explanatory variables. At each level of geographic scale, I interact "wave" with a variable indicating whether the respondent is a resident of the relevant "treatment" group, whether Lewiston at the municipal level, AC at the regional level, or the diverse block groups at the neighborhood level. The interactive variable can be interpreted as the differential effect of being a resident of the treatment group in 2006 as opposed to 2000, holding all else constant. In this way, the interactive variable identifies cases in which the treatment group has experienced a different social capital trajectory over the period. For continuous dependent variables, I use ordinary least squares; for binary dependent variables, I use probit; and for count dependent variables, I employ poisson regression.[11] Regression results for all levels of analysis are presented in the Appendix.

Findings

Following Putnam (2007) and others, I predict that a rapid increase in racial diversity in Lewiston will result in declines in inter- and intraracial trust, as well as increases in interracial friendships that can be attributed to increased opportunity for contact. As a first step toward understanding whether social capital indeed changed in response to the Somali migration, I first analyze changes in Lewiston over time, followed by analyses at the municipal, regional, and neighborhood levels.

Changes in Lewiston over time

As Table 4.3 demonstrates, being a resident of Lewiston in 2006 as opposed to 2000 is associated with lower levels of generalized social trust, increased anti-immigrant sentiment, and increases in interracial friendships (holding gender, age,

Table 4.3 Lewiston social capital change 2000–2006.

	2000	2006	Difference
Proportion agreeing strongly that immigrants too demanding	0.14	0.31	0.17***
Proportion agreeing most people can be trusted	0.57	0.42	−0.15**
Expected number of interracial friendships	0.74	1.10	0.36***

* p < 0.10, ** p < 0.05, *** p < 0.01

years of education, income, homeownership, and years of local residence at their means). For instance, all else constant, residence in Lewiston in 2006 is associated with a 15 percentage point decline in the likelihood of agreeing "most people can be trusted" and a 17 percentage point increase in the likelihood of agreeing that "immigrants have grown too demanding." On the other hand, residence in Lewiston in 2006 is also associated with increases in interracial friendship, including an increase of 0.36 interracial ties on the scale from zero to three. Analysis of Lewiston's social capital over time reveals some changes following the Somalis' arrival, but are these variations unique to Lewiston, given its increase in racial diversity?

Municipal level analysis

As compared to Auburn, Lewiston experienced few differential changes in social capital from 2000 to 2006. All else constant, the only marginally statistically significant change ($p = 0.07$) is that being a Lewiston resident in 2006 is associated with a 12 percentage point differential increase in the likelihood that the respondent strongly agrees that immigrants are growing too demanding. At the municipal level, we do not see evidence of declining social capital. Perhaps, however, a "treatment" of diversity operates at a broader geographic scale and comparing Lewiston to Auburn masks changes in social capital occurring throughout the local region.

Regional level analysis

At the regional level, Androscoggin County experienced few differential changes in social capital compared to the nation over this period. All else constant, residents of AC experienced a 7 percentage point differential increase in the likelihood of agreeing strongly that immigrants were too demanding. Other forms of inter- and intragroup trust did not experience differential declines. On the other hand, AC residents in 2006 did display a differential increase in interracial friendship, amounting to 0.22 additional interracial ties, on average. It is tempting to assume that these processes are related to the demographic shock of the Somali arrival, but to be confident in that assertion I need to show these differential changes were unique to AC and not evident in other samples from the SCCS.[12] Figure 4.2

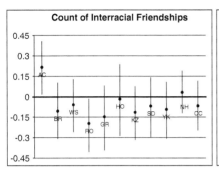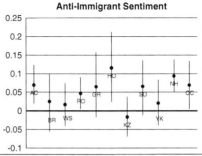

Figure 4.2 Differential change in social capital in Androscoggin County compared to the nation and ten placebo tests.

Note: Predicted differential change associated with being a resident of the sample in 2006, as compared to the nation. AC = Androscoggin County; BR = Baton Rouge, Louisiana; WS = Winston-Salem, North Carolina; RO = Rochester, New York; GR = Greensboro, North Carolina; HO = Houston, Texas; KZ = Kalamazoo, Michigan; SD = San Diego, California; YK = Yakima, Washington; NH = New Hampshire; CC = Cheshire County, NH.

presents the predicted differential change in anti-immigrant sentiment and interracial friendships associated with being a resident of each sample in 2006, as compared to the national sample, all else constant.

As the right-hand panel of Figure 4.2 demonstrates, differential increases in anti-immigrant sentiment are not unique to AC. Rochester (RO) and Houston (HO) also experienced differential increases in anti-immigrant sentiment as compared to the nation over this period, as did New Hampshire (NH) and Cheshire County within NH (CC), although these last two samples were fielded entirely in the post-immigration rally period. While AC experienced the greatest percent change in its ethnic and racial minority population between 2000 and 2010, Rochester's Monroe County experienced the least, and Houston's Harris County ranks fifth among the 11 samples. Given this pattern, it would be difficult to attribute the differential increase in AC wholly to the Somali migration. In terms of interracial friendships, however, the left-hand panel of Figure 4.2 demonstrates that AC's pattern of change as compared to the nation was entirely unique. None of the other 2000–2006 SCCS samples experienced a statistically significant differential increase in interracial friendships, with most experiencing directional differential declines.

While AC's increase in interracial friendship is unique, is it simply a matter of increased opportunity for contact? If so, we would expect the actual increase in the rate of interracial friendship to be no greater than the increase predicted randomly, given the increase in the out-group tie pool. De Souza Briggs' (2007) "random choice model of friendship selection" specifies that the probability of choosing at least one out-group friend can be calculated by the formula $1 - (1 - p)^N$, where p corresponds to the out-group proportion in the given context and N corresponds to the friendship network size. I set N to equal six, the average number of friends in the AC sample. Given AC's 2 percent ethnic/racial minority population in 2000, a random choice model would predict an 11 percent likelihood of having an interracial friend. In actuality, 51 percent of AC residents report an interracial friendship, a 40 percentage point difference. By 2006, when the AC ethnic/racial minority population amounts to six percent, a random choice model would predict a 31 percent likelihood of having an interracial friend. In reality, 63 percent of AC residents report an interracial tie. Given the 4 percentage point increase in ethnic minority population in Lewiston between 2000 and 2006, we would expect to see a 20 percentage point increase in the likelihood of having one interracial friend based on a random draw. In fact, we see a 12 percentage point increase in the likelihood of having one interracial friend. The increase is smaller than what a random opportunity model would predict, but levels of interracial friendship in AC far exceed predicted levels to begin with and increase even further in the presence of greater diversity. All the same, the increase in interracial friendships in AC over this period should not be interpreted as a flowering of interracial harmony, as the increase could be attributed to increased opportunity for contact.

In sum, five years after the Somalis' arrival in Lewiston, I find little evidence of broad-based change in social capital when comparing the town to a neighboring town or the county to areas elsewhere in the United States. It remains possible, however, that the neighborhoods where Somalis concentrated experienced changes in social capital that were obscured in analyses at the municipal and regional level. Thus, I next consider social capital change in neighborhoods of concentrated Somali settlement, as compared to similar neighborhoods that did not experience substantial changes in racial diversity over this period.

Neighborhood-level analysis

Looking first at the average levels of social capital in the concentrated and comparison block groups before and after the arrival of the Somali population, we see a striking pattern in Table 4.1. In 2000, the diverse neighborhoods were at least marginally greater in terms of social capital, save for slightly lower trust in blacks and higher anti-immigrant sentiment. In 2006, the relationship almost entirely reverses. While there are few statistically significant differences in simple post-treatment t-tests, average levels of social capital in the comparison group now exceed levels of social capital in the diverse neighborhoods on almost all measures.

In multivariate analyses, I find that living in the diverse neighborhoods in 2006 is associated with directional declines in interracial trust, intraracial trust, trust in neighbors, and generalized social trust, as well as statistically significant declines in perceptions of the likelihood of community cooperation and the number of interracial friendships. In its first panel, Figure 4.3 displays the predicted probability of saying that neighbors are very likely to cooperate to conserve resources across the two settings in 2000 and 2006. All else constant, living in a concentrated block group in 2006 is associated with a remarkable 41 percentage point differential

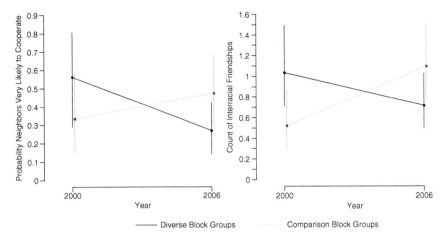

Figure 4.3 Predicted change in social capital in diverse and comparison neighborhoods, 2000–2006.

decline in the likelihood of saying that neighbors are very likely to cooperate (*p* = .04). In its second panel, Figure 4.3 illustrates the predicted count of the types of interracial friendships (a zero to three scale) across the two settings in 2000 and 2006. Holding other variables at their means, being a 2006 respondent in a diverse neighborhood is associated with a differential decline in interracial friendships of 1.65 (*p* = .01), despite the fact that these neighborhoods have the greatest opportunity for interracial contact.[13]

Of course, sample sizes are quite small here and results only rise to the level of statistical significance for two of seven dependent variables. Thus, I momentarily set aside the natural experiment design to instead look across all of Lewiston-Auburn at how the percentage of blacks in each block group in 2010 affects change in social capital. I find that a larger black population is associated with statistically significant differential declines in terms of interracial trust, intraracial trust, and all other trust measures, as well as statistically significant differential declines in interracial friendships (in all statistically significant declines in all the dependent variables, save for anti-immigrant sentiment).[14] This analysis, examining the full sample across the two towns, is less conducive to making causal claims than the preceding natural experiment design. Nonetheless, in combination, these two analyses suggest that long-term, white residents living in areas of concentrated Somali settlement experienced declines in trust and interracial friendship following the arrival of the Somali population.

The results with respect to interracial friendships are particularly robust and striking. The regional analysis demonstrates that residents of AC as a whole experienced differential increases in interracial friendships, which may be attributed to increased opportunity for contact. On the other hand, if we compare those living in highly diverse neighborhoods to those living in the otherwise similar neighborhoods that did not diversify, those in the diverse neighborhoods experienced substantial differential declines. Figure 4.4 illustrates the actual change

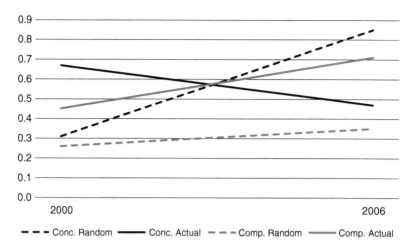

Figure 4.4 Change in interracial ties predicted by random model, versus actual change in concentrated and comparison block groups.

Note: "Conc." = Concentrated, "Comp." = Comparison.

in the likelihood of having one non-white friend in the diverse neighborhoods as compared to the predicted change given a random model of friendship selection. For residents of the diverse neighborhoods, where opportunity for contact with new Somali residents was greatest, the random model of friendship selection predicts a 54 percentage point increase in the likelihood of having at least one interracial friendship. Despite the increased opportunity for contact, residents of the diverse neighborhoods reported a 20 percentage point decline in the likelihood of having one interracial friendship. In contrast, residents of the comparison neighborhoods reported an increase in the likelihood of interracial friendships that exceeded the level predicted by the random model. Whereas the random model would have predicted a 9 percentage point increase in the likelihood of having an interracial friendship, residents of the comparison group experienced a 26 percentage point increase. Although some evidence suggests that interracial friendships may moderate the negative effect of diversity on social capital (Stolle *et al.*, 2008; Laurence, 2009), findings from Lewiston suggest that those who live in neighborhoods experiencing rapid diversification are less likely to form such friendships. Interestingly, however, those in nearby neighborhoods, including those only just across the river in Auburn, experience an increased likelihood of interracial friendship.

Recent studies have argued that some or even all of the relationship between racial diversity and declining social capital can be explained by socio-economic disadvantage in racially diverse areas (Laurence, 2009; Letki, 2008). Yet the more marked declines in social capital in the neighborhoods that experienced concentrated Somali settlement cannot be attributed to socio-economic status. First, in Lewiston and Androscoggin County as a whole, I find no interaction between individual level socio-economic status and changing levels of social capital following the Somalis' arrival. Second, the comparison group for the diverse neighborhoods was selected to have similar aggregate socio-economic characteristics prior to the Somalis' arrival, such that the diverse neighborhoods were not an area of distinct socio-economic disadvantage. Finally, between the 2000 and 2010 censuses, both areas experienced declining socio-economic status, but only the concentrated neighborhoods experienced increases in racial diversity and declines in social capital.

Discussion

Drawing on the findings of Putnam (2007) and others, I predicted that following the arrival of a substantial Somali population in previously homogeneous Lewiston, the area would experience declines in its levels of inter- and intraracial trust, and an increase in interracial friendship. To better understand the mechanisms through which diversity affects social capital, I analyzed changes at the municipal, regional, and neighborhood level. At the municipal and regional level, I find few changes in social capital unique to the Lewiston area. In placebo tests, the only unique change in Androscoggin County is a marked increase in interracial friendships. Given the substantial increase in racial diversity in the county over this period, the actual increase in interracial ties does not exceed what a random model would predict. At the county level, interracial friendships are forming, but these ties could be a sign of increased opportunity for contact, rather than necessarily increased interracial harmony.

At the neighborhood level, however, the picture is substantially different. The neighborhoods with the most concentrated Somali settlement experienced differential declines in the perceived likelihood of neighborhood cooperation, as compared to similar neighborhoods that did not diversify. Moreover, in contrast to the countywide increases in interracial friendship, diverse neighborhoods experienced substantial differential declines. The sample sizes at the neighborhood level of analysis are quite small, but an analysis of the full sample in Lewiston-Auburn provides additional support. Living in a block group that experienced higher levels of black settlement over this period is associated with statistically significant differential declines in six of the seven inter- and intraracial trust and friendship variables.

Taken as a whole, these results both challenge and support findings linking diversity and declining social capital. On the one hand, reviews of the literature suggested that the Somali migration to Lewiston presented a scenario in which social capital was especially likely to decline, given the high salience of ethnic boundaries as a racially, religiously, linguistically, and culturally distinct group arrived in a previously homogeneous white destination. Despite these predictions, at the municipal and regional level we see essentially no relationship between increasing diversity and declining social capital. Since previous studies have found social capital declines amid diversity at these geographic scales, declines at this level may only become visible over a longer span than five years. Alternatively, perhaps the relationship between diversity and social capital is only activated at a higher threshold of diversity than was present in Lewiston or AC as a whole.

On the other hand, reviews suggested that the strongest negative relationship between diversity and social capital was often found at the neighborhood level, as the evidence from Lewiston underscores. These findings provide suggestive evidence about which mechanisms may underpin the relationship between diversity and social capital. If we had seen declines in social capital primarily at the municipal or regional level where goods are distributed, it would have provided support for the out-group biases and divergent preferences mechanisms. Instead, the findings of declining social capital at the neighborhood level provide support for mechanisms that operate at the level of face-to-face contact, namely the coordination problems and social control mechanisms. In a previously homogeneous city that experienced a recent, rapid demographic shock, social capital appears to decline in response to challenges associated with face-to-face contact amid increasing diversity.

The findings also speak to the role of interracial contact in the relationship between diversity and social capital. Stolle *et al.* (2008) argue that, while contextual diversity generally has negative effects on trust, these effects are mitigated by intergroup interactions. The example of Lewiston suggests that interracial bridges are less likely to form among residents of rapidly diversifying neighborhoods, but more likely to form among residents of nearby neighborhoods that are not directly experiencing increasing racial diversity. These findings are actually consonant with Gordon Allport's (1954) contact theory, which argued that interracial contact could result in harmony only in the presence of stringent conditions, including that groups possesses similar status and work toward a shared goal. "Sheer" contact, Allport (1954: 263) wrote, "does not dispel prejudice; it seems more likely to increase it." Those slightly removed from changing racial diversity in Lewiston, can choose the extent of their exposure. The circumstances in which they encounter diversity may thus more closely fit the conditions of the contact theory. Those at the center of changes in racial diversity, however, do not get to choose their level of interaction. They navigate difference on a day-to-day basis and, at least in the short-term, they find that contact induces, if not outright animosity, still not harmony and friendship. Qualitative evidence from Lewiston provides further support for the idea that the initial valence of conflict in rapidly diversifying neighborhoods is negative. Informants spoke of fights among neighbors about different tolerance of noise and contrasting sexual mores in which disagreements quickly become attributed to race.

In combination, these findings suggest important directions for research and policy. First, the findings suggest that geographic scale shapes the impact of diversity on inter- and intragroup relations, a question that warrants further analysis beyond Lewiston. Second, the findings raise the question of the timeframe in which diversity affects social capital. Over time would contacts at the neighborhood level become more positive, while concerns beyond the neighborhood became more prevalent? If this pattern of findings proved robust to other settings and longer timeframes, it suggests that policy interventions should be aimed at facilitating positive contact at the neighborhood level in order to alleviate the challenges of cross-cultural communication.

Appendix

Asterisks in all appendix tables indicate the following p-values: $* p < 0.10$, $** p < 0.05$, $*** p < 0.01$.

Table 4.A1 Lewiston over time.

	Trust blacks	Anti-immigrant sentiment	Trust whites	Trust neighbors	General social trust	Cooperate with neighbors	Number interracial ties (0–3)
Model	oprobit	oprobit	oprobit	oprobit	probit	oprobit	poisson
Wave (2006=1)	-0.175	0.610***	-0.007	-0.214	-0.404**	0.113	0.355***
	(0.165)	(0.157)	(0.168)	(0.173)	(0.178)	(0.177)	(0.127)
Gender (Female=1)	0.075	-0.218	0.075	-0.095	-0.071	-0.175	-0.213
	(0.169)	(0.151)	(0.164)	(0.162)	(0.173)	(0.177)	(0.134)
Age	0.021***	0.002	0.022***	0.022***	0.008	0.011*	-0.003
	(0.006)	(0.005)	(0.006)	(0.006)	(0.006)	(0.007)	(0.004)
Years of Education	0.049	-0.127***	0.054	0.092***	0.122***	0.048	0.078***
	(0.033)	(0.033)	(0.034)	(0.034)	(0.040)	(0.038)	(0.027)
Income	0.000	0.000**	0.000	0.000	0.000**	0.000	0.000
	(0.000)	(0.000)	(0.000)	(0.000)	(0.000)	(0.000)	(0.000)
Homeownership (=1)	0.006	0.339*	-0.004	0.695***	-0.019	0.123	-0.349**
	(0.185)	(0.176)	(0.183)	(0.173)	(0.199)	(0.198)	(0.144)
Length of residence	-0.096	0.108	-0.151	-0.193**	-0.073	0.085	-0.085
	(0.090)	(0.080)	(0.092)	(0.089)	(0.092)	(0.098)	(0.065)
Constant / Cut 1	-0.614	-1.784	-0.981	-0.101	-1.781**	-0.310	0.548
	(0.598)	(0.611)	(0.588)	(0.636)	(0.694)	(0.684)	(0.484)
Cut 2	-0.155	-0.976	-0.505	0.501		0.340	
	(0.621)	(0.603)	(0.605)	(0.658)		(0.699)	
Cut 3	1.635	-0.867	1.464	1.655		0.373	
	(0.632)	(0.601)	(0.619)	(0.668)		(0.702)	
Cut 4		-0.138				2.041	
		(0.601)				(0.718)	
R-squared	0.049	0.061	0.053	0.118	0.092	0.030	0.109

Table 4.A2 Municipal comparison: Lewiston and Auburn.

Model	Trust blacks	Anti-immigrant sentiment	Trust whites	Trust neighbors	General social trust	Cooperate with neighbors	Number interracial ties (0–3)
	oprobit	oprobit	oprobit	oprobit	probit	oprobit	poisson
Lewiston*Wave	0.116	0.401*	0.176	-0.193	-0.132	0.028	-0.203
	(0.247)	(0.218)	(0.248)	(0.237)	(0.255)	(0.267)	(0.227)
Lewiston	-0.181	-0.038	-0.242	0.249	-0.134	-0.161	0.113
	(0.191)	(0.156)	(0.193)	(0.179)	(0.185)	(0.215)	(0.194)
Wave (2006=1)	-0.209	0.116	-0.108	0.011	-0.162	-0.003	0.588***
	(0.192)	(0.166)	(0.195)	(0.174)	(0.196)	(0.201)	(0.178)
Gender (Female=1)	-0.077	-0.096	-0.061	0.029	-0.188	-0.031	-0.141
	(0.123)	(0.111)	(0.122)	(0.118)	(0.130)	(0.131)	(0.102)
Age	0.011***	0.006*	0.013***	0.019***	0.000	0.011**	-0.006*
	(0.004)	(0.004)	(0.004)	(0.004)	(0.004)	(0.004)	(0.003)
Years of education	0.048*	-0.125***	0.045*	0.105***	0.140***	0.035	0.065***
	(0.024)	(0.024)	(0.025)	(0.026)	(0.029)	(0.027)	(0.021)
Income	0.000	0.000	0.000	0.000	0.000	0.000	0.000**
	(0.000)	(0.000)	(0.000)	(0.000)	(0.000)	(0.000)	(0.000)
Homeownership (=1)	0.001	0.183	-0.040	0.644***	-0.074	0.157	-0.300**
	(0.141)	(0.132)	(0.139)	(0.131)	(0.150)	(0.149)	(0.116)
Length of residence	-0.031	0.007	-0.032	-0.099*	0.035	-0.031	-0.022
	(0.060)	(0.057)	(0.061)	(0.058)	(0.066)	(0.066)	(0.049)
Constant / Cut 1	-1.032	-1.908	-1.193	0.601	-1.743***	-0.963	-0.795**
	(0.455)	(0.456)	(0.463)	(0.472)	(0.521)	(0.560)	(0.402)
Cut 2	-0.651	-1.122	-0.773	1.263		-0.424	
	(0.461)	(0.449)	(0.462)	(0.478)		(0.558)	
Cut 3	1.099	-1.009	1.096	2.456		-0.361	
	(0.455)	(0.447)	(0.455)	(0.490)		(0.556)	
Cut 4		-0.293				1.292	
		(0.444)				(0.550)	
R-Squared	0.021	0.043	0.025	0.106	0.079	0.029	0.049

	Trust blacks	Anti-immigrant sentiment	Trust whites	Trust neighbors	General social trust	Cooperate with neighbors	Number interracial ties (0–3)
Model	oprobit	oprobit	oprobit	oprobit	probit	oprobit	poisson
Androscoggin*Wave	−0.194	0.244***	0.011	0.007	0.004	0.045	0.187**
	(0.129)	(0.093)	(0.118)	(0.100)	(0.120)	(0.123)	(0.090)
Androscoggin County	0.382***	−0.259***	0.222**	0.019	0.055	−0.133	−0.278***
	(0.092)	(0.075)	(0.093)	(0.079)	(0.071)	(0.099)	(0.073)
Wave (2006=1)	0.103*	0.170***	0.064	−0.017	−0.104*	−0.084	0.142***
	(0.055)	(0.050)	(0.056)	(0.056)	(0.059)	(0.064)	(0.034)
Gender (Female=1)	0.106**	−0.098**	0.093**	0.123***	0.009	0.148***	−0.074**
	(0.043)	(0.040)	(0.044)	(0.044)	(0.047)	(0.048)	(0.029)
Age	0.011***	0.007***	0.013***	0.012***	0.006***	0.011***	−0.005***
	(0.002)	(0.001)	(0.002)	(0.002)	(0.002)	(0.002)	(0.001)
Years of education	0.042***	−0.111***	0.025***	0.062***	0.092***	0.026**	0.042***
	(0.009)	(−0.009)	(0.009)	(0.010)	(0.010)	(0.011)	(0.006)
Income	0.000**	0.000	0.000***	0.000***	0.000***	0.000	0.000***
	(0.000)	(0.000)	(0.000)	(0.000)	(0.000)	(0.000)	(0.000)
Homeownership (=1)	0.028	0.087	0.102	0.385***	0.073	0.143*	−0.074*
	(0.063)	(0.060)	(0.063)	(0.058)	(0.070)	(0.078)	(0.044)
Length of residence	−0.004	0.050**	0.042*	0.030	0.020	−0.054*	−0.035**
	(0.023)	(0.024)	(0.025)	(0.024)	(0.024)	(0.031)	(0.016)
Post-rally (= 1)	−0.098	0.213***	−0.109*	−0.079	−0.072	−0.041	−0.032
	(0.066)	(0.067)	(0.066)	(0.068)	(0.072)	(0.065)	(0.041)
Constant / Cut 1	−0.751	−2.081	−0.397	0.536	−3.091***	−0.742	1.266***
	(0.695)	(0.626)	(0.677)	(0.624)	(0.668)	(0.725)	(0.330)
Cut 2	0.040	−1.236	0.430	1.197		−0.191	
	(0.689)	(0.625)	(0.667)	(0.623)		(0.723)	
Cut 3	1.931	−1.136	2.300	2.358		−0.127	
	(0.689)	(0.625)	(0.668)	(0.624)		(0.722)	
Cut 4	0.030	−0.449				1.526	
		(0.625)				(0.721)	
R-Squared	0.030	0.044	0.033	0.062	0.055	0.024	

Note: Each regression includes census tract level contextual controls for population density, percent in same town as five years earlier, percent Bachelor's degree, poverty rate, a Herfindahl index of diversity, Gini index of inequality, average commute time, percent renters, and percent citizens.

Table 4.A4 Neighborhood comparison: concentrated block groups and comparison block groups.

	Trust blacks	Anti-immigrant sentiment	Trust whites	Trust neighbors	General social trust	Cooperate with neighbors	Number interracial ties (0–3)
Model	oprobit	oprobit	oprobit	oprobit	probit	oprobit	poisson
Concentrated*Wave	0.079	0.258	-0.259	-0.258	-0.325	-1.172**	-1.131***
	(0.537)	(0.478)	(0.550)	(0.516)	(0.543)	(0.581)	(0.423)
Conc. block group	-0.378	-0.090	0.048	0.600	0.122	0.629	0.712**
	(0.423)	(0.303)	(0.392)	(0.403)	(0.393)	(0.475)	(0.350)
Wave (2006=1)	-0.987**	0.282	-0.370	-0.452	-0.392	0.376	0.756**
	(0.419)	(0.385)	(0.392)	(0.403)	(0.406)	(0.409)	(0.329)
Gender (Female=1)	-0.508	0.003	-0.447	0.125	-0.615**	0.118	-0.209
	(0.332)	(0.250)	(0.294)	(0.270)	(0.295)	(0.285)	(0.226)
Age	0.019**	-0.008	0.026***	0.038***	0.011	0.021**	0.004
	(0.009)	(0.008)	(0.010)	(0.009)	(0.010)	(0.009)	(0.006)
Years of education	0.127*	-0.154***	0.085	0.120*	0.293***	0.022	0.047
	(0.069)	(0.057)	(0.066)	(0.062)	(0.069)	(0.064)	(0.045)
Income	0.000	0.000	0.000	0.000***	0.000	0.000	0.000
	(0.000)	(0.000)	(0.000)	(0.000)	(0.000)	(0.000)	(0.000)
Homeownership (=1)	-0.238	0.372	-0.393	0.101	-0.483	0.397	-0.124
	(0.346)	(0.282)	(0.327)	(0.319)	(0.338)	(0.359)	(0.251)
Length of residence	0.002	0.153	0.038	-0.284**	0.044	-0.093	-0.133
	(0.121)	(0.108)	(0.127)	(0.117)	(0.132)	(0.126)	(0.095)
Constant / Cut 1	-1.007	-2.227	-0.811	0.589	-3.471***	-0.477	-0.852
	(1.080)	(0.890)	(1.020)	(0.960)	(0.989)	(1.124)	(0.710)
Cut 2	-0.491	-1.436	1.993	1.573		-0.352	
	(1.008)	(0.873)	(0.983)	(0.933)		(1.137)	
Cut 3	1.637	-1.352		3.002		-0.243	
	(1.045)	(0.872)		(0.943)		(1.133)	
Cut 4		-0.672				1.676	
		(0.861)				(1.109)	
R-Squared	0.119	0.049	0.094	0.185	0.161	0.073	0.055

Table 4.A5 Effect of 2010 percent block group black on social capital indicators.

Model	Trust blacks	Anti-immigrant sentiment	Trust whites	Trust neighbors	General social trust	Cooperate with neighbors	Number interracial ties (0–3)
	oprobit	oprobit	oprobit	oprobit	probit	oprobit	poisson
Percent black 2010*Wave	-3.338***	0.764	-2.113**	-2.593***	-3.463**	-2.506***	-2.323**
	(0.666)	(0.733)	(0.999)	(0.684)	(1.440)	(0.954)	(0.897)
Percent black 2010	1.407*	0.306	2.241***	1.688**	1.621*	1.294	1.313**
	(0.745)	(1.291)	(0.786)	(0.735)	(0.949)	(1.313)	(0.600)
Wave (2006=1)	-0.042	0.433***	0.077	0.049	-0.030	0.034	0.403***
	(0.125)	(0.091)	(0.134)	(0.095)	(0.118)	(0.119)	(0.095)
Gender (Female=1)	-0.036	-0.106	-0.034	0.013	-0.193**	0.069	-0.159*
	(0.099)	(0.091)	(0.099)	(0.090)	(0.098)	(0.097)	(0.090)
Age	0.012***	0.006**	0.017***	0.014***	0.002	0.010***	-0.007***
	(0.004)	(0.003)	(0.004)	(0.005)	(0.004)	(0.003)	(0.002)
Years of education	0.039**	-0.120***	0.030*	0.095***	0.129***	0.049**	0.049***
	(0.018)	(0.021)	(0.018)	(0.026)	(0.024)	(0.021)	(0.016)
Income	0.000	0.000	0.000	0.000	0.000	0.000	0.000**
	(0.000)	(0.000)	(0.000)	(0.000)	(0.000)	(0.000)	(0.000)
Homeownership (=1)	0.049	0.189*	0.047	0.464***	0.008	0.099	-0.165
	(0.113)	(0.111)	(0.120)	(0.096)	(0.116)	(0.170)	(0.104)
Length of residence	-0.043	0.044	-0.048	-0.043	0.026	-0.025	-0.043
	(0.043)	(0.050)	(0.050)	(0.046)	(0.048)	(0.062)	(0.042)
Median HH income 2000	0.000	0.000	0.000	0.000***	0.000	0.000	0.000
	(0.000)	(0.000)	(0.000)	(0.000)	(0.000)	(0.000)	(0.000)
% change med. HH income	-0.052	-0.358	0.131	0.517*	-0.071	-0.196	0.025
	(0.274)	(0.304)	(0.290)	(0.311)	(0.296)	(0.280)	(0.276)
Constant / Cut 1	-1.048	-1.705	-0.963	0.823	-1.991***	-0.510	-0.255
	(0.374)	(0.330)	(0.354)	(0.434)	(0.433)	(0.412)	(0.392)
Cut 2	-0.596	-0.930	-0.501	1.412		0.010	
	(0.382)	(0.322)	(0.360)	(0.439)		(0.392)	

Table 4.A5 (cont.)

	Trust blacks	Anti-immigrant sentiment	Trust whites	Trust neighbors	General social trust	Cooperate with neighbors	Number interracial ties (0–3)
Cut 3	1.163	−0.833	1.440	2.632		0.051	
	(0.370)	(0.321)	(0.340)	(0.464)		(0.391)	
Cut 4		−0.093				1.596	
		(0.317)				(0.386)	
R-squared	0.027	0.046	0.033	0.095	0.073	0.028	

Notes

1 Respondents were recruited via random-digit dialing achieving an overall AAPOR RR3 response rate of 27.4 percent in 2000 and 19.3 percent in 2006. The AAPOR RR3 response rate in the Androscoggin County sample was 26.8 in 2000 and 25.4 in 2006.

2 Among the ten other samples in the 2000 and 2006 SCCS, most are rejected because of regional differences or because they were not racially homogeneous in 2000. Cheshire County, New Hampshire remains a plausible comparison group, although it cannot be considered entirely "untreated" by diversity over this period, with a doubling of its racial and ethnic minority population over this period to comprise 3 percent of the county. Analysis comparing AC and Cheshire County finds no differential changes in social capital in AC over this period. I do not present these results since, as I shall discuss below, the timing of the interviews in New Hampshire compromises their comparability. Nearly all 2006 interviews in AC occurred before the 2006 immigration rallies and all 2006 New Hampshire interviews occurred in the post-rally period.

3 While not all blacks in the area are Somalis, municipal estimates of the population suggest that roughly 95 percent of local blacks are Somali and not native-parentage African-American (Cullen, 2011).

4 The second wave of the SCCS took place in 2006, so the 2010 data will not perfectly represent the Somali settlement patterns in 2006. Fieldwork in Lewiston suggests that Somali settlement patterns within the region did not change in any notable way from 2006 to 2010.

5 Survey respondents are classified by their 2000 census block location, but 2010 block definitions do not differ markedly. Mapping the 2010 proportion black onto the 2000 block definitions includes some residents in the "treatment" group (in the areas labelled "TG" on Figure 4.1) that actually live amid lower levels of diversity, thus understating the effect of diversity on social capital.

6 All of the comparison neighborhoods are in Auburn, while most of the "treatment" neighborhoods are in Lewiston, raising the possibility that the changes in social capital are the result of municipal residence rather than changing levels of racial diversity. To address this possibility, I conduct additional analyses described below that allow me to probe neighborhood-level change independent of municipal residence.

7 The first asks to what extent the respondent trusts "people in your neighborhood." The canonical "generalized trust" question asks "Would you say that most people can be trusted or that you can't be too careful?" The collective action question reads: "If public officials asked everyone to conserve water or electricity because of some emergency, how likely is it that people in your community would cooperate?" Five response categories range from "very unlikely" to "very likely."

8 Controlling for the year 2000 Herfindahl index allows me to hold constant the effect of baseline diversity on social capital across the different settings, while an interactive variable indicating that the respondent is a resident of AC in 2006 aims to capture the effect of change in diversity resulting from the Somali migration. Including or omitting the Herfindahl index from analyses does not alter the results.

9 To address methodological issues resulting from analyzing variables at the individual and census tract level, I employ clustered standard errors (see Primo *et al.*, 2007).

10 In Lewiston-Auburn, only 14 of 246 interviews took place after news of the rallies broke on the national scene. At the municipal and neighborhood levels of analysis, including or omitting this variable does not change results and I present them with it omitted. In the national sample, however, 35 percent of interviews took place after news of the rallies was widely known, so in comparisons of AC and the nation and the placebo tests, I include it in analyses.

11 To address concerns related to interaction terms in non-linear models (Ai and Norton, 2003), I checked results using the method described in Norton *et al.* (2004) and employed CLARIFY (Tomz *et al.*, 2003) to calculate predicted effects.

12 The Appendix presents regression results from the comparison of AC to the nation. Regression results from the placebo tests comparing each of the other ten 2000–2006 samples to the national sample are available upon request.
13 All of the comparison block groups are located in Auburn, while all but one of the concentrated block groups is in Lewiston, raising the possibility that the changes in social capital result from factors associated with municipal residence and not just the increase in racial diversity. To address this concern, I relaxed the conditions for what constituted a "control" neighborhood and ran additional analyses comparing the concentrated block groups to all center city block groups in Lewiston and Auburn that by 2010 still had a black population of less than 5 percent. The comparison group for these analyses was thus 15 center city block groups, with five in Lewiston. Comparing the center city neighborhoods that did not experience marked increases in racial diversity to the concentrated neighborhoods produced substantively identical results, with the concentrated neighborhoods experiencing statistically significant differential declines in the likelihood of cooperation and the number of interracial ties. This analysis, in combination with examining how the 2010 percent black in neighborhoods across both cities affects social capital, suggests that the findings result from residence in a diverse neighborhood and not whether the respondent lives in Auburn as opposed to Lewiston.
14 To reduce the possibility that these results stem from increasing socio-economic disadvantage rather than increasing racial diversity, this analysis controls for block group level median household income and change in median household income from 2000 to 2010 and employs clustered standard errors.

References

Ai, C. and Norton, E. C. (2003) Interaction terms in logit and probit models. *Economics Letters*, 80(1): 123–129.

Allport, G. W. (1954) *The Nature of Prejudice*. Reading, MA: Addison-Wesley.

Braga, P. D. (2003) *City of Portland Health and Human Services Department Division of Social Services Refugee and Immigrant Services Year End Report FY 2002*.

Cook, T. D., Shadish, W. R., and Wong, V. C. (2008) Three conditions under which experiments and observational studies produce comparable causal estimates: new findings from within-study comparisons. *Journal of Policy Analysis and Management*, 27(4): 724–750.

Cullen, A. (2011) Struggle and progress: ten years of Somalis in Lewiston. *Lewiston Sun Journal*, December 18.

De Souza Briggs, X. (2007) "Some of my best friends are…": interracial friendships, class, and segregation in America. *City & Community*, 6(4): 263–290.

Dunning, T. (2008). Improving causal inference strengths and limitations of natural experiments. *Political Research Quarterly*, 61(2): 282–293.

Eric Oliver, J. and Wong, J. (2003) Intergroup prejudice in multiethnic settings. *American Journal of Political Science*, 47(4): 567–582.

Hopkins, D. J. (2010) Politicized places: explaining where and when immigrants provoke local opposition. *American Political Science Review*, 104(1): 40–60.

Laurence, J. (2009) The effect of ethnic diversity and community disadvantage on social cohesion: a multi-level analysis of social capital and interethnic relations in UK communities. *European Sociological Review*, 27(1): 70–89.

Letki, N. (2008) Does diversity erode social cohesion? Social capital and race in British neighbourhoods. *Political Studies*, 56(1): 99–126.

McPherson, M., Smith-Lovin, L., and Cook, J. M. (2001) Birds of a feather: homophily in social networks. *Annual Review of Sociology*, 27: 415–444.

Norton, E. C., Wang, H., and Ai, C. (2004) Computing interaction effects and standard errors in logit and probit models. *Stata Journal*, 4: 154–167.

Office of Refugee Resettlement (2009) *Annual Report to Congress*. www.acf.hhs.gov/sites/default/files/orr/fy_2009_annual_report_to_congress.pdf.

Primo, D. M., Jacobsmeier, M. L., and Milyo, J. (2007) Estimating the impact of state policies and institutions with mixed-level data. *State Politics and Policy Quarterly*, 7(4): 446–459.

Putnam, R. D. (2007) *E pluribus unum*: diversity and community in the twenty-first century. *Scandinavian Political Studies*, 30(2): 137–174.

Schaeffer, M. (2014) *Ethnic Diversity and Social Cohesion: Immigration, Ethnic Fractionalization and Potentials for Civic Action*. Aldershot: Ashgate.

Stolle, D., Soroka, S., and Johnston, R. (2008) When does diversity erode trust? Neighbourhood diversity, interpersonal trust and the mediating effect of social interactions. *Political Studies*, 56(1): 57–75.

Sturgis, P. and Smith, P. (2010) Assessing the validity of the generalized trust question: what kind of trust are we measuring? *International Journal of Public Opinion Research*, 22: 74–92.

Tomz, M., Wittenberg, J., and King, G. (2003) CLARIFY: software for interpreting and presenting statistical results. *Journal of Statistical Software*, 8(1): 1–30.

Torpe, L. and Lolle, H. (2011) Identifying social trust in cross-country analysis: do we really measure the same? *Social Indicators Research*, 103: 481–500.

United Nations High Commission on Refugees (2013) 2013 UNHCR country operations profile – Somalia. www.unhcr.org/pages/49e483ad6.html.

Uslaner, E. M. (2010) Segregation, mistrust and minorities. *Ethnicities*, 10(4): 415–434.

US Refugee Admissions Program (2010–2011) *Annual Reports to Congress*. www.wrapsnet.org/Documents/RefugeeProgramInformation/tabid/300/ItemId/1580/Default.aspx.

Part II

The moderating role of interethnic contacts, identities, and policies

5   Diversity, segregation, and trust

Eric M. Uslaner

Introduction

Every Western society is becoming more diverse. For some, this is a blessing. Our horizons are expanded when we interact with people of different backgrounds. For others, it is a deep-seated problem. Many, if not most, immigrants don't look like or act like the majority (white) population. When immigrants fail to assimilate, they may be perceived as threats to the dominant culture. Many people see immigrants as too dependent on the welfare state and not as hardworking or deserving as members of the majority population. Diversity, for many, is less an opportunity to learn about new cultures than to worry about the fate of one's "old" culture.

Studying diversity's effects has become a mini-industry among scholars and social critics more broadly defined (including political leaders). As outlined in Chapter 1, there is a dizzying array of findings about diversity's effects—positive, negative, or null—on a wide range of outcomes and attitudes. Can we make any sense out of these results? And is diversity really the problem? I argue that residential segregation is more important than diversity. The causal mechanism between diversity and any number of outcomes is often unclear. Segregation has much more straightforward negative implications for a wide variety of outcomes and attitudes, as I shall argue below.

Diversity and segregation are not the same thing. They are measured differently and are only modestly correlated (see below). More critically, diversity measures tell us nothing about how close people of different backgrounds live to each other. Diversity is a measure of potential isolation. The commonly used measure of fractionalization (Herfindahl index) indicates the probability that members of different groups will interact with each other (Alesina *et al.*, 2003). Many studies use simpler measures such as the minority share of population—but this is not of major concern since the two measures are largely interchangeable (Alesina *et al.*, 1999: 1270–1271). This index is strongly dependent upon the size of each group and how members are distributed within that area. It is a measure of the probability of contact with people of different backgrounds. The most commonly employed measure of segregation is the dissimilarity index. It measures how evenly groups are spread out across metropolitan areas. What proportion of each group in a neighborhood would have to move to make the area representative of the larger metropolitan area (in the United States, the standard metropolitan statistical area, or SMSA)? The dissimilarity index is designed for just two groups, but there is an extension to multiple groups, the entropy measure (Iceland and Weinberg with Steinmetz, 2002). Segregation and diversity are *not* the same thing. Across 325 American communities, the simple correlation for the two measures in 2000 is just .297 (and .231 for 1990 and .270 for 1980).[1]

What might diversity and segregation affect? The most common answer is tolerance of people who are different from ourselves. There are longstanding findings that people are most comfortable when they are surrounded by people of their own background. Advocates of "contact theory" maintain that if we interact with people of different backgrounds, we will become more tolerant of their group—and of "outsiders" more generally. "Conflict theory," on the other hand, would lead us to believe that interactions with people of different backgrounds will lead to greater hostility—or perhaps being surrounded by many people who are different from ourselves would lead us to become less tolerant—since we feel threatened. Even the most positive outcome—from "contact theory"—leads to modest results. Tolerance is a low bar, it does not mean that we are welcoming toward others, only that we accept them as members of our society.

Trust is more demanding than tolerance Generalized (or "moralistic") trust, the belief that "most people can be trusted," is the assumption that people from diverse backgrounds can still be part of your "moral community": People unlike yourself nevertheless share your fundamental moral values and should be treated as you would wish to be treated by them. What happens to them affects you (Uslaner, 2002: 1–3). This is much stronger than tolerance, the difference between someone being a member of your community versus being part of your "moral community." And it is much more difficult to build trust than to create tolerance. Trust in your own kind (in-group trust) is common, even "natural." Trust in people more generally—and this means trust in strangers who are likely to be different from yourself (Uslaner, 2002: ch. 3)—is far less common. Across 69 countries in the 1981–1990–1995 World Values Surveys, only 30 percent of respondents agreed that "most people can be trusted." In only a handful of countries did more than half of the respondents agree: Norway, Sweden, Denmark, the Netherlands, and Canada (with Australia added in a later survey).

Trust involves stronger ties than "mere" tolerance. It is also more difficult to "move." For most people, trust is developed early in life—learned from one's parents and stable over time (Uslaner, 2002: 57–68). While contact theory is all about how to develop tolerance, building trust is much more difficult. Generalized trust is not shaped by most forms of adult experience, be it membership in voluntary associations; life events such as divorce, unemployment, and short-term fluctuations in your economic circumstances; or how often you socialize with your friends, family, and neighbors (Uslaner, 2002: ch. 5). As I shall argue below, context may indeed shape trust—and the sort of context that matters is segregation, isolation from people of different background.

Why should we care about trust? Generalized trust *does* connect us to people who are different from ourselves: Trusters are more likely to be tolerant of minorities and supportive of equal rights for blacks, gays, and women (among other groups).

They give more to charities and volunteer more for causes that link them to people who are different from themselves. High trust societies have higher growth rates, less corruption and crime, and are more likely to redistribute resources from the rich to the poor. Generalized trust leads people of different backgrounds to work with each other—to less polarization in our political life and to greater legislative productivity over time in the United States.

Trusters are more willing to admit immigrants to their countries and are less worried that immigrants will take their jobs. This sense of unity of identity under-lies the provision of universal social welfare benefits, where all are entitled to receive benefits such as education from the state *simply because they are members of a political and social community* (see Chapter 7 for more on the linkage between diver-sity, trust and national identity). Governments in high trusting societies also have greater commitments to policies that promote equality among their publics (Algan and Cahuc, 2010; LaPorta *et al.*, 1997; Rothstein and Uslaner, 2005; Uslaner, 1993, 2002: chs. 5, 7).

I review the literature on contact and conflict, on diversity and segregation, and trust. Why is trust important and why does it seem so resistant to adult experi-ence? How does the environment lead to greater or lower levels of trust? How does segregation contribute to lower trust more than diversity does? And what, if anything, can we do about it? It is not easy (at best) to "rearrange" neighborhoods to make them more integrated or diverse. Negative attitudes toward minorities by the majority white populations work against integrated neighborhoods. So does the fear of discrimination that grips minorities contemplating moving to majority white communities. People with low levels of trust, as well as negative attitudes toward minorities, are less likely to favor living in integrated neighborhoods. So the causal link does not go simply from integrated neighborhoods with diverse social connections to trust, but also from trust to preferring mixed neighborhoods in the first place. Once we take into account this reverse causality—from trust to neighborhood choice—the effects of integration on trust are much smaller (often insignificant). I suggest that we shift our focus to young people, who are more pre-disposed toward favorable attitudes about minorities, although I acknowledge that this may not be readily accomplished.

Contact and conflict theories

Contact theory, as summarized in Koopmans, Lancee, and Schaeffer (Chapter 1, this volume), is the claim that exposure to people of different backgrounds leads to less prejudice. Conflict theory is based upon the argument that interactions among people of different backgrounds is likely to lead to more hostility—or, more likely, withdrawal.

This is the syndrome of increasing diversity that Putnam found characteristic of contemporary American society:

> Inhabitants of diverse communities tend to withdraw from collective life, to distrust their neighbors, regardless of the color of their skin, to withdraw even from close friends, to expect the worst from their community and its

leaders, to volunteer less, give less to charity and work on community projects less often, to register to vote less, to agitate for social reform more, but have less faith that they can actually make a difference, and to huddle unhappily in front of the television… this pattern encompasses attitudes and behavior, bridging and bonding social capital, public and private connections. Diversity, at least in the short run, seems to bring out the turtle in all of us.

(Putnam, 2007: 150–151)

The evidence that "mere" contact will lead to greater tolerance or trust is too simple. Not just any contact is sufficient to overcome prejudice. "Superficial" contact is likely to reinforce negative stereotypes. Simply having a friend of a different race is insufficient, at least for trust; I show that having a friend of a different race does not lead to greater trust in any of the five countries I analyzed: the United States, Canada, the United Kingdom, Australia, and Sweden (Uslaner, 2012: 32–36). It may be too easy to have a friend of a different group—and to argue that they are different from others of that background.

The contact that matters is *positive, deeply-seated, and persistent*: "Only the type of contact that leads people to *do* things together is likely to result in changed attitudes" (Allport, 1958: 276). Allport formulated conditions of "optimal contact": equal status between the groups, common goals, cooperation between the groups; and a supportive institutional and cultural environment (Allport, 1958: 263, 267; Pettigrew, 1998: 66). In a meta-analysis of 513 studies of contact theory, Pettigrew and Tropp (2006: 760) found that *any* contact was likely to reduce prejudice, but that optimal contact had considerably greater effects. Williams (1964: 185–190), Ihlanfeldt and Scafaldi (2002: 633), Dixon (2006: 2194–2195), and McClelland and Linnander (2006: 107–108) find that whites develop more favorable attitudes about minorities only if they know and feel close to a minority group member.

Hewstone (2009) summarizes a large body of research demonstrating that *contact alone* (regardless of the context) will lead to a reduction in prejudice, but finds that the strongest effects occur when interactions are "sustained, positive contact between members of the two previously antipathetic groups." Since trust is more demanding than "mere" prejudice reduction, so will be the conditions of boosting this stable value that doesn't change much over one's lifetime. Here, context matters, as I shall argue and support.

What constitutes a positive environment? Context is critical—and the most important context is the nature of your community. Residential segregation leads to isolation, "exaggerate[s] the degree of difference between groups" (Allport, 1958: 18–19) and makes the out-group "seem larger and more menacing than it is" (Allport, 1958: 256). Contacts in segregated communities are most likely to be "frozen into superordinate-subordinate relationships"—exactly the opposite of what is essential for the optimal conditions to be met (Allport, 1958: 251). Integrated neighborhoods "remove barriers to effective communication" (Allport, 1958: 261) and may lead to more contact with people of different backgrounds, especially among young people (Phinney *et al.*, 2006: 94; Quillian and Campbell, 2003: 560).

Forbes goes further, arguing that

> [t]he more frequent and the more intimate the contacts among individuals belonging to different tribes or nations, the more these groups come to resemble each other culturally or linguistically. [...] Different languages, religions, customs, laws, and moralities—in short, different cultures—impede economic integration, with all its benefits. [...] Isolation and subordination, not gore and destruction, seem to be the main themes in linguistic conflict.
>
> (Forbes, 1997: 144, 150)

Some support for Allport's thesis came before he refined contact theory. Deutsch and Collins (1951) surveyed occupants of public housing in four projects in New York City and Newark, two of which were integrated and two segregated. "Neighborly contacts" between whites and blacks were almost non-existent in segregated projects but were common in integrated units—and contact in integrated units led to less prejudiced racial feelings among both Whites and African-Americans regardless of their levels of education, ideology, or religion (Deutsch and Collins, 1951: 57, 86, 97). A similar design in cities in the northeast in 1951 also found that respondents (all white women) in integrated housing projects had far more contact with African-Americans, were far more approving of integrated housing than those in segregated units, and were more likely to report that their views had changed to become more positive toward blacks (Wilner *et al.*, 1955: 86, 92, 99). Self-selection was not an issue in either study (cf. Hemét, Chapter 2, this volume). In surveys conducted in Elmira, New York form 1949 through 1951, more "intimate" ties between Jews and African-Americans led to more positive views of the other (Williams, 1964: 185).

Many studies have provided support for the argument that contact with people of different backgrounds leads to less prejudice in neighborhoods that are integrated or even simply diverse. Anglos living in integrated neighborhoods have more favorable attitudes toward Latinos (Rocha and Espino, 2009). Closer contact with people of different backgrounds—approximating Allport's optimal conditions—leads to more positive attitudes toward out-groups (McClelland and Linnander, 2006: 108; McKenzie, 1948), especially if that contact occurs in more diverse and integrated neighborhoods (Dixon, 2006: 2194–2195; Stein *et al.*, 2000: 298–299; Valentova and Berzosa, 2010: 29; Wagner *et al.*, 2006: 386).

Diversity and segregation

The problem of contact versus conflict theories only arises when there is a substantial minority population. When an area is all-majority (all white in most cases), there are few opportunities to interact with people of different backgrounds. This is hardly surprising. There is an almost universal, perhaps even genetic, proclivity to bond with, and trust, our own kind more than we put faith in out-groups (Brewer, 1979). Messick and Brewer review experiments on cooperation and find that "members of an in-group tend to perceive other in-group members in generally favorable terms, particularly as being *trustworthy, honest, and cooperative*" (Messick and Brewer, (1983: 27–28, emphasis in original). The Maghribi of Northern Africa relied on their extended Jewish clan—and other Jews in the Mediterranean area—to establish a profitable trading network in the twelfth century (Greif, 1993). Models from evolutionary game theory suggest that favoring people like ourselves is our best strategy (Hamilton, 1964: 21; Masters, 1989: 169; Trivers, 1971: 48).

Alesina and LaFerrara argue that in-group preference leads to both demobilization and to negative social attitudes toward minorities, especially in more diverse areas (similar to Putnam's argument, but made five years earlier):

> individuals prefer to interact with others who are similar to themselves in terms of income, race, or ethnicity [...] diffuse preferences for homogeneity may decrease total participation in a mixed group if fragmentation increases. However, individuals may prefer to sort into homogenous groups. [...] For eight out of nine questions concerning attitudes toward race relations, the effect of racial heterogeneity is strongest for individuals more averse to racial mixing.
> (Alesina and LaFerrara, 2004: 850, 889)

There are many studies showing how people react negatively when confronted with diversity (Schaeffer, 2014; Van der Meer and Tolsma, 2014). Some of the negative consequences of racial and ethnic diversity include:

- greater corruption, infant mortality, and illiteracy and lower rates of governmental transfers (Alesina *et al.*, 2003, p. 171);
- lower long-term growth (Alesina and LaFerrara, 2004);
- less support for racial integration among Americans in the early 1970s as well as perceptions of threat (Fossett and Kielcolt, 1989) and anti-black sentiment (Taylor, 1998);
- lower levels of transfer payments adjusted for gross domestic product across nations (Alesina *et al.*, 2003, p. 171) but more transfer payments in American municipalities (Alesina, Baqir, and Easterly, 1999, p. 1264);
- less spending on welfare and on roads in American municipalities (Alesina *et al.*, 1999: 1259, 1263).
- less support for public education in more heterogeneous urban areas in the United States from 1910 to 1928 than in more homogeneous small towns (Goldin and Katz, 1999: 718);
- public goods production across a wide variety of measures (Baldwin and Huber, 2010);
- lower support for school funding, the quality of school facilities, and ownership of textbooks across Kenyan communities as well as for the maintenance of community water wells and fewer threats against parents who do not pay their school fees or participate in school projects (Miguel and Gugerty, 2005);
- the failure to maintain infrastructure in Pakistan (cited in Putnam, 2007: 143);

- less favorable views of neighborhoods and lower levels of participation in community improvement projects (Guest *et al.*, 2008: 512; Rice and Steele, 2001);
- lower rates of voting and participation in civic organizations for whites and African-Americans (but not Hispanics) across American cities (Oliver, 2001: 120); and
- higher rates of civil conflict (Matuszeski and Schneider, 2006).

Since minority groups everywhere and especially blacks in the United States and immigrants in other Western countries are far more likely to be poor and to receive government assistance than are the majority populations, greater minority populations may lead to less support for public spending, especially on welfare. Joppke argues that diversity strains the welfare state in Europe:

> Because a majority of [...] migrants are unskilled and (with the exception of France) not proficient in the language of the receiving societies, and often directly become dependent on welfare, they pose serious adjustment problems.
> (Joppke, 2007: 18–19)

Yet, the findings on diversity are not all negative. Woolever (1992) finds no connection between neighborhood diversity and community attachment or participation in Indianapolis. Collier *et al.* (2001) find that ethnic group dominance, rather than simple ethnic diversity, leads to a greater likelihood of civil conflict (cf. Bros, 2010). Even in the very diverse society of Uganda, ethnicity had only minimal effects on how people valued the welfare of others in experimental games (Habyarimana *et al.*, 2009: 23).

David Goodhart (2004), editor of *Prospect* in the United Kingdom, argued that "[a] generous welfare state is not compatible with open borders and possibly not even with [...] mass immigration." Yet, the negative reaction has not led to retrenchment everywhere. Even as Swedish policy-makers realized that the generosity of welfare benefits to immigrants could lead to resentment, they redoubled their efforts to integrate immigrants into Swedish society—and support for welfare programs remained high (Crepaz, 2008: 225–226; Kumlin and Rothstein, 2010: 69–70). There was a reaction in the 2010 election when support for the anti-immigrant Swedish Democrats reached an all-time high, but it was still less than 6 percent. In Canada, diversity seems to increase support for the welfare state (Soroka *et al.*, 2007). Finseraas (2009) finds no support for the argument that increasing diversity leads to less support for redistribution in a cross-national analysis of European Social Survey data.

Heterogeneous networks often lead to positive outcomes, such as more productive job searches (Granovetter, 1973) and more creativity (Burt, 2000). Diversity is associated with increased wages and higher prices for rental housing (Ottaviano and Peri, 2005), greater profits and market share for firms that have more diverse work forces (Herring, 2006), and greater problem-solving capacities (Gurin *et al.*, 2004). Florida *et al.* (2009) find higher levels of overall well-being in more diverse states.

More critical than diversity is segregation. In Uslaner (2012) I consider how diversity and segregation affect trust in five countries, selected by the availability of data on segregation and trust. However, these countries also differ on levels of segregation, diversity, trust, and equality. The United States is by far the most segregated and is also the most unequal—with the lowest level of trust. Sweden and Australia are the most trusting, the least segregated, and the most equal. Canada is highly trusting, with moderate levels of segregation, and less inequality. Britain has greater inequality than does Canada (but less than the United States) and moderate levels of both trust and equality.

Inequality matters because across time and space (years and the states), the level of inequality is the strongest determinant of generalized trust in the United States. Across nations without a legacy of communism, inequality is also the most important determinant of trust (Uslaner, 2002: chs. 6, 7; Uslaner and Brown, 2005). Segregation is also a key determinant of inequality, both across American communities and cross-nationally. There is both a direct and indirect negative relationship (through inequality) between segregation and trust (Uslaner, 2012: 48–56; cf. Alesina and Zhuravskaya, 2011, for cross-national evidence as well).

Segregation is also linked to a wide range of social ills: higher crime, perceptions of community well-being, low incomes, lack of jobs, drug use, teenage pregnancies, unmarried parents, low birth-weight babies, higher levels of AIDS infections, lower rates of education fostered by less government spending on schools, lower levels of entrepreneurship, more crime, and deteriorating public housing (Uslaner, 2012: 53–56; Massey and Denton, 1993: 13; LaFerrara and Mele, 2005; De Souza Briggs, 2005; Fischer and Massey, 2000; Cutler and Glaeser, 1997; Carter *et al.*, 1998: 1906). The causal link between segregation and these negative outcomes seems more firmly established than the ties between diversity and the consequences listed above. There are both positive and negative effects for diversity but only negative consequences for segregation.

In most Western countries, there isn't much diversity *or* segregation. The most diverse country is the United States. The minority shares of the populations of Western countries are small outside of the United States. Thirty percent of Americans are minorities—most are not immigrants (they are African-Americans). Only 9 percent of British are minorities (Goodhart, 2004).

In the United States, African-Americans are highly segregated, with whites and blacks living apart from each other—although Hispanics and especially Asian-Americans being better integrated into majority white neighborhoods.

Even as racial residential segregation has declined somewhat in recent decades, American neighborhoods are more segregated by income (Iceland, 2009: 113; Uslaner, 2012: 78–79; Wilson, 1987). Segregation is much lower in Australia and Sweden (Uslaner, 2012: 145–149, 164–165). Canada is somewhat less segregated than the United States, although this varies by ethnic group, with blacks and Vietnamese more isolated than other "visible minorities" (Uslaner, 2012: 101). There is strong debate over the level of segregation in Britain (Johnston *et al.*, 2002; Simpson, 2004). There is general agreement that segregation is lower in

Britain, but this reflects the mixture of different minorities (blacks, South Asians, East Asians, Arabs, and even Greeks and Turks) in "minority districts," largely away from where whites live (Uslaner, 2012: 116–123).

Whether people live in integrated or segregated neighborhoods, their social lives revolve around people like themselves. We choose people very much like ourselves to form our social networks (Marsden, 1987; McPherson *et al.*, 2001). As Allport argues:

> People mate with their own kind. They eat, play, and reside in homogeneous clusters. They visit with their own kind, and prefer to worship together. We don't play bridge with the janitor.
>
> (Allport, 1958: 17–18; cf. Uslaner, 2002: 40–42)

Even in integrated neighborhoods, people largely stay close to their own kind. Bradburn, Sudman, and Gockel report few cross-racial friendships in the most comprehensive survey of race relations in integrated and segregated neighborhoods across 100 segregated and 100 integrated neighborhoods in 35 cities in 1967:

> Eighty-one per cent of Whites in integrated neighborhoods report that neither they nor any member of their family has even stopped and talked with a Negro neighbor in the past few months, and 95 per cent also report no equal-status interracial contact in the home or at parties, movies, or neighboring meetings. These figures are particularly striking since they refer to interracial contact in integrated neighborhoods. But the great bulk of Americans live in segregated neighborhoods.
>
> (Bradburn *et al.*, 1970: 394–396)

Much may have changed since 1967 but there is little reason to believe that the overall pattern is markedly different.

Both segregation and preferences for socializing with people like ourselves limit the impact of contact theory. If we live apart from people who are different from ourselves, we will not have the opportunity to interact with them and to develop trust in them. Even if we do have friends of different backgrounds, this may not be sufficient to boost either tolerance or trust. Allport's "optimal conditions" and Hewstone's "positive contact" are both more demanding than simply knowing people from diverse backgrounds. It is more common for people to have friends of their own background, whether they live in integrated or segregated neighborhoods, whether their communities are diverse or dominated by one race or ethnic group. Integrated neighborhoods *do* provide greater opportunities for having friends of diverse backgrounds, whereas segregated neighborhoods do not (although greater opportunities will not necessarily result in more actual contact; see Chapter 3).

It is not surprising that generalized trust does *not* depend upon experience— or at least adult experience. You can't develop faith in people of different backgrounds if you rarely encounter them. And there is little rationale or evidence for the argument of Putnam and his co-authors that trust is "transitive": Clark, Putnam, and Fieldhouse suggest otherwise:

> Stronger intra-racial bonds and stronger interracial bridges can be positively, rather than negatively, correlated. [...] The same American or Brit who has more ties to others of their *own* racial and ethnic group is actually *more* likely, not less likely, to have more social bridges to other racial or ethnic groups. [...] American Whites who trust Whites more tend also to trust Latinos more, not less than Whites who distrust Whites. [...] Our research tends to support public policies which foster the building of strong bonds within ethnic groups [...] because that could be an important prelude to the broader social bridging we seek. [...] A social salad bowl is thus a better ideal than a homogenizing melting pot [...].
>
> (Clark *et al.*, 2010: 142–143)

This argument pays little heed to how trust is developed and "expands." If I trust people who are very different from myself, I will surely trust my wife, my son, and my close friends. But if I trust my wife, this says nothing about trust in people who are different from myself (Uslaner, 2002: 145–148). So a positive correlation does not imply anything about *the direction of causality*.

Stolle (1998: 500) shows that longstanding membership in voluntary associations leads to greater trust, but only for members of the group and not to the larger society. The extension of trust from your own group to the larger society occurs through "mechanisms not yet clearly understood." Rosenblum calls the purported link "an airy 'liberal expectancy'" that remains "unexplained" (Rosenblum, 1998: 45, 48). Uslaner (2002: 52–56, 142–148) shows that in-group and out-group trust form distinct clusters in people's minds and that trust in people you know does not lead to trust in strangers. The notion that we transfer any trust we develop in group members to people unlike ourselves is "a simplistic 'transmission belt' model of civil society, which says that the beneficial formative effects of association spill over from one sphere to another" (Rosenblum, 1998: 48).

In Putnam's Social Capital Benchmark Survey, I examined the interrelationship among generalized trust and dichotomized measures of trusting one's neighbors and trusting your own race. For whites, the modal category is trusting other whites and your neighbors but not "most people" (43.7 percent). Only 3 percent have faith in "most people" but not in their neighbors. The simple correlation between the two measures is modest (tau-b = .225), at least in part because so many people trust their neighbors (85 percent). About two-thirds of whites trust other whites, but less than half (46 percent) of those who trust people of their own race believe that "most people can be trusted." Eighty-nine percent of whites have faith in others of their race and 86 percent of them also trust their neighbors.

Forty-six percent of African-Americans trust their neighbors but not people in general, while 30 percent do not trust either their neighbors or "most people." Two-thirds of African-Americans trust blacks but not "most people," while almost 60 percent trust blacks *and* trust their neighbors. For whites and especially for blacks, the modal pattern is to trust their neighbors and their own racial group but not people in general. The same pattern holds across ethnic groups in Britain: people trust their own race and their own neighbors, but not "most people" (Uslaner, 2012: 66). Since most people don't have friends of different backgrounds and most people don't live in integrated and diverse neighborhoods, there is less room for contact to matter.

Putnam's arguments are not only unsupported, they are inconsistent. When confronted with diversity, we "hunker down" into our own world of ethnic and racial uniformity (Putnam, 2007). So diversity leads to less out-group contact and lower trust. Yet, he also argues that in-group trust can lead to out-group trust, even when we restrict our contacts to people like ourselves (Clark *et al.*, 2010). Diversity thus leads us to withdraw into our own communities. Yet contact only with people like ourselves somehow leads us to trust people of different backgrounds.

How contact and context matter

Intergroup contact may matter for trust because it is *not* the norm. We can develop trust when we have social contacts that fulfill Allport's "optimal conditions." There are few opportunities to measure how deep friendships are across racial or ethnic groups, but it is possible to consider the context of friendships. I argue in Uslaner (2012) that living in an integrated and diverse community *and* having friends of diverse backgrounds (as Allport's "optimal conditions" would suggest) leads to increased trust. Neither diverse friendship networks nor living in an integrated neighborhood alone suffices. Moreover, the effects are greatest in the United States and the United Kingdom, the two countries in my study with the most segregation (Johnston *et al.*, 2002; Jupp, 2002).

The impact of living in an integrated and diverse community and having friends of different backgrounds is strongest in the most highly segregated country, the United States, where meeting the "optimal conditions" boosts trust by almost 30 percent. In Britain, the effects are much smaller—between 5 and 10 percent depending upon the ethnic/racial group. In Australia and Canada, there are much stronger effects for whites than for minorities—about 10 percent for whites and 5 percent or less for minorities. In most countries, the effects are stronger for whites than for minorities since whites are more likely to be socially isolated. The majority population is already highly trusting, but whites have fewer friends of different ethnicities.

Diversity is important in moderating the connection between integrated neighborhoods and trust in the United States. The dissimilarity/entropy indices tell us the share of people who would have to move to make a neighborhood representative of the larger community. Overwhelmingly, white communities such as Portsmouth, New Hampshire, or Lewiston, Maine, are among the least segregated, since there are so few minorities there. So for the United States, it is important to interact segregation and diversity.

For the five countries, diversity only matters in the United States—where it does lead to less trust. But diversity's depressing effect is far smaller than the impact of living in an integrated and diverse neighborhood with friends of different backgrounds. And this result is general. Diversity is not the culprit in reducing trust. Segregation and social isolation lie at the root of the problem.

Yet, segregation is not an "unmoved mover." We can't build trust simply by putting people in different neighborhoods. For many years, racial residential segregation in the United States was enforced by both formal statutes and informal norms among realtors and the sellers of homes (Massey and Denton, 1993). Even when these laws were replaced by fair housing statutes, the government often did little to enforce integration. And even when enforcement became more effective, there was a reluctance of whites to move into neighborhoods with even one-third black population (Farley *et al.*, 1978). The "ideal" neighborhood for whites (in the 2000 General Social Survey in the United States) has a majority of whites and just 17 percent blacks; a quarter of whites preferred no blacks at all in their immediate area (Massey, 2007: 71–72). Blacks fear that whites will "treat them as unwelcome intruders" (Krysan and Farley, 2002: 969–970; Charles, 2006: 55).

Views of out-groups are what matters—and blacks are the least liked group for whites, Asians, and Hispanics. Whites, on the other hand, have positive views of Asians and want them as neighbors (Charles, 2006: 127, 139). Whites are the group with the highest favorability ratings among minorities and thus are the most desirable neighbors (Bobo and Massagli, 2001). But all minorities see whites as dominant and not welcoming (Charles, 2006: 181).

Crowder, Hall, and Tolnay (2011) claim that both whites and African-Americans prefer to live in "better neighborhoods," with lower crime rates, more highly ranked schools, and better services. They argue that it is not race that predominantly shapes residential preferences, but rather neighborhood quality (see also Frey, 1979: 439; Ellen, 2000: 99–100, 121–122). Yet negative racial attitudes— notably stereotypes about minorities—seem to be more critical in shaping housing preferences. Ellen admits:

> the segregation levels of blacks are so much higher than that of other ethnic groups that we would have to assume, implausibly it seems, that their desire for clustering is exceptional – far beyond that of even recent immigrants, such as Mexicans and Koreans, whose foreign language and customs make such clustering natural and perhaps even advantageous.
>
> (Ellen, 2000: 57)

In 100 segregated and integrated neighborhoods in 1967, Bradburn *et al.* (1970: 136) found that most white residents of integrated neighborhoods did not choose to live among blacks because they had more liberal views on race: these poor neighborhoods were all they could afford.

In 1962, six out of ten Americans believed that whites could keep African-Americans out of their neighborhoods (Massey and Denton, 1993: 49). As the American civil rights leader and politician Jesse Jackson said of whites' opposition to busing children across town to achieve racial balance in the public schools in the 1970s: "It's not the bus, it's us" (quoted in Davis, 2007: 60).

In the United States and the United Kingdom—the only countries for which questions on residential preferences are included in national surveys—I found that it is people who trust others, and who have positive views of minorities, that are the most likely to choose to live in an integrated and diverse neighborhood (Uslaner, 2012: ch. 8). So you need trust to get to the optimal conditions that seem to build trust. Once I take this into account—through a multiple equation model predicting both trust and residential choice simultaneously—the effect of Allport's "optimal conditions" on trust become weak. There are no statistically significant effects for any ethnic, racial, or religious group in Britain and only marginally significant effects for whites in the United States.

Whither diversity?

In one sense, diversity does matter a lot. When people have negative views of minorities and low levels of trust in out-groups, they will shy away from both contact with people of different backgrounds and especially neighborhoods with substantial minority populations. They shy away from diversity.

In this sense, Putnam is right—we do avoid people who are different from ourselves. However, arguing that we need to put limits on immigration to avoid the negative effects of diversity—or, more particularly, segregation—seems to put the blame on the wrong culprit. Most immigrants move out of segregated communities after a generation and have a desire to assimilate, if not for themselves, then at least for their children. Immigrants may be lower trusting since they come to their host countries with levels of trust of their native land (Uslaner, 2008). In some countries, immigrants are highly trusting, when there are strict criteria for education and training to admit them to their new country, as in Canada or Australia. Negative attitudes toward diversity are mostly confined to the majority population.

If people don't want to move to integrated and diverse neighborhoods, the likelihood of building trust through contact is small. Is there any way to increase trust?

While adults will have relatively fixed levels of trust, young people's attitudes are more malleable by their experiences. I have elsewhere shown that people who had friends of a different race in secondary school were less likely to trust only their own in-groups as adults and became more trusting in general over the course of their lives (Uslaner, 2002: 105, 169–171).

In each of the five countries I examine young people (under 30) from the majority are considerably more likely to have friends of other races, ethnicities (Canada), or who speak other languages (Sweden) than are their elders.[2] Dinesen (2011) shows that native Danish elementary students develop more out-group trust if their school populations are *more* diverse.[3] Stolle and Harrell (2009) show that young Canadians whose social networks are more racially and ethnically heterogeneous *in diverse neighborhoods* have higher levels of trust, even as older people become *less* trusting when they live among people who are different from themselves.

It may not be easy to bring young people of different backgrounds together. Many schools are even more segregated than neighborhoods (Orfield, 2009: 6). However, this seems to be the best route to building trust and tolerance.

Notes

1 The P* indices for Asian-American and Hispanic isolation from whites, as well as white isolation from minorities, are all highly correlated with Iceland's diversity (Herfindahl) index (between –.73 and –.76). The correlations of the P* indices for Asian-Americans, Hispanics, and whites are only modestly correlated with segregation (–.22 and –.23) and the P* index for Asian-Americans is barely correlated with segregation (–.04). The index for African-American isolation from whites is strongly correlated with both diversity and the entropy index of Iceland (–.66 and –.70, respectively), which is hardly surprising since African-Americans are hyper-segregated (segregated on multiple dimensions). The N is 239 for all correlations (P* is available for fewer SMSAs than are the segregation and diversity measures). Diversity and segregation are not the same thing across Australian neighborhoods either, although the correlation is somewhat higher (r = .405).

2 In the Social Capital Benchmark Survey, an implausibly high 79 percent of whites under 30 say that they have friends of a different race (compared to 61 percent of older people, also too high). In the UK, the figures are 25 percent and 15 percent; for Canada, 82 percent of younger respondents and 73 percent of older people have friends of different ethnicities (a less demanding criterion). In Sweden, 53 percent of younger respondents have a friend who speaks a different language, compared to 43 percent of older people. In Australia, 47 percent of younger people visit friends of different ethnic groups compared to 33 percent of older people (the age ranges are 18–34 for Australia since the exact age is not available).

3 There is, surprisingly, only an increase in out-group trust, not generalized trust.

References

Alesina, A. and LaFerrara, E. (2004) Ethnic diversity and economic performance. *National Bureau of Economic Research Working Paper 10313*. www.nber.org/papers/w10313.

Alesina, A. and Zhuravskaya, E. (2011) Segregation and the quality of government in a cross-section of countries. *American Economic Review*, 101(5): 1872–1911.

Alesina, A., Baqir, R., and Easterly, W. (1999) Public goods and ethnic divisions. *Quarterly Journal of Economics*, 114(4): 1243–1284.

Alesina, A., Devleeschauwer, A., Easterly, W., Kurlat, S., and Wacziarg, S. (2003) Fractionalization. *Journal of Economic Growth*, 8: 155–194.

Algan, Y. and Cahuc, P. (2010) Inherited trust and growth. *American Economic Review*, 1000: 2060–2092.

Allport, G. (1958) *The Nature of Prejudice* (Abridged). Garden City, NY: Doubleday.

Baldwin, K. and Huber, J. (2010) Economic versus cultural differences: forms of ethnic diversity. *American Political Science Review*, 104: 644–662.

Bobo, L. and Massagli, M. (2001) Stereotyping and urban inequality. In A. O'Connor, C. Tilly, and L. Bobo (eds) *Urban Inequality*. New York: Russell Sage Foundation. pp. 89–162.

Bradburn, N., Sudman, S., and Gockel, G. with the assistance of Noel, J. (1970) *Racial Integration in American Neighborhoods: A Comparative Survey*. Chicago: National Opinion Research Corporation.

Brewer, M. (1979) In-group bias in the minimal intergroup situation: a cognitive-motivational analysis. *Psychological Bulletin*, 86: 307–324.

Bros, C. (2010) Social fragmentation and public goods. *Working Paper 2010. 26, Centre d'Economie de la Sorbonne*. http://ideas.repec.org/p/mse/cesdoc/10026.html.

Burt, R. (2000) Structural holes versus network closure as social capital. In N. Lin, C. S. Cook, and R. S. Burt (eds) *Social Capital: Theory and Research*. New York: Aldine, pp. 31–79.

Carter, W., Schill, M., and Wachter, S. (1998) Polarisation, public housing and racial minorities in US cities. *Urban Studies*, 35: 1889–1911.

Charles, C. Z. (2006) *Won't You Be My Neighbor? Race, Class and Residence in Los Angeles*. New York: Russell Sage Foundation.

Clark, T., Putnam, R., and Fieldhouse, E. (2010) *The Age of Obama*. Manchester: Manchester University Press.

Collier, P., Honahan, P., and Moene, K. (2001).Implications of ethnic diversity. *Economic Policy*, 16: 129–166.

Crepaz, M. (2008) *Trust Beyond Borders: Immigration, the Welfare State, and Identity in Modern Societies*. Ann Arbor: University of Michigan Press.

Crowder, K., Hall, M., and Tolnay, S. (2011) Neighborhood immigration and native out-migration. *American Sociological Review*, 76: 25–47.

Cutler, D. and Glaeser, E. (1997) Are ghettos good or bad? *Quarterly Journal of Economics*, 112: 827–872.

Davis, L. (2007) *Scandal: How "Gotcha" Politics is Destroying America*. New York: Palgrave Macmillan.

De Souza Briggs, X. (2005). More *pluribus*, less *unum*? The changing geography of race and opportunity. In X. De Souza Briggs (ed.) *The Geography of Opportunity*. Washington: Brookings Institution Press, pp. 17–44.

Deutsch, M. and Collins, M. (1951) *Interracial Housing: A Psychological Evaluation of a Social Experiment*. Minneapolis: University of Minnesota Press.

Dinesen, P. (2011) *When in Rome, Do as the Romans Do? An Analysis of the Acculturation of Generalized Trust of Non-Western Immigrants in Western Europe*. Unpublished PhD dissertation, University of Aarhus.

Dixon, J. (2006) The ties that bind and those that don't: toward reconciling group threat and contact theories of prejudice. *Social Forces*, 84: 2179–2804.

Ellen, I. G. (2000). *Sharing America's Neighborhoods: The Prospects for Stavle Racial Integration*. Cambridge, MA: Harvard University Press.

Farley, R., Schuman, H., Bianchi, S., Colastano, D., and Hatchett, S. (1978) "Chocolate city, vanilla suburbs": will the trend toward racially scparate communities continue? *Social Science Research*, 7: 319–344.

Finseraas, H. (2009) *Xenophobic Attitudes, Preferences for Redistribution, and Partisan Alignments in Europe*. Presented at the Workshop on Diversity and Democratic Politics: Canada in Comparative Perspective, Queens University, Kingston, Ontario, Canada, May.

Fischer, M. and Massey, D. (2000) Residential segregation and ethnic enterprise in US metropolitan areas. *Social Problems*, 47: 408–424.

Florida, R., Mellander, C., and Rentfrow, P. (2009) Happy states of America: a state-level analysis of psychological, economic, and social well-being. *Martin Prosperity Institute Working Paper 003*. http://research.martinprosperity.org.

Forbes, H. (1997) *Ethnic Conflict: Commerce, Culture, and the Contact Hypothesis*. New Haven: Yale University Press.

Fossett, M. and Kielcolt, K. (1989) The relative size of minority populations and white racial attitudes. *Social Science Quarterly*, 70: 820–835.

Frey, W. H. (1979) Central city white flight: racial and nonracial causes. *American Sociological Review*, 44: 425–448.

Goldin, C. and Katz, L. (1999) Human capital and social capital: the rise of secondary schooling in America, 1910–1940. *Journal of Interdisciplinary History*, 29: 683–723.

Goodhart, D. (2004) Too diverse? *Prospect*, February 20. www.prospectmagazine. co.uk/2004/02/too-diverse-david-goodhart-multiculturalism-britain-immigration-globalisation.

Granovetter, M. (1973) The strength of weak ties. *American Journal of Sociology*, 78: 1360–1380.

Greif, A. (1993) Contract enforceability and economic institutions in early trade: the Maghribi Traders' Coalition. *American Economic Review*, 83: 525–578.

Guest, A., Kubrin, C., and Cover, J. (2008) Heterogeneity and harmony: neighbouring relationships among whites in ethnically diverse neighbourhoods in Seattle. *Urban Studies*, 45: 501–526.

Gurin, P., Nagda, B., and Lopez, G. (2004) The benefits of diversity in education for democratic citizenship. *Journal of Social Issues*, 60: 17–34.

Habyarimana, J., Humphreys, M., Posner, D., and Weinstein, J. (2009) *Coethnicity: Diversity and the Dilemmas of Collective Action*, New York: Russell Sage Foundation.

Hamilton, W. (1964) The genetical evolution of social behavior, II. *Journal of Theoretical Biology*, 7: 17–52.

Herring, C. (2006) Does diversity pay? Racial composition of firms and the business case for diversity. Unpublished paper, University of Illinois at Chicago.

Hewstone, M. (2009) Living apart, living together? The role of intergroup contact in social integration. *Proceedings of the British Academy*, 162: 243–300.

Iceland, J. (2009) *Where We Live Now: Immigration and Race in the United States*. Berkeley: University of California Press.

Iceland, J. and Weinberg, D. with Steinmetz, E. (2002) Racial and ethnic residential segregation in the United States: 1980–2000. www.census.gov/hhes/www/housing/resseg/pdf/paa_paper.pdf.

Ihlanfeldt, K. and Scafaldi, B. (2002) The neighbourhood contact hypothesis: evidence from the multicity study of urban inequality. *Urban Studies*, 39: 619–641.

Johnston, R., Forrest, J., and Poulsen, M. (2002) Are there ethnic enclaves/ghettos in English cities? *Urban Studies*, 39: 591–618.

Joppke, C. (2007) Beyond national models: civic integration policies for immigrants in western Europe. *Western European Politics*, 30: 1–22.

Jupp, J. (2002) *From White Australia to Woomera: The Story of Australian Immigration*. Cambridge: Cambridge University Press.

Krysan, M. and Farley, R. (2002) The residential preferences of blacks: do they explain persistent segregation? *Social Forces*, 80: 937–980.

Kumlin, S. and Rothstein, B. (2010) Questioning the new liberal dilemma immigrants, social networks, and institutional fairness. *Comparative Politics*, 43(1): 63–89.

LaFerrara, E. and Mele, A. (2005) Racial segregation and public school expenditure. Unpublished paper, Bocconi University. http://ideas.repec.org/p/cpr/ceprdp/5750.html.

LaPorta, R., Lopez-Silanes, F., Schleifer, A., and Vishney, R. (1997) Trust in large organizations. *American Economic Review Papers and Proceedings*, 87: 333–38.

Marsden, P. (1987) Core discussion networks of Americans. *American Sociological Review*, 52: 122–131.

Massey, D. S. (2007) *Categorically Unequal: The American Stratification System*, New York: Russell Sage Foundation.

Massey, D. S. and Denton, N. (1993) *American Apartheid: Segregation and the Making of the Underclass*, Cambridge, MA: Harvard University Press.

Masters, R. D. (1989). *The Nature of Politics*. New Haven: Yale University Press.

Matuszeski, J. and Schneider, F. (2006) Patterns of ethnic group segregation and civil conflict. Unpublished paper, Harvard University. http://isites.harvard.edu/fs/docs/icb.topic637173.files/Matuszeski_061003.pdf.

McClelland, K. and Linnander, E. (2006) The role of contact and information in racial attitude change among white college students. *Sociological Inquiry*, 76: 81–115.

McKenzie, B. (1948) The importance of contact in determining attitudes toward Negroes. *Journal of Abnormal Social Psychology*, 43: 417–441.

McPherson, M., Smith-Lovin, L. and Cook, J. (2001) Birds of a feather: homophily in social networks. *Annual Review of Sociology*, 27: 415–444.

Messick, D. and Brewer, M. (1983) Solving social dilemmas: a review. In L. Wheeler and P. Shaver (eds) *Review of Personality and Social Psychology*, Vol. IV. Beverly Hills: Sage, pp. 11–44.

Miguel, E. and Gugerty, M. (2005) Ethnic diversity, social sanctions, and public goods in Kenya. *Journal of Public Economics*, 89: 2325–2368.

Oliver, J. E. (2001) *Democracy in Suburbia*. Princeton: Princeton University Press.

Orfield, G. (2009) *Reviving the Goal of an Integrated Society: A 21st Century Challenge*. Los Angeles, CA: The Civil Rights Project/Proyecto Derecjos Civiles at UCLA.

Ottaviano, G. I. and Peri, G. (2005) Rethinking the gains from immigration: theory and evidence from the US (No. w11672). National Bureau of Economic Research.

Pettigrew, T. (1998) Intergroup conflict theory. *Annual Review of Psychology*, 49: 65–85.

Pettigrew, T. and Tropp, L. (2006) A meta-analytic test of intergroup contact theory. *Journal of Personality and Social Psychology*, 90: 751–783.

Phinney, J., Berry, J., Vedder, P., and Liebkind, P. (2006) The acculturation experience: behaviors of immigrant youth. In J. Berry, J. Phinney, D. Sam, and P. Vedder (eds) *Immigrant Youth in Cultural Transition: Acculturation, Identity, and Adaptation Across National Contexts*. Mahwah, NJ: Psychology Press, pp. 71–116.

Putnam, R. D. (2007) *E pluribus unum*: diversity and community in the twenty-first century. *Scandinavian Political Studies*, 30(2): 137–174.

Quillian, L. and Campbell, M. (2003) Beyond black and white: the present and future of multiracial friendship segregation. *American Sociological Review*, 68: 540–566.

Rice, T. and Steele, B. (2001) White ethnic diversity and community attachment in small Iowa towns. *Social Science Quarterly*, 82: 397–407.

Rocha, R. and Espino, R. (2009) Racial threat, residential segregation, and the policy attitudes of Anglos. *Political Research Quarterly*, 62: 415–426.

Rosenblum, N. (1998) *Membership and Morals*. Princeton: Princeton University Press.

Rothstein, B. and Uslaner, E. (2005) All for all: equality, corruption, and social trust. *World Politics*, 58: 41–72.

Schaeffer, M. (2014) *Ethnic Diversity and Social Cohesion: Immigration, Ethnic Fractionalization and Potentials for Civic Action*. Aldershot: Ashgate.

Simpson, L. (2004) Statistics of racial segregation: measures, evidence and policy. *Urban Studies*, 41(3): 661–681.

Soroka, S., Johnston, R., and Banting, K. (2007) Ties that bind? Social cohesion and diversity in Canada. In K. Banting, T. Courchene, and F. Seidle (eds) *Belonging? Diversity, Recognition and Shared Citizenship in Canada*. Montreal: Institute for Research on Public Policy, pp. 561–600.

Stein, R., Post, S., and Rinden, A. (2000) Reconciling context and contact effects on racial attitudes. *Political Research Quarterly*, 53: 285–303.

Stolle, D. (1998) Bowling together, bowling alone. *Political Psychology*, 19: 497–526.

Stolle, D. and Harrell, A. (2009) Social capital and ethno-racial diversity: learning to trust in a diverse society. Presented at the Workshop on Diversity and Democratic Politics: Canada in Comparative Perspective, Queens University, Kingston, Ontario, Canada, May.

Taylor, M. (1998) How white attitudes vary with the racial composition of local populations. *American Sociological Review*, 63: 512–535.

Trivers, R. (1971) The evolution of reciprocal altruism. *Quarterly Review of Biology*, 46: 35–57.

Uslaner, E. (1993) *The Decline of Comity in Congress*, Ann Arbor: University of Michigan Press.

—— (2002) *The Moral Foundations of Trust*. New York: Cambridge University Press.

—— (2008) Where you stand depends upon where your grandparents sat: The inheritability of generalized trust. *Public Opinion Quarterly*, 72: 1–14.

—— (2012) *Segregation and Mistrust: Diversity, Isolation, and Social Cohesion*. New York: Cambridge University Press.

Uslaner, E. and Brown, M. (2005) Inequality, trust, and civic engagement. *American Politics Research*, 33(6): 868–894.

Valentova, M. and Berzosa, G. (2010) Attitudes toward immigrants in Luxembourg – do contacts matter? *CEPS Instead Working* Paper 2010–20. http://econpapers.repec.org/paper/irscepswp/2010–20.htm.

Van der Meer, T. and Tolsma, J. (2014) Ethnic diversity and its supposed detrimental effects on social cohesion. *Annual Review of Sociology*, 40.

Wagner, U., Christ, O., Pettigrew, T., Stellacher, J., and Wolf, C. (2006) Prejudice and minority proportion. *Social Psychology Quarterly*, 69: 380–390.

Williams, R. Jr. in collaboration with Dean, J. and Shuchman, E. (1964) *Strangers Next Door: Immigration, Migration and Mission*. Englewood Cliffs, NJ: IVP Books.

Wilner, D., Walkley, R., and Cook, S. (1955) *Human Relations in Interracial Housing*. New York.

Wilson, W. J. (1987) *The Truly Disadvantaged*. Minneapolis: University of Minnesota Press.

Woolever, C. (1992) A contextual approach to neighbourhood attachment. *Urban Studies*, 29: 99–116.

6 The consequences of ethnic diversity

Advancing the debate

Dietlind Stolle and Allison Harell

Introduction

Increasing levels of ethnic and racial diversity in industrialized democracies have given rise to the perception that such diversity is eroding various forms of social solidarity. Skeptics of diversity are worried that diverse societies are more prone to all kinds of problems and pathologies: the assumption is that they are more likely to breed ethnic conflict, less likely to develop into stable democracies, less likely to enact a solidaric social welfare system, and less likely to have widespread generalized trust. While some of these earlier concerns have been refuted, pessimism lingers, both within academic circles, and certainly within the broader public debate. If societies depend on immigration and diversity, more research on the conditions that create beneficial rather than detrimental effects of diversity deserves our attention.

In this chapter we focus on how we can advance the debate about the consequences of ethnic diversity. In particular, we suggest three important innovations in the research agenda. First, we propose to move away from purely contextual studies to examine more closely actual experiences with diversity, namely through interethnic contact. Second, we suggest that the beneficial effects of diverse networks should be strongest in a society where diversity is normalized in everyday life, particularly when young generations experience this normalization during their childhood and adolescence. The policy context is one particularly promising avenue for understanding differences in how diversity is experienced across societies. Finally, we argue that we need to shift away from general measures that focus solely on out-group attitudes and generalized trust in standard survey settings. The chapter collates evidence supporting these points and concludes with ideas for future research on what is required for diversity to have favorable consequences.

The literature to date: context and mixed results

Much of the research on the consequences of diversity was spurred by Putnam's (2007) much-cited work where he argues that, in the short run, racial diversity is likely to reduce various aspects of social capital, defined as dense social networks and the norms of trust and reciprocity that facilitate collective action. His study finds that in racially diverse areas in the US, citizens tend to trust each other less and are less able to cooperate with one another to address shared problems. He even finds that trust in one's own group members is reduced when facing ethnic and racial diversity. Since then numerous follow-up studies attempted to ascertain whether the effect holds outside the US. A recent meta-analysis including the latest 90 articles on the topic addressed this relationship directly (Van der Meer and Tolsma, 2014; see also Schaeffer, 2014). They find that about 26 articles tend to support Putnam's findings, however, the same number of studies reject his findings (25), and 39 studies provide mixed or neutral findings.

Clearly, then, the results can only be described as divergent, but the question remains as to why. For one thing, most of these studies focus on measuring the diversity of neighborhoods or often larger regional contexts and do not include intergroup contact at all. While it is generally believed that diverse contexts bring about more intergroup contact (Joyner, 2000; McPherson *et al.*, 2001), the possibility exists that not all diverse areas score equally on this account. The puzzle about diversity may therefore not be as much about the presence or absence of minority groups as such, but about the level of segregation in each area (Massey and Denton, 1993; Uslaner, Chapter 5, this volume) and variance in interethnic social interaction patterns (Danzer and Yaman, 2013). If the most diverse areas and neighborhoods are also the most segregated, then the potential for intergroup contact to counteract group conflict is minimized. So, including interethnic contact into the analyses is a fundamental necessity.

Although informal socializing in the neighborhood may be a particularly important source of social capital, especially for women and families with children more generally (Lowndes, 2006: 234), the nearly exclusive focus on neighborhoods (and especially larger regional units) is, in our opinion, not warranted. While this emphasis certainly corresponds to Putnam's original concern, it is not really clear why the neighborhood or even larger geographic units dominate the discussion (see also Esaiasson, 2014). The neighborhood as a focus of social relations has declined over the last decades, especially as commuting times have increased and in as much as neighborhoods have simply become a place where houses are located rather than a focus of community life (Leyden, 2003). Other types of contexts have become more important sites for social interactions, such as work (Mutz and Mondak, 2006) or online communities (Valenzuela *et al.*, 2012). It is possible that in these contexts people encounter diversity in ways that may differ from simply sharing geographic space. For example, Mutz and Mondak (2006) find in several surveys that the workplace provided respondents with the greatest percentage (between 28 and 48 percent) of their discussion partners compared to other arenas, such as groups and meeting people through friends. Additionally, they claim that exposure to political disagreement in the work place is greater relative to all other social contexts. We believe similar dynamics lead this to be true for ethnic diversity as well.

Furthermore, how geographic space itself is experienced can change as the diversity of a context does. For example, Gorny and Toruńczyk-Ruiz (2013) find that diversity in a neighborhood has a negative impact on neighborhood attachment, but that natives with high levels of diverse ethnic interaction are immune to this effect, whereas migrants are insulated from the negative effect if they have mostly mono-ethnic ties. In other words, to understand the impact of diversity, we need to understand more precisely how diversity is *experienced*. Is there actually interaction between different groups and what is the nature and context in which this interaction occurs? Clearly, one way to do this is to study more closely the relation between social context and social interaction, as we (Harell and Stolle, 2010) and others (Schmid *et al.*, Chapter 8, this volume) have argued.

It also requires that we take social context more seriously. We suggest that the norm environment and socialization experiences of generational groups should play a role in shaping whether diversity will have beneficial consequences. In societies where diversity has become normalized in everyday life during the prime socialization period for young adults, diversity will be perceived and experienced very differently than in societies where the diversity of the context is changing rapidly (Hopkins, 2010). In addition, different compositions of diversity and different types of ethnic cleavages in societies will make it difficult to find universal patterns. For example, hyper-diversity—where several ethnic groups mix with majority groups—should be distinguished from other societal models where a smaller number of ethnic minority groups are present (e.g., blacks and Hispanics in the United States).

Integration policies are also one of the important societal features that can moderate how threatening out-groups are perceived to be. While such policies are all meant to bring minority and majority groups closer together, they are based on different principles and beliefs (Howard, 2009) and thus might not be able to achieve similar results. In short, different contexts and policies are important conditions under which diversity might have beneficial outcomes (Hopkins, 2010).

A final major reason for the divergent results is the use of different dependent variables across various studies. While they all are meant to capture some aspect of social cohesion, social capital, or social solidarity, they range from various types of trust, out-group attitudes, neighborhood feelings, to problem-solving in the neighborhood and other behavioral measures. While these are certainly relevant aspects of social cohesion, the literature has so far not included many measures of policy attitudes that seem to have important repercussions. So, our fourth and final suggestion is to include support for solidarity based policies in the study of diversity.

Advancing the debate: research examples

In this section, we explore what the newest research suggests about the three different conditions that in our view should be considered more closely in the debate about the consequences of ethnic diversity.

Interethnic contact as a moderating effect

Studies on the relationship between diversity and social capital have not sufficiently integrated the insights of the contact hypothesis, which claims that positive interactions between people of different ethnic backgrounds can help to establish inclusive intergroup feelings (see Hewstone *et al.*, Chapter 11, this volume; Schmid *et al.*, Chapter 8, this volume; as well as Schlueter and Scheepers, 2010). This is particularly astounding, as the essence of the social capital literature has been that "social relationships have value." Originally there were high hopes for so-called bridging contacts with people who are different from oneself (Putnam, 2000: ch, 1). These beneficial contacts between people of different backgrounds were expected to happen, for example, in voluntary associations where people also learn to cooperate and trust each other. While social capital research has already highlighted the importance of diverse social interactions, the direct measurement of interethnic contact has not entered most of the empirical analyses on the consequences of ethnic diversity for social cohesion.

Contact theory has a longer history and has provided much evidence that interethnic contact matters for lowering prejudice and negative out-group attitudes (Allport, 1954; Hewstone, 2009; Pettigrew and Tropp, 2006). The question is why the insights of the contact hypothesis have received such little attention in this debate? When diversity is measured, contact is often not taken into account (see exceptions in Fieldhouse and Cutts, 2010; Gundelach and Freitag, 2013; Marschall and Stolle, 2004; Semyonov and Glikman, 2009; Stolle *et al.*, 2008; Stolle and Harell, 2013; Uslaner, 2010). Putnam (2007), for example, has assumed that the composition of local communities and at times census tracts is a good proxy for actual contact experiences. This is, however, a fundamental misunderstanding of what intergroup contact denotes (i.e., actually engaging in face-to-face interaction with one or more members of an out-group—at best getting to know them and thus moving beyond stereotypes—but not merely co-existing with them in the same neighborhood, school, or organization, *without engaging in such interaction;* see Hewstone, 2009, Stolle *et al.*, 2013).

In order to ascertain the effects of contact with diverse others one needs to measure both the quantity and, ideally, the quality of diverse contacts, rather than merely consider contextual diversity. This distinction is important because potentially negative effects of facing diversity in one's surroundings might be entirely or at least partially overcome when people have the opportunity to interact with each other in a positive environment (Barlow *et al.*, 2012).[1] In short, while diversity (without contact) may (or may not) diminish interpersonal trust and other aspects of social cohesion, the question is whether positive personal experiences with individuals of immigrant background might have additional, positive effects (see also Stolle *et al.*, 2008; Stolle and Harell, 2013), and moreover, whether they can moderate the potential negative effects of diversity? Where should such contacts take place in order to have beneficial outcomes?

The contact theory specifies that under certain conditions of equality and cooperation such contact can have positive effects on out-group prejudice (Allport, 1954). In particular, as the chapters by Schmid *et al.* and Hewstone *et al.* (Chapters 8 and 11, this volume) show, feelings of threat might be reduced by the experience of out-group contact. There is evidence that contact with one type of out-group can have consequences for attitudes towards another out-group (Tausch *et al.*, 2010). That is, people who have contact with Hindus, for example, might transfer their reduced prejudices to other religious out-groups such as Muslims. Furthermore, contact does not have to be direct but could also be extended, that is, the interethnic contact that your friends or family members have might also shape your own prejudices (Christ *et al.*, 2010; Wright *et al.*, 1997). The question for us here is whether and how interethnic contact can influence social cohesion, and how the context in which this diversity is experienced affects such interactions and their consequences for social solidarity.

While much research on the contact hypothesis has focused on prejudice, these insights travel also to classic indicators of social cohesions, such as generalized trust. While the measurement of census tract diversity relates negatively to trust in the United States, we were able to show that talking to neighbors in diverse neighborhoods, although not in homogeneous neighborhoods, is related to higher levels of generalized trust (Stolle *et al.*, 2008). Recently this idea was tested again in a German dataset. The data comes from the study "Diversity and Contact" (DivCon), conducted at the Max Planck Institute for the Study of Religious and Ethnic Diversity in Göttingen. The study sampled individuals from neighborhoods instead of other regional units (Petermann *et al.*, 2012), as it is based on the assumption that the immediate context in which people live and potentially interact is an important determinant of their social networks and an important site of everyday experiences. The data set allows us to link detailed contextual variables of the neighborhood context with individual measures of social interactions and particularly contact between immigrants and non-immigrants (see more details in Stolle *et al.*, 2013).

In the analysis we found that neighborhood diversity does not seem to have the same negative effects on trust as in North America and some other European countries. For generalized trust as well as out-group trust, diversity exhibits insignificant negative relations. In addition, we found that, similarly as in the US, neighborhood contact that entails conversations with immigrants as well as other interethnic weak ties are both significantly related to higher trust levels, whereas intergroup strong tie relations are not. This is interesting, as traditionally, contact theory has focused on closer and strong ties. However, this research suggests that the ethnic composition of weaker ties is key. While we maintain that interaction must be generally positive, with whom this interaction occurs seems as important. The generalizing effect, in other words, may be more likely when the out-group member with whom we interact is less well-known to us (and therefore not as individuated in our thinking). That is, knowing several acquaintances from diverse backgrounds does contribute to the generalization that most people (including immigrants) can be trusted.

While the inclusion of contact did not change the overall effect of neighborhood diversity significantly in the German sample, the intergroup contact effects seem to overpower the weak and unstable effects of neighborhood diversity on trust, at least in this sample of German natives. Furthermore, they seem to become stronger in more diverse neighborhoods; indeed contact moderated the effects of diversity. These results indicate that the consideration of neighborhood diversity as context is incomplete without considering the moderating effects of intergroup contact. Indeed further research shows that similar results could be obtained in the UK where the inclusion of intergroup ties completely overwhelmed the negative consequences of ethnic diversity (Fieldhouse and Cutts, 2014). In sum, contacts work as buffers or vaccines—people with interethnic contact seem to become immune against adverse diversity effects. The question is how to create more positive interethnic contacts that will have these stabilizing effects.

While we need more confirmation of the moderating power of interethnic contact for a variety of outcomes, there are also two additional problems to be addressed. First, of course, the research discussed is unable to fully address the endogeneity issue. That is we do not truly know whether inter-ethnic contact affects prejudice, or whether non-prejudiced people entertain more interethnic contact. Most likely a bit of both is true, however, research designs which include longitudinal and experimental studies would be better able to disentangle the causal mechanism here (see Chapters 3, 4, and 9 in this volume for such approaches to studying the effects of diversity).

The second issue concerns the type and locations of interethnic contact and diversity experiences. We need to move away from self-selected contexts (such as neigborhoods or even schools) toward arenas such as the workplace where prior prejudicial attitudes are less likely to determine whether one is part of a certain context. We should also concentrate on types of contact that are not self-selected, e.g., moving away from a focus on friendships towards the study of more fleeting encounters as at the post office, in shops, doctors' offices, etc. However, these arenas, such as work, might also pose other analytical problems. Work relations are often hierarchical, and many positions entail power differentials, a condition which does not fulfill one of the requirements of the contact hypothesis. What is the role of clients or customers, for example? How does the size of a company relate to the effects of diversity? Similarly, other informal contacts are much more difficult to study and measure. Many questions remain open here and their future research will need to indicate whether the pre-conditions of the contact hypothesis remain important for other indicators of social cohesion.

Context matters: the role of discourse, norm environment, and policy

Second, we assume that the effect of diverse networks should be stronger in a society where diversity is normalized in everyday life (Stolle and Harell, 2013). Since the phenomenon of ethnic diversity in Western democracies is relatively recent, the norms should be particularly important for younger generations who are socialized into diverse surroundings and who do not know homogeneous contexts. These generations then should be immune to any potential threats perceived to result from diversity. Do such normalized contexts exist and how do they affect the consequences of diversity?

Diversity is not experienced in a vacuum. Political discourse and nation-wide (or at least regionwide) value systems influence and shape whether and

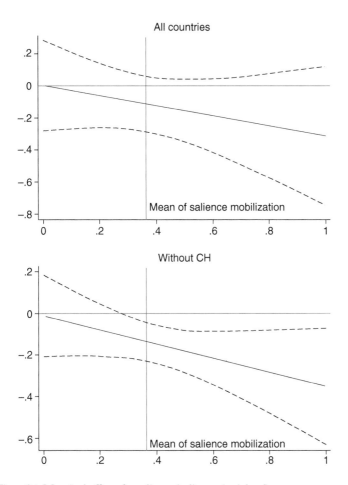

Figure 6.1 Marginal effects for salience indicator (weighted).

Note: The graphs display the marginal effects of immigration rates on trust (y-axis) for different levels of mobilization (x-axis). Source: ESS 2002/03, reproduced from Helbling *et al.* (2013).

how diversity might affect any aspect of social cohesion (Laxer, 2013). In other words, it makes a difference whether diversity increases in a context in which we see, for example, strong radical right parties (on the rise) with the ability to dominate the political discourse with anti-immigration agendas, compared to a context where the recognition of ethnic minorities is enshrined in law. These differences can even be measured when just exploring the character of the party discourse on national and immigration issues more generally. In an article with Marc Helbling and Tim Reeskens (Helbling *et al.*, 2013), we show that it is the combination of the higher proportion of foreigners and the political mobilization of immigration in national party discourses which diminishes generalized trust, not diversity on its own. The more often political parties mentioned the topic of immigration in a diverse country, the more this became threatening to trust in society (similarly to Hopkins' findings on immigration attitudes, 2010).

Discourses about immigration issues and nationality are not the only ones that matter. Canada has a very diverse population, with about one in five of its residents being foreign born, the highest percentage in the G8 (20.6 percent; Statistics Canada, 2013: 6–7). The population, largely due to immigration, is ethnically diverse and relatively young, meaning that in the past 40 years, the ethno-cultural makeup of Canada has changed drastically. While this rising diversity has clearly created some tension, in general the official discourse has been one of acceptance. The principle of multiculturalism was enshrined in the constitution in 1982, and since the 1990s, Canadians have increasingly been supportive of immigration and ethnic diversity (Harell and Deschatelêts, 2014). This kind of norm environment should condition the diversity-social cohesion nexus, especially for the youngest generation.[2]

As diversity becomes more normalized in a country or region, we expect that progressive generations of citizens will experience diversity differently.[3] Specific generational circumstances shape these experiences and related consequences of diversity. Younger generations in diverse and multicultural societies should be much less influenced by increasing diversity around them and in their networks compared to generations who were socialized into a homogeneous time period with little government policy in place that supports and underlines the normalcy of immigration and rising diversity in the population.

In our previous work, we look at how younger Canadian age groups react differently to their diverse social networks compared to older age groups (Stolle and Harell, 2013). Our argument is that the different norm environment and different opportunities to build interethnic contact will condition how these young people react to diversity. Indeed, while older generations in Canada react negatively to diversity in their surroundings and even in their social networks, the young generation consistently benefits in terms of trust. As Figure 6.2 shows, in the Canadian context, young people receive positive effects from diverse networks, unlike their older counterparts. In other words, we find asymmetrical effects with young Canadians not experiencing any adverse effects of the diversity of their surroundings and benefiting positively from their interethnic contacts. Again, such an approach combines contextual diversity with actual contact and considers how *both* can influence attitudes across generations.

The norm environment, and how it influences progressive generations, may partly account for the variance in country-level findings. As we discussed before, the negative effects of increasing diversity are not found everywhere. According to Van der Meer and Tolsma's (2014) meta-analysis, Putnam's constrict theory holds better in the United States, where there is a negative relation between diversity and trust, whereas fewer studies find this to be the case for Europe. Other work in the European context, however, challenges this assessment. With data spanning three

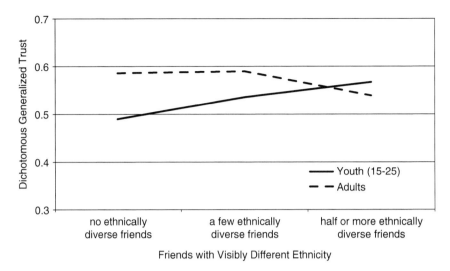

Figure 6.2 Predicted probabilities of generalized trust by network diversity and youth.
Source: Canadian GSS 2003, reproduced from Stolle and Harell (2013).

decades, Dinesen and Sønderskov (2012) find that immigration-related diversity at the municipality level depresses generalized social trust in Denmark; and so does Schaeffer (2013) with data from 55 cities and regions in Germany. Similar findings are reported for the Netherlands by Lancee and Dronkers (2011) for contact with neighbors. In Canada, results are mixed. While Canadians who live in ethnically diverse environments are also less trusting overall (Soroka *et al.*, 2007a), their attitudes of social solidarity in terms of supporting social welfare policies that benefit others, are completely unaffected (Soroka *et al.*, 2007b). Overall the tally collected by Van der Meer and Tolsma shows that 50 percent of US studies, but only 26 percent of European studies (and only 11 percent of European cross-national), and 17 percent of Anglo-Saxon studies outside of the US and Europe, support the negative relationship between diversity and trust.

So, there seems to be some cross-national variation in the consequences of ethnic diversity. While US neighborhood studies often find that diversity negatively shapes views of others and out-groups; the results in European cases and in Canada are much less homogeneous. Of course, when contact is taken into account, more positive effects emerge overall. Yet, what we are arguing here is that larger contextual factors—including the level of diversity present, the dynamics of diversity development, and how public discourses react to it—may together determine how diversity is experienced on the ground. Our analyses of the divergent effects of diversity on different age groups in Canada are just showing a glimpse of how such different contexts shape the diversity-contact-cohesion nexus.

This calls for a more nuanced consideration in cross-national research that does not rely simply on aggregate percentages of foreign-born statistics. Instead, the nature of the diversity present and how it is being received needs to be taken into account. For example, studies should pay more attention to whether a country's diversity comes from multiple sources (often referenced as hyper-diversity such as in Canada) or whether certain immigrant groups shape immigration flows (e.g., Hispanics in the US, Turks in Germany, etc.). We must also pay more attention to the types of immigrants (asylum seekers, family reunification, economic class) and the related socio-economic and cultural backgrounds that such immigrants bring with them. This is especially important because we know people perceive immigrants differently based on where they come from and their socio-economic status, and to a lesser extent whether they are bringing families with them (Iyengar *et al.*, 2013; Harell *et al.*, 2012) This suggests that the policy context may have important implications for how diversity is experienced.

The question here is about the characteristics of policies that are most beneficial for the relationship between native-borns and immigrants. Integration policies in particular could help to moderate the public perception of diversity, facilitate interethnic contact between native-borns and immigrants, provide hands-on integration help for immigrants and so on. Several policy candidates have been studied, e.g., ethnic versus civic citizenship policies, welfare state policies, multicultural policies, integration policies, etc. Research finds that civic citizenship policies, stronger integration regimes, multicultural policies and universal welfare states fare better on overall indicators of social cohesion and social capital, but also particularly for immigrants' social and political participation, and have overall lower gaps between immigrants and native-borns (Kesler and Bloemraad, 2010; Helbling *et al.*, 2014; see also the discussion of various policy effects in Koopmans and Veit, 2014). We consider particularly the latter point as important because the social and political gaps between societal groups, specifically between majorities and minorities, can be interpreted as indicators of social cohesion (Harell and Stolle, 2010).

In our cross-national research we found that countries with more inclusive integration policies (measured by the Mipex index) demonstrate smaller immigrant-native born gaps for political and social participation (Helbling *et al.*, 2014). For example, Wright and Bloemraad (2012) explore how multicultural and citizenship policies affect trust, discrimination, identity, political interest, and non-electoral participation across three different kinds of policy regimes. While they focus on absolute levels and gaps between majorities and minorities, they find no signs that these policies do any harm to immigrant integration, to the contrary, immigrants in these regimes are often more trusting and more engaged *vis-à-vis* their majority counterparts.

However, not only minorities themselves are affected. Majorities also benefit from certain integration policies. Johnston *et al.* (2010) identify links between Canadian public policies, Canadian identity and support for immigration and universal access to health care for everyone. Identification with Canada increases tolerance for immigrants and support for the welfare state especially among the affluent. Schlueter *et al.* (2013) also look at how majorities are affected by integration policies. They explore how pre-existing immigrant integration policies are associated with subsequent perceptions of threatened group interests. They find evidence that more permissive integration policies seem to be related to diminished perceived group threat.

In sum, many cross-national studies suggest ways of how public policy might help to intervene in the diversity-social cohesion nexus. While some types of integration policies have been related to either higher indicators of overall trust, lower group threat and smaller gaps between majorities and minorities, the research agenda has still to disentangle the causal effects behind this relationship. Obviously it is likely that more cohesive societies are able to implement different types of integration policies. Measurements of integration policies and indicators of social cohesion and solidarity over time should allow researchers to better understand what comes first.

Beyond trust and out-group attitudes

Finally, we argue that we need to shift away from general measures of social cohesion that focus largely on out-group attitudes and generalized trust in standard survey settings. While important, such questions are prone not only to social desirability biases, but they fail to capture the real political consequences of rising levels of diversity. We thus propose to shift away from the heavy focus on out-group attitudes and trust to include more behavioral or situational measures of social solidarity. This can be accomplished by examining more closely how ethnic diversity is influencing policy attitudes, especially those attitudes that benefit others. By using innovative experimental designs and asking citizens to make concrete decisions about resources, research will be better able to focus on the micro-mechanisms that lead citizens toward solidaric behavior and attitudes in the face of diversity.

There has been a lot of focus on attitudinal measures of social solidarity, especially on various forms of trust among social capital scholars and on out-group attitudes among those drawing from social psychological research on intergroup conflict and contact. One of the challenges of such measures is that they are general, and even within concepts of trust, there are several measures, such as out-group trust, generalized trust, and neighborhood trust that are often used as if interchangeable.

We believe strongly that a focus on more behavioral and situational measures of social cohesion may also help to more strongly ground this research in a theoretically-driven definition of what we mean by social cohesion. Social solidarity, social cohesion and social capital are all concepts that tend to focus on how a society's members feel about and interact with each other, yet all of these terms are used in a variety of ways in current research, and their measurement is often inconsistent and theoretically vague.

> Social cohesion, in effect, is about how well people get along with each other and, importantly, on what terms interaction between people take place…

social cohesion is defined by a set of social relations that are characterized by people's ability to collaborate with one another to solve collective issues and to conduct dialogue in a way that does not privilege one social group's identity or perspective over another. Given the limitations with current conceptualizations of social cohesion, we propose a refined definition of social cohesion as *cooperative relations among individuals and groups of individuals that are based on mutual recognition, equality and norms of reciprocity.*

(Harell and Stolle, 2011: 17, emphasis in original)

While trust and attitudes toward various groups in society are important measures in their own right, we think it is essential to also focus on how intergroup attitudes transfer to the political realm, especially through policy attitudes. The contemporary state that manages today's diverse societies includes a broad range of policies that are designed to protect its citizens. The welfare state, for example, puts in place protections for citizens against adversity (job loss, hunger, disability, etc.). All citizens are supposed to contribute certain amounts through their tax dollars in order to ensure that those who need such programs are looked after

Rising diversity, it has been argued (Goodhart, 2004), is putting such expressions of social solidarity at risk because those in need of such programs are increasingly being viewed as "outsiders." This is one area, then, in which we might expect intergroup experiences and attitudes to have a direct impact on political attitudes about redistribution. Indeed, some findings support that notion, and confirm that citizens have a hard time supporting programs that benefit "other" people who are viewed as different (Wolfe and Klausen, 1997; Sanderson, 2004; Alesina and Glaeser, 2004; Shayo, 2009). Sanderson (2004: 74) argues that "[e]thnically heterogeneous societies should have less public spending because people are more reluctant to incur costs to provide for others when those others are much less likely to belong to their own ethnic group." In other words, the presence of ethnic and racial diversity is seen as an impediment to shared public goods. According to a recent and widely read social commentator, this tension between "sharing and solidarity" and diversity is "one of the central dilemmas of political life in developed societies" (Goodhart, 2004). Both economists (Easterly *et al.*, 2006; Alesina and Ferrara, 2002) and welfare state scholars (Sanderson, 2004) have posited a negative relationship between racial and ethnic diversity and indicators of social cohesion, and Soroka and colleagues (2007b) find that greater changes in diversity are linked to smaller increases in social spending, although this effect does not hold within Canada, where people in diverse areas are not less supportive of welfare state policies than in homogeneous places.

Empirical findings at the individual level, however, are much more limited. There is a large literature in the US that demonstrates that Americans' low support for welfare is largely due to its association with minorities, in particular blacks (e.g., Gilens, 2000). It is little-known, however, if these findings can be extended to diversity driven by immigration and to other contexts outside the US. Recent work in this area suggests that out-group attitudes in Canada, the US, and the UK have a direct negative impact on support for redistribution (Soroka *et al.*, 2014a) and that this relationship extends beyond just welfare (Soroka *et al.*, 2013). Furthermore, when citizens are asked to make direct assessments of the level of benefits, those with pre-existing prejudicial attitudes become less solidaric when confronted with a minority welfare recipient (Soroka *et al.*, 2014a, 2014b).

This is a potentially fruitful avenue for future research on the consequences of diversity because it looks at the political implications, and goes a step beyond general out-group attitudes. It puts diversity in context by asking citizens to make specific decisions in real monetary and symbolic terms with respect to the diverse others in society. The next step is obviously to take the other insights of this chapter and apply them to such measures of diversity by addressing how changes in the demographic reality of a society can translate into concrete shifts in policy support, in part through the ways in which citizens experience that diversity in their everyday lives. This can also be extended through other behavioral measures that directly address helping behaviors between groups (see Koopmans and Veit, 2014).

Implications and concluding thoughts

The debate about the consequences of ethnic diversity on social cohesion has reached a stalemate. While a high number of studies continue to be published, they seem to highlight the problem, with at best mixed results. The argument of this chapter has been that instead of adding more analyses that prove or disprove Putnam's findings we should move toward a rigorous study of the conditions that facilitate (or perhaps hinder) the beneficial consequences of ethnic diversity. First and foremost we believe that we have looked too exclusively for the effects of diversity in neighborhoods or even larger geographic units. Diversity is, however, experienced in a myriad of ways: at work and in fleeting encounters in shops, restaurants, and doctors' offices. These might also be the places where interethnic contact has powerful moderating effects. Future research should at least try to encompass these places and at least include interethnic contact in the analyses. Beyond this, we have argued that the larger context in which diverse interactions occur needs to be studied more consistently. Experiences of diversity likely differ with changing media and party discourses and in various types of welfare state or integration regimes. Several of these system characteristics might also be able to moderate the effects between diversity and social cohesion. Finally, we argue that we should look beyond general levels of intergroup attitudes and trust as indicators of social cohesion. General support for solidaric policies or actual gaps between immigrants and native-borns in their social, political, and economic participation might be even better measures. Research should move to include such attitudes and related behaviors on the consequences of diversity.

Of course, our research agenda does not come without problems. For example, if interethnic ties matter in the explanation of the diversity-social cohesion nexus, it will be a challenge to create conditions where everyone has access. While segregation can be actively prevented, it is much more difficult, or rather impossible, to legislate interethnic friendship networks. The tasks for policy must be more modest and should focus on increasing the possibilities of horizontal interethnic contact. Second, the research on integration policies and their effects is in its infancy. While correlations between type of policy and outcome have been identified, it is much harder to determine a causal path from policy to political benefits. It could simply be that certain types of diverse, immigrant-receiving countries are more likely to implement certain types of policies (see Crepaz, 2007). Not to mention that the implementation of new integration policies is not always simple. Institutional inertia and path dependency prevent radical policy change (Esping-Andersen, 1990; Howard, 2009). And even if research identifies better solutions, they might never make it to the parliaments of Western democracies. Finally, focusing on attitudes of solidarity, policy support, and behavioral measures of social cohesion has its own set of problems. Often this research is undertaken in experiments that might lack external validity. Nevertheless, the research agenda needs to take the conditions that shape the effects of diversity more into account.

Notes

1 While there is some evidence that negative experiences may be more important in increasing prejudice than positive experiences are in reducing prejudice (Barlow *et al.*, 2012; see also Bekhuis *et al.*, 2013), other research has found the opposite (Pettigrew, 2008).
2 Just and Anderson (2014) analyze positive and negative opinion climates towards immigrants, and find that positive opinion climate increase immigrant political engagement.
3 While Putnam's work is often cited to show the negative effects of diversity, he also suggests that these effects may diminish as diversity becomes normalized.

References

Alesina, A. and Ferarra, E. L. (2002) Who trusts others? *Journal of Public Economics*, 85(20): 207–234.
Alesina, A. and Glaeser, E. (2004) *Fighting Poverty in the US and Europe: A World of Difference*. Oxford: Oxford University Press.
Allport, G. W. (1954) *The Nature of Prejudice*. Cambridge, MA: Addison-Wesley.
Barlow, F. K., Paolini, S., Pedersen, A., Hornsey, M. J., Radke, H. R. M., Harwood, J., Rubin, M., and Sibley, C. G. (2012) The contact caveat: negative contact predicts increased prejudice more than positive contact predicts reduced prejudice. *Personality and Social Psychology Bulletin*, 38(12): 1629–1643.
Bekhuis, H., Ruiter, S., and Coenders, M. (2013) Xenophobia among youngsters: the effect of inter-ethnic contact. *European Sociological Review*, 29(2): 229–242.
Christ O., Hewstone M., Tausch N., Wagner U., Voci A., Hughes J., and Cairns E. (2010) Direct contact as a moderator of extended contact effects: cross-sectional and longitudinal impact on outgroup attitudes, behavioral intentions, and attitude certainty. *Personality and Social Psychology Bulletin*, 36(12): 1662–1674.

Crepaz, M. M. L. (2007) *Trust Beyond Borders: Immigration, the Welfare State and Identity in Modern Societies*. Ann Arbor: University of Michigan Press.

Danzer, A. M. and Yaman, F. (2013) Do ethnic enclaves impede immigrants' integration? Evidence from a quasi-experimental social-interaction approach. *Review of International Economics*, 21(2): 311–325.

Dinesen, P. T. and Sønderskov, K. M. (2012) Trust in a time of increasing diversity: on the relationship between ethnic heterogeneity and social trust in Denmark from 1979 until today. *Scandinavian Political Studies*, 35(4): 273–294.

Easterly, W., Ritzen, J., and Woolcock, M. (2006) Social cohesion, institutions, and growth. *Economics & Politics*, 18(2): 103–120.

Esaiasson, P. (2014) Ethnic diversity in schools and work places – its effects on tolerance and trust. Ongoing research project.

Esping-Andersen, G. (1990) *Three Worlds of Welfare Capitalism*. Princeton: Princeton University Press.

Fieldhouse, E. and Cutts, D. (2010) Does diversity damage social capital? A comparative study of neighbourhood diversity and social capital in the US and Britain. *Canadian Journal of Political Science*, 43: 289–318.

—— (2014) Comparing the effects of neighbourhood diversity and inter-ethnic ties in the US and UK. Unpublished manuscript.

Gilens, M. (2000) The black poor and the 'liberal press'. *Civil Rights Journal*, 5(1): 18–26.

Goodhart, D. (2004) Discomfort of strangers. *Prospect*, 24 February. Republished in *The Guardian*. http://dinwww.guardian.co.uk/politics/2004/feb/24/race.eu.

Gorny, A. and Toruńczyk-Ruiz, S. (2013) Neighbourhood attachment in ethnically diverse areas: the role of interethnic ties. *Urban Studies*, 51(5): 1000–1018.

Gundelach, B. and Freitag, M. (2013) Neighbourhood diversity and social trust: an empirical analysis of interethnic contact and group-specific effects. *Urban Studies*, 51(6): 1236–1256.

Harell, A. and Deschatelêts, L. (2014) Political culture(s) in Canada: orientations to politics in a pluralist, multicultural federation. In A. Gagnon and J. Bickerton (eds) *Canadian Politics* (6th edition). Toronto: University of Toronto Press, pp. 229–247.

Harell, A. and Stolle, D. (2010) Diversity and democratic politics: an introduction. *Revue Canadienne de Science Politique*, 43(3): 235–256.

—— (2011) Reconciling diversity and community? Defining social cohesion in diverse democracies. In M. Hooghe (ed.) *Social Cohesion: Interdisciplinary Theoretical Perspectives on the Study of Social Cohesion and Social Capital*. Brussels: Royal Flemish Academy of Belgium for Science and the Arts, pp. 8–43.

Harell, A., Soroka, S., Iyengar, S., and Valentino, N. (2012) The impact of economic and cultural cues on support for immigration in Canada and the US. *Canadian Journal of Political Science*, 45(3): 499–530.

Helbling, M., Reeskens, T., and Stolle, D. (2013) Political mobilization, cultural diversity and social cohesion. the conditional effect of political parties. *Political Studies*.

Helbling, M., Reeskens, T., Stark, C., Stolle, D., and Wright, M. (2014) Enabling immigrant participation: redirecting our attention to the role of integration regimes. Book chapter under review.

Hewstone, M. (2009) Living apart, living together? The role of intergroup contact in social integration. *Proceedings of the British Academy*, 162: 243–300.

Hopkins, D. (2010) Politicized places. *American Political Science Review*, 104(1): 40–60.

Howard, M. M. (2009) *The Politics of Citizenship in Europe*. Cambridge: Cambridge University Press.

Iyengar, S., Jackman, S., Messing, S., Valentino, N., Aalberg, T., Duch, R., Soroka, S., Harell, A., and Kobayashi, T. (2013) Do attitudes about immigration predict willingness to admit individual immigrants? A cross-national test of the person-positivity bias. *Public Opinion Quarterly*, 7(3): 641–665.

Johnston, R., Banting, K., Kymlicka, W., and Soroka, S. (2010) National identity and support for the welfare state. *Canadian Journal of Political Science*, 43(2): 349–377.

Joyner, K. (2000) School racial composition and adolescent racial homophily. *Social Science Quarterly*, 81: 810–825.

Just, A. and Anderson, C. J. (2014) Opinion climates and immigrant political action: a cross-national study of 25 European democracies. *Comparative Political Studies*, 47(7): 935–965.

Kesler, C. and Bloemraad, I. (2010) Does immigration erode social capital? The conditional effects of immigration-generated diversity on trust, membership, and participation across 19 countries, 1981–2000. *Canadian Journal of Political Science*, 43(2): 319–347.

Koopmans, R. and Veit, S. (2014) Cooperation in ethnically diverse neighborhoods: a lost-letter experiment. *Political Psychology*, 35(3): 379–400.

Lancee, B. and Dronkers, J. (2011) Ethnic, religious and economic diversity in Dutch neighbourhoods: explaining quality of contact with neighbours, trust in the neighbourhood and inter-ethnic trust. *Journal of Ethnic and Migration Studies*, 37(4): 597–618.

Laxer, E. (2013) Integration discourses and the generational trajectories of civic engagement in multi-nation states: a comparison of the Canadian provinces of Quebec and Ontario. *Journal of Ethnic and Migration Studies*, 39(10): 1577–1599.

Leyden, K. (2003) Social capital and the built environment: the importance of walkable neighborhoods. *American Journal of Public Health*, 93(9): 1546–1551.

Lowndes, V. (2006) It's not what you've got but what you do with it: women, social capital and political participation. In B. O'Neill and E. Gidengil (eds) *Gender and Social Capital*. New York: Routledge, pp. 213–240.

McPherson, M., Smith-Lovin, L., and Cook, J. M. (2001) Birds of a feather: homophily in social networks. *Annual Review of Sociology*, 27: 415–444.

Marschall, M. J. and Stolle, D. (2004) Race and the city: neighborhood context and the development of generalized trust. *Political Behaviour*, 26(2): 125–153.

Massey, D. and Denton, N. A. (1993) *American Apartheid: Segregation and the Making of the Underclass*. Cambridge: Harvard University Press.

Mutz, D. C. and Mondak, J. J. (2006) The workplace as a context for cross-cutting political discourse. *Journal of Politics*, 68(1): 140–155.

Petermann, S., Heywood, M., Huettermann, J., Schmid, K., Schmitt, T., Schönwälder, K., Stolle, D., and Vertovec, S. together with Emnid, T. N. S. (2012) The "Diversity and Contact" (DIVCON) Survey.

Pettigrew, T. (2008) Future directions for intergroup contact theory and research. *International Journal of Intercultural Relations*, 32(3): 187–199.

Pettigrew, T. and Tropp, L. (2006) A meta-analytic test of intergroup contact theory. *Journal of Personality and Social Psychology*, 90(5): 751–783.

Putnam, R. D. (2000) *Bowling Alone: The Collapse and Revival of American Community*. New York: Simon and Shuster.

——(2007) *E pluribus unum*: diversity and community in the twenty-first century. *Scandinavian Political Studies*, 30(2): 137–174.

Sanderson, S. K. (2004) Ethnic heterogeneity and public spending: testing the evolutionary theory of ethnicity with cross-national data. In F. Salter (ed.) *Welfare, Ethnicity, and Altruism: New Findings and Evolutionary Theory*. London: Frank Cass, pp. 4–87.

Schaeffer, M. (2013) Can competing diversity indices inform us about why ethnic diversity erodes social cohesion? A test of five diversity indices in Germany. *Social Science Research*, 42(3), 755–774.

—— (2014) *Ethnic Diversity and Social Cohesion*. Aldershot: Ashgate.

Schlueter, E. and Scheepers, P. (2010) The relationship between outgroup size and anti-outgroup attitudes: A theoretical synthesis and empirical test of group threat and intergroup contact theory. *Social Science Research*, 39(2): 285–295.

Schlueter, E., Meuleman, B., and Davidov, E. (2013) Immigrant integration policies and perceived group threat: a multilevel study of 27 Western and Eastern European countries. *Social Science Research*, 42: 670–682.

Semyonov, M. and Glikman, A. (2009) Ethnic residential segregation, social contacts, and anti-minority attitudes in European societies. *European Sociological Review*, 25(6): 693–708.

Shayo, M. (2009) A model of social identity with an application to political economy: nation, class, and redistribution. *American Political Science Review*, 103(2): 147–174.

Soroka, S., Helliwell, J. F., and Johnston, R. (2007a) Measuring and modelling trust. In F. Kay and R. Johnston (eds) *Social Capital, Diversity and the Welfare State*. Vancouver: University of British Columbia Press, pp. 95–132.

Soroka, S., Johnston, R., and Banting, K. (2007b) Ethnicity, trust and the welfare state. In F. Kay and R. Johnston (eds) *Social Capital, Diversity and the Welfare State*. Vancouver, BC: University of British Columbia Press, pp. 279–304.

Soroka, S., Harell, A., and Iyengar, S. (2013). Racial Cues, Prejudice and Attitudes Toward Redistribution: A Comparative Experimental Approach. In APSA 2013 Annual Meeting Paper.

—— (2014a) Race, prejudice and attitudes toward redistribution: a comparative experimental approach. Unpublished manuscript.

Soroka, S., Harell, A., and Ladner, K. (2014b) Public opinion, prejudice and the racialization of welfare in Canada. *Ethnic and Racial Studies*.

Statistics Canada (2013) *Immigration and Ethnocultural Diversity in Canada: National Household Survey 2011*. Catalogue no. 99-010-X1011001. Ottawa: Ministry of Industry.

Stolle, D. and Harell, A. (2013) Social capital and ethno-racial diversity: learning to trust in an immigrant society. *Political Studies*, 61(1): 42–66.

Stolle, D., Soroka, S., and Johnston, R. (2008) When does diversity erode trust? Neighbourhood diversity, interpersonal trust, and the mediating effect of social interactions. *Political Studies*, 56(1): 57–75.

Stolle, D., Peterman, S., Schmid, K., Schönwälder, K., Hewstone, M., and Heywood, J. (2013) Immigration-related diversity and trust in German cities: the role of intergroup contact. *Journal of Elections, Public Opinion and Parties*, 23(3): 279–298.

Tausch, N., Hewstone, M., Kenworthy, J. B., Psaltis, C., Schmid, K., Popan, J. R., Cairns, E., and Hughes, J. (2010) Secondary transfer effects of intergroup contact: alternative accounts and underlying processes. *Journal of Personality and Social Psychology*, 99(2): 282–302.

Uslaner, E. M. (2010) Segregation, mistrust and minorities. *Ethnicities*, 10(4): 415–434.

Valenzuela, S., Kim, Y., and Gil de Zúñiga, H. (2012) Social networks that matter: exploring the role of political discussion for online political participation. *International Journal of Public Opinion Research*, 24(2): 163–184.

Van der Meer, T. and Tolsma, J. (2014) Ethnic diversity and its supposed detrimental effects on social cohesion. *Annual Review of Sociology*, 40.

122   *D. Stolle and A. Harell*

Wolfe, A. and Klausen, J. (1997) Identity politics and the welfare state. *Social Philosophy and Policy*, 14(2): 213–255.

Wright, M. and Bloemraad, I. (2012) Is there a trade-off between multiculturalism and socio-political integration? Policy regimes and immigrant incorporation in comparative perspective. *Perspectives on Politics*, 10(1): 77–95.

Wright, S. C., Aron, A., McLaughlin-Volpe, T., and Ropp, S. A. (1997) The extended contact effect: knowledge of cross-group friendships and prejudice. *Journal of Personality and Social Psychology*, 73(1): 73–90.

7 Ethnic heterogeneity, ethnic and national identity, and social cohesion in England

Dingeman Wiertz, Matthew R. Bennett, and Meenakshi Parameshwaran

Introduction

This chapter investigates to what extent ethnic identity and national identity mediate the relationship between ethnic heterogeneity and social cohesion in England. Scholars argue that a shared superordinate national identity is necessary to foster trust, cooperation, and solidarity among diverse sub-groups in a society (Miller, 1995; Reeskens and Wright, 2013). Some commentators assert that ethnic heterogeneity undermines the trust and solidarity necessary for cohesive societies (cf. Goodhart, 2013; Scheffer and Waters, 2011) because it reinforces separate ethnic (subordinate) identities rather than promotes a shared national (superordinate) identity. In line with such arguments, social identity theory suggests that ethnic heterogeneity can lead individuals to identify more strongly with other ethnic in-group members rather than with members of society more broadly, which could thereby restrict the development of a shared superordinate identity and therefore harm social cohesion. As such, besides the mechanisms discussed in Chapter 1, the strength of ethnic and national identities represents an additional mechanism that may explain the relationship between ethnic heterogeneity and social cohesion. Indeed, we argue that several of the previously discussed mechanisms could operate via the strength of ethnic and national identification.

Reasoning along the lines of social identity theory, as outlined in Chapter 1, increasing ethnic heterogeneity represents a threat to original national cultures, making people lose their general sense of belonging, as they are confronted with increased ethnic and cultural diversity in their surroundings. Looking for security and familiarity, people in response develop stronger feelings of identification with their own ethnic group, at the cost of their identification with the nation, to which they feel less akin and in which they find it harder to recognize themselves. These stronger identifications with one's own ethnic group and the concomitant weaker feelings of sharing a national identity may subsequently dilute social cohesion. At first, this may predominantly manifest itself in terms of more negative attitudes towards and fewer contacts with ethnic out-group members, but in the longer run this may extend to ethnic in-group members as well, leading to a more general retraction from social life (cf. Putnam, 2007). A similar chain of events is a crucial building block in the arguments developed by many critics of multiculturalism (cf. Goodhart, 2013; Scheffer and Waters, 2011).

However, contrary to this bleak narrative, there is reason to believe that social cohesion can be maintained in the presence of stronger ethnic identities. The common identity model, for example, suggests that individuals can simultaneously uphold both strong subordinate as well as strong superordinate group identities, thereby reducing in-group bias and intergroup conflict (Gaertner *et al.*, 1993). According to this model, there is no inevitable trade-off between ethnic and national identity. It therefore remains the question whether ethnic heterogeneity does indeed raise the salience of subordinate in-group identities and correspondingly decreases the salience of superordinate overarching identities, and whether these changes in turn reduce levels of social cohesion.

This chapter addresses this question and examines to what extent the strength of ethnic and national identities can explain the relationship between ethnic heterogeneity and social cohesion. We test whether higher levels of ethnic heterogeneity are associated with a stronger sense of ethnic identity, and whether a stronger sense of ethnic identity is associated with levels of lower social cohesion. We simultaneously test whether higher levels of ethnic heterogeneity are associated with a weaker sense of national identity, and whether a weaker sense of national identity is associated with lower social cohesion. In doing so, we investigate two dimensions of ethnic heterogeneity and three measures of social cohesion, as the relationships between our concepts of interest are likely to depend on how they are conceptualized.

Analytical framework: the mediating role of identity in explaining the link between ethnic heterogeneity and social cohesion

According to social identity theory, identity provides people with distinct social categories to classify their social worlds in terms of in-groups—*"us"*—and out-groups—*"them"* (Tajfel, 1978; Tajfel and Turner, 1979). Identity can be flexible as opposed to fixed and static, and can be influenced by salient features of a context such as the presence of out-group members, which can result in cognitive biases favoring the in-group (for reviews of in-group bias see Brewer, 1979; Hewstone *et al.*, 2002). In this study, in-group bias refers to the identification with a subordinate ethnic identity, at the expense of a shared superordinate national identity. Biases towards the subordinate ethnic identity are thought to undermine social cohesion because people move away from shared superordinate national identities that bind people from different ethnic sub-groups together. We investigate the effects of ethnic heterogeneity on the importance of national (superordinate) identification and ethnic/racial (subordinate) identity, which is a commonly used measure of identity strength in the literature (Ashmore *et al.*, 2004).

We derive testable hypotheses by building on the popular narratives discussed above and the theories referred to in Chapter 1 (see also Van der Meer and Tolsma, 2014). We focus on two main pathways through which ethnic identity and national identity could explain a negative association between ethnic

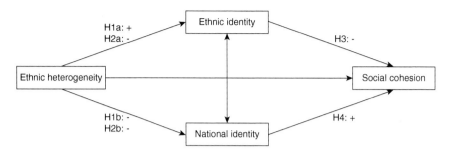

Figure 7.1 Schematic overview of hypotheses.

heterogeneity and social cohesion, both of which are related to different under-lying mechanisms and different dimensions of ethnic heterogeneity (cf. Van der Meer and Tolsma, 2014; Koopmans and Schaeffer, 2013). Analyzing these dif-ferent pathways is a valuable contribution to the scholarly literature in this field given that the role of identity as potential mediator of the relationship between ethnic heterogeneity and social cohesion thus far remains underinvestigated. Figure 7.1 provides a schematic overview of our hypotheses.

Ethnic out-group density and identity

The first pathway stresses the importance of in-group biases and is grounded in conflict theory (Blalock, 1967; Blumer, 1958). This pathway suggests that the relative out-group size, also referred to as ethnic out-group density, in a locality stimulates perceptions of material, symbolic, and cultural threat. This argument relates directly to the out-group density dimension of ethnic heterogeneity because the degree of perceived threat to one's in-group is not premised on the distribution of out-groups in a locality (i.e., one large out-group or many small out-groups), but instead on the presence of ethnic out-group members in general, irrespective of the amount of heterogeneity among these out-group members. On the basis of conflict theory we expect that a larger relative out-group size increases the salience of ethnic identity for people's sense of who they are and stimulates in-group biases, translating into stronger subordinate ethnic identification and consequently weaker superordinate national identification. This relationship assumes that ethnic and national identities are mutually exclusive and thus constitute a zero-sum game, in line with the prediction of classical social identity theory that a rise in salience of one identity comes at the expense of another identity. Our first hypotheses thus read:

H1a: Ethnic out-group density is positively associated with the strength of ethnic (subordinate) identity.
H1b: Ethnic out-group density is negatively associated with the strength of national (superordinate) identity.

Ethnic diversity and identity

The second pathway concerns social disorganization mechanisms and feelings of anomie. Of the mechanisms referred to in Chapter 1, all those related to diversity in preferences, coordination problems, and a lack of social control can essentially be classified as expressions of social disorganization due to high degrees of ethnic diversity. In a similar vein, Van der Meer and Tolsma (2014: 463) argue that higher degrees of ethnic diversity elicit feelings of anomie, which they define as "anxiety about the existence of shared societal norms and moral values." Both Chapter 1 and Van der Meer and Tolsma (2014) argue that, in an environment in which multiple ethnic groups reside, it is harder for people to reach consensus, obtain knowledge, and achieve successful enforcement with regard to shared social norms, which breeds feelings of exclusion, alienation, and up-rootedness. As a result, people become increasingly uncertain about how to relate to other people, even if these others are from their own ethnic group. In line with the constrict theory outlined by Putnam (2007), which states that cohesion diminishes both between as well as within ethnic groups in ethnically heterogeneous areas, the social disorganization and anomie pathway predicts increased normlessness and aimlessness (Smith and Bohm, 2008). This causes individuals to engage less with in-groups and with out-groups because people "no longer know how to behave in public, they are hesitant to meet and mingle with others, regardless of the ethnicity of their co-residents" (Van der Meer and Tolsma, 2014: 464). Under such circumstances, the strength of both people's national identification *and* their ethnic identification is expected to diminish. The composition of the out-group is very important according to these arguments: people living in neighborhoods where the out-group is homogenous still know what to expect from this out-group, whereas in ethnically diverse areas multiple out-groups evoke feelings of anomie. In line with this pathway we hypothesize:

> H2a: Ethnic diversity is negatively associated with the strength of ethnic (subordinate) identity.
>
> H2b: Ethnic diversity is negatively associated with the strength of national (superordinate) identity.

Linking identities to social cohesion

Our final set of hypotheses connects ethnic identity and national identity to social cohesion. These hypotheses relate directly to claims that stronger subordinate ethnic identities erode social cohesion (Goodhart, 2013; Scheffer and Waters, 2011), whereas the maintenance of a strong superordinate national identity strengthens social cohesion (Miller, 1995). The underlying assumption behind these claims is that stronger ethnic identification goes together with a stronger focus on one's ethnic in-group, at the expense of feelings of solidarity, trust, and cooperation that extend beyond these in-group boundaries, while a stronger national identity is allegedly associated with a higher commitment to solidarity, trust, and cooperation at a more comprehensive scale. In short, strong ethnic identification is considered to be a dividing force in society, as opposed to the unifying role of strong national identification.

It is important to recognize here that social cohesion is a multifaceted phenomenon: it has an attitudinal as well as a behavioral dimension; it can refer to formal and informal bonds between people; it can concern attitudes towards and relationships with in-group members, out-group members, as well as people in general; and it can also be conceptualized at different geographic levels. Despite this multifaceted nature/character of the concept of social cohesion, there is little theoretical guidance from the social psychological literature regarding the different impacts that ethnic and national identity may have across various measures of social cohesion. As such, we hypothesize uniform effects of ethnic identity and national identity across different measures of cohesion, but emphasize that differences are likely to be observed, just like the direct effect of ethnic heterogeneity on social cohesion is found to vary depending on the measure of cohesion used (Van der Meer and Tolsma, 2014). Our final set of hypotheses can be summarized as follows:

H3: The strength of ethnic (subordinate) identity is negatively associated with social cohesion.
H4: The strength of national (superordinate) identity is positively associated with social cohesion.

Figure 7.1 contains two additional arrows alongside those discussed as part of our main hypotheses. First, the bidirectional arrow between ethnic identity and national identity takes into account that the strength of ethnic and national identities may co-vary. These concepts could be either negatively correlated, as in a zero-sum game, or positively, as posited by the common identity model (Gaertner *et al.*, 1993). The second arrow runs directly from ethnic heterogeneity to social cohesion, and assesses whether ethnic and national identity fully mediate the relationship between ethnic heterogeneity and social cohesion or whether there are additional factors at work. Observing a significant direct effect of ethnic heterogeneity, having accounted for the potential mediating impact of the strength of ethnic and national identification, indicates that this relationship cannot be *fully* explained via the previously discussed identity mechanisms.

Finally, we stress that, while our hypotheses are phrased in general terms, it is plausible that some of the hypothesized relationships vary across ethnic subgroups. For example, increases in ethnic out-group density may increase the salience of ethnic identity to a greater extent among the white British majority, who may perceive higher levels of economic and symbolic threat as the currently dominant sub-population in England than ethnic minority groups that are accustomed to the presence of larger ethnic out-groups and are thus less affected by this aspect of geographic context. For this reason, we have conducted additional analyses for white British and ethnic minority respondents separately.

Data and measurement

We test our hypotheses with data from the 2008–2009 Citizenship Survey, which features a large representative sample of approximately 10,000 adults living in England and Wales, alongside a boost sample of 5,000 ethnic minority respondents. The survey captures information on a wide range of demographics, attitudes, and behaviors, including large batteries of questions on identity and social cohesion. Respondents living in Wales are excluded from the analysis because we have been unable to obtain information on the ethnic composition of smaller geographic areas in Wales. Furthermore, respondents are only selected if they have complete data for our dependent and independent variables, and if they consider their national identity to be British and/or English, accounting for a total of 8,750 respondents. We restrict our analyses to people reporting a British or English national identity, since these identities represent the relevant superordinate identities in English communities, having the potential to bind together people of different ethnic origin.[1]

We match the 2001 Census Small Area Microdata Sample (SAMS) to the Citizenship Survey 2008–2009 to create our contextual-level variables of interest. Local authorities are used as our geographic contextual-level units because they represent the smallest geographical areas for which we can match the Citizenship Survey and SAMS data. Local authorities are local administrative areas and contain on average approximately 330,000 people. The 8,750 respondents in our sample live in 300 different local authorities.

Our contextual-level variables of substantive interest measure ethnic out-group density (the threat, conflict, and cognitive biases pathway) and ethnic diversity (the social control and anomie pathway) of a local authority.[2] *Ethnic out-group density* is defined as the proportion of individuals in the local authority who report an ethnic affiliation that is different from the individual's own ethnic affiliation. Ethnic out-group density ranges from 0 (all individuals in the local authority have the same ethnic affiliation as the individual in question) to 1 (all individuals in the local authority have a different ethnic affiliation to the individual in question). This variable has a bimodal distribution, reflecting that most ethnic minority respondents have a high ethnic out-group density, while most white British respondents have a low ethnic out-group density. The separate analyses we additionally run for white British and ethnic minority respondents serve as a sensitivity check of how this bimodal distribution affects our results. *Ethnic diversity* is defined as the ethnic fractionalization index of a local authority, which is the inverse of the Herfindahl Index. Ethnic diversity varies from 0 to 1, where scores of 1 indicate the highest level of ethnic diversity. For the construction of our measures of ethnic out-group density and ethnic diversity, we use a nine-category classification of ethnicity contained in the Census, consisting of the following categories: white British, white Other, mixed, Indian, Pakistani, Bangladeshi, black Caribbean, black African, and other.[3]

We use three measures of social cohesion captured in the Citizenship Survey. First, we look at neighborhood trust, which is measured with the question "Would you say that: (1) many of the people in your neighborhood can be trusted, (2) some can be trusted, (3) a few can be trusted, (4) or that none of the people in your neighborhood can be trusted?" A fifth and less-informative answering option— "just moved here"—is excluded from our analysis (approximately 2 percent of the respondents opted for this answer). Second, we analyze levels of generalized trust, which scope extends beyond the neighborhood and which is measured using the question "Generally speaking, would you say that most people can be trusted, or that you can't be too careful in dealing with people?" In addition to the two core answering options "People can be trusted" and "You can't be too careful" about 8 percent of the respondents spontaneously reply "It depends," which represents an intermediate answer between the two extremes. We treat both neighborhood trust and generalized trust as ordinal variables in our analysis. Our third measure concerns the behavioral dimension of social cohesion by examining civic participation. This variable is constructed as a factor score on the basis of four measures capturing the yearly instance of 1) formal volunteering; 2) informal volunteering; 3) civic activism; and 4) general civic participation.

Our indicators of ethnic (subordinate) and national (superordinate) identity measure the strength of ethnic and national identification, based on the questions "How important is your ethnic or racial background to your sense of who you are?" and "How important is your national identity to your sense of who you are?"[4] The response categories for both questions are "(1) not at all important," "(2) not very important," "(3) quite important," and "(4) very important." We treat the strength of ethnic and national identity as ordinal variables in our analysis.

Table 7.1 presents descriptive statistics for the core variables in our analyses, i.e., ethnic heterogeneity, social cohesion, and the importance of ethnic and national identity.

We control for a number of variables at the individual level captured in the Citizenship Survey 2008–2009. Ethnicity/race is included as a categorical variable measuring whether a respondent is white (57 percent of our sample), Asian (24 percent), black (12 percent), or other (7 percent). Religious affiliation is included via a categorical variable measuring whether the respondent is Christian, Muslim, or another denomination, or has no religion at all. Religious practice is captured via a dummy variable coded 1 for respondents who report active religious participation and 0 otherwise. We treat educational attainment as a continuous measure, ranging from 0 (no qualifications) to 4 (university degree). Housing tenure is included via dummy variables for outright homeownership, ownership via a mortgage, and renting. We control for whether the respondent is born in Great Britain with a dummy indicator. Our marital status indicator measures whether the respondent is married or cohabiting, single without ever having cohabited or been married, or separated, divorced, or widowed. Gender is included as a dummy variable (1 is female; 0 is male). Age is measured in years.

In addition to these individual-level controls, we control at the local authority level for the degree of socio-economic deprivation of the area and whether it is an urban or rural area. For socio-economic deprivation we include the Index of Multiple Deprivation (IMD), which is a composite poverty measure created using the rankings of the local authority according to the following characteristics: income, employment, health deprivation and disability, educational skills and training, barriers to

Table 7.1 Descriptive statistics for social cohesion, identity, and ethnic heterogeneity (n = 8,750).

Neighborhood trust	Percentage
Many of the people in one's neighborhood can be trusted	40.1%
Some of the people in one's neighborhood can be trusted	38.6%
A few of the people in one's neighborhood can be trusted	18.5%
None of the people in one's neighborhood can be trusted	2.8%

Generalized trust	Percentage
Most people can be trusted	35.1%
You can't be too careful in dealing with people	56.6%
It depends (as spontaneous answer)	8.4%

Civic participation	Percentage
Any formal volunteering in the past 12 months	40.3%
Any informal volunteering in the past 12 months	61.3%
Any civic activism in the past 12 months	11.4%
Any other civic participation in the past 12 months	37.8%

Importance of ethnic/racial identity	Percentage
Very important	40.4%
Quite important	33.2%
Not very important	19.6%
Not at all important	6.9%

Importance of national identity	Percentage
Very important	45.4%
Quite important	38.2%
Not very important	13.2%
Not at all important	3.2%

Ethnic heterogeneity	Mean	SD
Ethnic out-group density 2008	0.485	0.398
Percentage change in ethnic out-group density 2001–2011	37.1	43.2
Ethnic diversity 2008	0.395	0.262
Percentage change in ethnic diversity 2001–2011	49.0	32.8

housing and services, crime, and the living environment. The urban/rural character of the local authority is controlled for via a dummy variable that equals 1 if the respondent lives in an urban area and 0 if the respondent lives in a rural area.

Estimation strategy

We test our hypotheses by estimating structural equation models that take into account the clustering of respondents in different local authorities. Structural equation modelling allows us to simultaneously model various pathways, with the outcome variables in some equations (i.e., ethnic and national identity) being used as predictor variables in other equations (i.e., social cohesion). Although structural equation modelling does not enable us to make firm claims regarding the exact *causal* pathways between our concepts of interest, it does enable us to assess the *plausibility* of the hypothesized pathways by examining to what extent they fit the associations that are present in our data.

We initially estimated two-level hierarchical path models to account for the clustering of respondents in local authorities, but we encountered convergence difficulties in some models. These convergence problems are likely due to the complexity of our models, and previous studies estimating similar models have run into the same problem (e.g., Savelkoul *et al.*, 2011). Instead, we therefore correct for the clustering in our data using the COMPLEX estimation method in Mplus 7, which employs WLSMV estimation (Muthén and Muthén, 1998–2012). This robust weighted least squares estimator estimates probit coefficients for all our regression equations with a categorical dependent variable (i.e., ethnic identity, national identity, neighborhood trust, and generalized trust), and a simple linear coefficient for the regression equations with the factor score for civic participation as the dependent variable. In addition to the hypothesized pathways outlined in Figure 7.1, our models also estimate the direct path from ethnic heterogeneity to social cohesion, and allow ethnic identity and national identity to be correlated with each other. Finally, we include all of our individual-level and contextual-level control variables in the regressions for all of the endogenous variables in our models (i.e., ethnic identity, national identity, and social cohesion).

Results

Figures 7.2, 7.3, and 7.4 present the results of path models that estimate the effects of ethnic heterogeneity, via ethnic and national identity, on our three measures of social cohesion: neighborhood trust, generalized trust, and civic participation. Each of these figures summarizes two path models: one that uses ethnic out-group density as measure of ethnic heterogeneity (in bold), and another that uses our measure of ethnic diversity (in italics). The figures also display the associations between socio-economic area deprivation with ethnic and national identity and social cohesion, since prior studies demonstrate this is a crucial control variable (Laurence, 2011; Letki, 2008; Twigg *et al.*, 2010). We do not present the coefficient estimates for our other control variables, but they are in line with previous research (results available upon request).

Before discussing our core hypotheses we first stress two other findings. To start with, there is a strong positive correlation between ethnic and national identity in all of our models (0.556), suggesting that these two identities do *not* constitute a zero-sum game from a cross-sectional perspective, thus supporting the common identity model. Separate analyses for the white British and the ethnic minority sub-populations in our sample indicate that this holds true for both majority *and* minority groups, with estimated correlations of approximately 0.575 and 0.520, respectively. Second, our finding that socio-economic area deprivation has a powerful negative direct impact on all of our social cohesion indicators

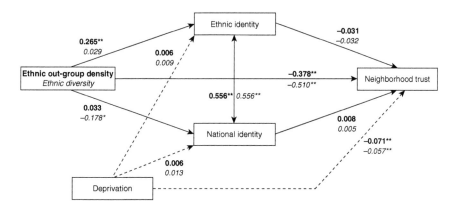

Figure 7.2 Results of path analyses of the identity-mediated effects of ethnic heterogeneity on neighborhood trust.

Note: Bold coefficients: path model with ethnic out-group density as measure of ethnic heterogeneity. The estimated indirect effect of ethnic out-group density on neighborhood trust via ethnic identity is –0.008 (p = 0.146), and the estimated indirect effect via national identity is smaller than 0.001 (p = 0.792). Italic coefficients: path model with ethnic diversity as measure of ethnic heterogeneity. The estimated indirect effect of ethnic diversity on neighborhood trust via ethnic identity is –0.001 (p = 0.742), and the estimated indirect effect via national identity equals –0.001 (p = 0.808). n = 8750. † p<0.10, * p<0.05, ** p<0.01.

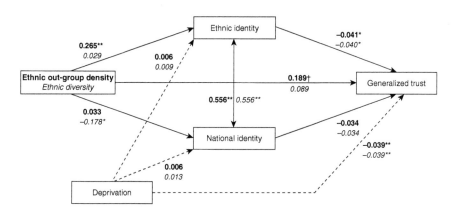

Figure 7.3 Results of path analyses of the identity-mediated effects of ethnic heterogeneity on generalized trust.

Note: Bold coefficients: path model with ethnic out-group density as measure of ethnic heterogeneity. The estimated indirect effect of ethnic out-group density on generalized trust via ethnic identity is –0.011 (p = 0.067), and the estimated indirect effect via national identity is –0.001 (p = 0.692). Italic coefficients: path model with ethnic diversity as measure of ethnic heterogeneity. The estimated indirect effect of ethnic diversity on generalized trust via ethnic identity is –0.001 (p = 0.734), and the estimated indirect effect via national identity equals –0.006 (p = 0.210). n = 8750. † p<0.10, * p<0.05, ** p<0.01.

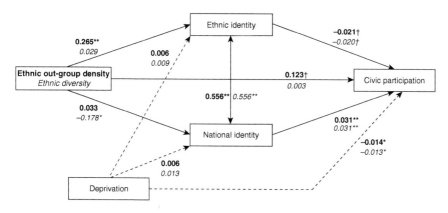

Figure 7.4 Results of path analyses of the identity-mediated effects of ethnic heterogeneity on civic participation.

Note: Bold coefficients: path model with ethnic out-group density as measure of ethnic heterogeneity. The estimated indirect effect of ethnic out-group density on civic participation via ethnic identity is −0.005 (p = 0.112), and the estimated indirect effect via national identity is 0.001 (p = 0.679). For this model, RMSEA = 0.019 and CFI = 0.953. Italic coefficients: path model with ethnic diversity as measure of ethnic heterogeneity. The estimated indirect effect of ethnic diversity on civic participation via ethnic identity is −0.001 (p = 0.736), and the estimated indirect effect via national identity equals −0.006 (p = 0.104). For this model, RMSEA = 0.019 and CFI = 0.957. n = 8750. † p<0.10, * p<0.05, ** p<0.01.

corroborates the findings from previous studies on the UK (Laurence, 2011; Letki, 2008; Twigg *et al.*, 2010). Conversely, area deprivation does not affect the strength of ethnic and national identification.

Ethnic out-group density and identity

With respect to our hypotheses that ethnic out-group density is positively associated with the importance of ethnic identity (hypothesis 1a) and negatively with the importance of national identity (hypothesis 1b), we find the strongest support for hypothesis 1a: people living in local authorities with higher concentrations of people from a different ethnicity than themselves do have a stronger sense of ethnic identity (estimated coefficient equals 0.265). This finding is in line with the conflict, threat, and cognitive bias mechanisms that have been discussed earlier on in this chapter and volume. Conversely, we do not find supportive evidence for the second implication of these mechanisms: the relationship between ethnic out-group density and the strength of national identification is non-significant in all of our models, suggesting that the rising salience of ethnic identity in communities with higher stocks of ethnic out-group members does not come at the expense of a loss of national identity. Hence, hypothesis 1b is refuted.

Ethnic diversity and identity

On the basis of social disorganization and anomie mechanisms, we hypothesized that higher degrees of ethnic diversity in localities are associated with a weakening of both ethnic and national identities (hypotheses 2a and 2b). As can be seen in Figures 7.2–7.4, we find support for hypothesis 2b, with an estimated negative effect of ethnic diversity on national identity (–0.178). However, we do not find any evidence that people in more ethnically diverse areas also have a weaker sense of ethnic identity due to general feelings of exclusion and alienation. Instead, we observe a statistically insignificant effect of ethnic diversity on ethnic identity, causing us to reject hypothesis 2a.

Linking identities to social cohesion

Hypotheses 3 and 4 concern the impact of ethnic and national identity on social cohesion, whereby stronger ethnic identification leads to lower levels of social cohesion (hypothesis 3), while stronger national identification is supposed to have the opposite effect (hypothesis 4). These hypotheses presume that ethnic identity plays a dividing role in society whereas national identity is believed to be a unifying force.

The results demonstrate the importance of making a distinction here between different measures of social cohesion. Firstly, Figure 7.2 shows that hypotheses 3 and 4 are not supported in terms of neighborhood trust. Although the signs of the estimated coefficients for the effects of ethnic and national identity on neighborhood trust are in line with our hypotheses, both coefficients are insignificantly different from zero. This suggests that the strength of ethnic and national identification does not influence localized attitudinal measures of social cohesion.

In Figure 7.3, however, a different pattern emerges. While the effect of national identity on social cohesion (measured by generalized trust in this model) is non-significant, resulting in the rejection of hypothesis 4 once again, we do find that people with a stronger sense of ethnic identity tend to report lower levels of generalized trust, supporting hypothesis 3. This latter finding stands in sharp contrast with the lack of association between ethnic identity and neighborhood trust observed in Figure 7.2. One potential explanation for this contrast lies in the confounding impact of ethnic residential segregation. After all, if different ethnic groups are segregated across or even within neighborhoods, this likely strengthens their identification with their own ethnic group. However, this does not have to express itself in lower levels of neighborhood trust, as one's neighbors probably belong to one's ethnic in-group in such a scenario. On the other hand, generalized trust, which also encompasses trust towards ethnic out-groups, is likely to be damaged. Further investigation is required to untangle the negative association between ethnic identity and generalized trust, but at first glance this result supports the narrative of identity as mediator of the relationship between ethnic heterogeneity and social cohesion. We also observe a negative indirect effect (–0.011) of ethnic out-group density on generalized trust via ethnic identity, which is significant at the 10 percent level. This indirect effect results from the positive direct effect of ethnic out-group density on ethnic identity strength combined with the negative direct effect of ethnic identity strength on generalized trust.

Lastly, for civic participation (Figure 7.4) we find support for both hypotheses 3 and 4: ethnic identity has a marginally significant negative effect on civic participation (–0.021), while national identity has a strong positive effect (.031). The former finding suggests that people who identify more strongly with their ethnic group are poorer in terms of formal social capital, which may or may not be offset with larger stocks of informal social capital. The latter finding is interesting because it is the only significant link between national identity and our social cohesion indicators. Apparently, the strength of national identity is less important for attitudinal measures of cohesion, but is a strong predictor of civic behavior. Altogether, the right-hand half of Figure 7.4 is consistent with the claim that subordinate, ethnic-based identities are detrimental to social cohesion, whereas stronger superordinate, national identities tend to be associated with higher levels of social cohesion. Nevertheless, if we combine the coefficient estimates of the right-hand half of the figure with those of its left-hand half, neither the indirect paths from ethnic heterogeneity via ethnic identity to civic participation, nor their counterparts via national identity, are statistically significant.

The direct effects of ethnic heterogeneity on social cohesion

While the direct path from ethnic heterogeneity to social cohesion is not the focus of this chapter, it is interesting to pay some attention to our estimates for these direct paths. In short, our results demonstrate that ethnic out-group density and ethnic diversity have strong negative associations with neighborhood trust, that ethnic out-group density has a weak but significant positive relationship with generalized trust and civic participation, while ethnic diversity is unrelated to generalized trust and civic participation. These results are reasonably consistent with the existing British literature on the direct relationship between ethnic heterogeneity and social cohesion. Most studies on Great Britain suggest that while ethnic heterogeneity does have a negative impact on neighborhood attitudes and local trust (Laurence, 2013; Letki, 2008; Twigg *et al.*, 2010), its effects on generalized trust and civic participation are non-existent or even positive (Laurence, 2013; Letki, 2008; Sturgis *et al.*, 2011). This is the exact same pattern as we find here.

The strong direct effects of ethnic heterogeneity on neighborhood trust that remain after accounting for the role of ethnic and national identity as potential mediators of this relationship underline the fairly weak mediating impact of identity.[5] This also suggests that there must be other mechanisms underlying this relationship than the identity-related ones that we focus on in this chapter. Various alternative mechanisms have already been mentioned in Chapter 1, including more general versions of the cognitive bias and social disorganization mechanisms, but also mechanisms related to communication problems and diversity in terms of socio-political preferences. Another alternative explanation concerns the confounding impact of residential stability, which tends to be lower in more ethnically heterogeneous areas (Laurence, 2011, 2013). Nonetheless, previous research on the UK indicates that strong negative direct effects of ethnic heterogeneity on neighborhood trust persist after controlling for residential turnover (Laurence, 2011, 2013). Finally, contact mechanisms (see Chapter 8) and residential ethnic segregation (see Chapter 5) are also often cited as prominent mediators and/or moderators of the ethnic heterogeneity-social cohesion nexus.

Changes in ethnic heterogeneity

In recognition of arguments that most claims on the impact of ethnic heterogeneity on social cohesion are fundamentally dynamic in nature, we have rerun our models to estimate the effects of changes in ethnic out-group density and ethnic diversity. The idea here is that social cohesion is probably most strongly affected by changes in the ethnic composition of local areas rather than by stable levels of ethnic heterogeneity with which people are familiar (e.g., Hopkins, 2009). Therefore, we have replaced our static ethnic heterogeneity measures for the year 2008 with variables measuring the change in these indicators on the basis of the ethnic composition of the local authorities in 2001 and 2011 (i.e., the years that the Census survey took place). Table 7.2 presents the estimated effects of these changes in ethnic heterogeneity on the strength of people's ethnic and national identification, as well as on our three measures of social cohesion.

Table 7.2 reinforces our previously established conclusion that ethnic and national identity have little or no mediating power when it comes to the relationship between ethnic heterogeneity and social cohesion. Indeed these models for the *changes* in ethnic heterogeneity convey an even more optimistic message than the models for the *levels* of ethnic heterogeneity. The majority of models presented in Table 7.2 show that increases in ethnic out-group density as well as ethnic diversity are associated with stronger national identification. Moreover, if we ignore outliers for whom ethnic out-group density has risen by more than 100 percent, increases in ethnic out-group density go together with weaker identification with one's own ethnic group. In other words, to the extent that we found evidence that higher ethnic heterogeneity is associated with stronger ethnic and weaker national identification; this evidence largely evaporates when looking at changes in ethnic heterogeneity over time. Interestingly, the strong negative direct effects of ethnic heterogeneity on neighborhood trust in Figure 7.3 also disappear when shifting our focus from levels of heterogeneity to changes in heterogeneity.

Differential effects across ethnic groups

As pointed out earlier in this chapter, one may expect the effect of ethnic heterogeneity on identity, but also the effects of ethnic and national identification on social cohesion, to be different for ethnic majority than for ethnic minority groups. To allow for such differential effects, we have rerun our path models separately for all white British people (n = 4,859) and all ethnic minorities (n = 3,891) in our sample.

Table 7.2 Results of path analyses of the identity-mediated effects of changes in ethnic heterogeneity on social cohesion.

Social cohesion measure	Ethnic heterogeneity measure	Effect of 10 percentage point change in ethnic heterogeneity on:		
		Ethnic identity	National identity	Social cohesion
Neighborhood trust	Ethnic out-group density	**−0.005**	**0.014****	**0.003**
		−0.020*	*0.003*	*0.019**
	Ethnic diversity	**0.001**	**0.019****	**0.007**
		−0.008	*0.017**	*0.021**
Generalized trust	Ethnic out-group density	**−0.005**	**0.014****	**−0.003**
		−0.020*	*0.003*	*−0.018†*
	Ethnic diversity	**0.001**	**0.019****	**−0.005**
		−0.008	*0.017**	*−0.014†*
Civic participation	Ethnic out-group density	**−0.005**	**0.014****	**−0.006**
		−0.020*	*0.003*	*0.000*
	Ethnic diversity	**−0.001**	**0.018****	**−0.003**
		−0.008	*0.017**	*0.000*

Note: Only the estimates for the effects of changes in ethnic heterogeneity are displayed. Bold coefficients: full sample (n = 8,750); italic coefficients: restricted sample for which the change in ethnic heterogeneity is less than 100 percent (n = 8,072 for the ethnic out-group density models, and n = 8,130 for the ethnic diversity models). † p<0.10, * p<0.05, ** p<0.01.

The key insight obtained from these analyses (results available upon request) is that there is indeed considerable variation across these two groups. In terms of the association between ethnic heterogeneity and identity, both ethnic out-group density and ethnic diversity are related to stronger ethnic identification for white British people, while these factors do not seem to be related in any way to the strength of their national identity. On the other hand, we observe that for ethnic minority respondents the relative size of ethnic out-groups is neither associated with their ethnic nor national identification, but that higher degrees of ethnic diversity go together with both weaker ethnic as well as national identification.[6] Thus, we observe partial support for the conflict/threat/cognitive bias mechanism among white British people as far as the effect of ethnic out-group density and diversity on ethnic identification are concerned, while the effects of ethnic diversity on ethnic and national identification for ethnic minority respondents is in accordance with the social disorganization/anomie mechanism. These cross-ethnic differences are masked in our general analyses summarized in Figures 7.2–7.4.

With respect to the relationship between ethnic and national identity and social cohesion, we find that for white British people a stronger ethnic identity is associated with lower civic participation and to a lesser extent lower neighborhood trust. Among ethnic minority respondents we observe a negative relationship between ethnic identity and generalized trust and a strong positive relationship between national identity and civic participation. Altogether, these associations imply a strong significant negative indirect effect of ethnic diversity on civic participation via national identity for ethnic minority respondents, as well as a negative indirect effect of both measures of ethnic heterogeneity on civic participation and to a lesser extent neighborhood trust via ethnic identity for the white British subpopulation. From this perspective identity seems to have more mediating power when we look at the white British and ethnic minority sub-populations separately than in a pooled analysis.

Discussion and conclusion

This chapter refines the literature investigating the link between ethnic heterogeneity and social cohesion by exploring the extent to which ethnic and national identity mediate these relationships in England. This is a timely contribution given popular claims that ethnic heterogeneity causes people to identify more strongly with other ethnic in-group members rather than with members of society more broadly, thereby restricting the development of social cohesion (cf. Goodhart, 2013; Scheffer and Waters, 2011)—claims that have thus far eluded any systematic empirical scrutiny. We test the pathways that may exist between ethnic heterogeneity, ethnic and national identities, and social cohesion, incorporating recommendations that the effects of ethnic heterogeneity may be different depending on the exact measures of heterogeneity and social cohesion used (Koopmans and Schaeffer, 2013; Van der Meer and Tolsma, 2014).

Our first hypothesis, founded on arguments related to ethnic conflict and cognitive out-group biases, states that the proportion of ethnic out-groups in an area is positively associated with the strength of ethnic identity, and negatively associated with the strength of national identity. Despite finding that larger ethnic out-groups stocks are associated with a stronger ethnic identity (mainly for white British people, as additional analyses suggest), we do not find that national identity is weakened in favor of this stronger ethnic identity. In line with social disorganization and anomie mechanisms, we hypothesize that the ethnic diversity in an area is negatively associated with the strength of national identity *and* ethnic identity. Our analysis finds that ethnic diversity is associated with a weaker national identity at the 10 percent significance level; in contrast, there is no effect of ethnic diversity on ethnic identity. Nevertheless, these results mask the fact that ethnic diversity is associated with significantly weaker ethnic as well national identification for ethnic minorities, as additional analyses indicate.

We also test hypotheses that stronger ethnic identification is associated with lower levels of social cohesion, while stronger national identification is associated with higher levels of social cohesion. We fail to find support for these claims with regard to our local attitudinal measure of neighborhood trust. Neither do we find evidence for an association between national identity and generalized trust, but we do find that ethnic identity is negatively associated with generalized trust. Finally, we do find that stronger ethnic identification correlates with lower levels of civic participation, while stronger national identification correlates with higher levels of civic participation.

We thus find partial support, depending on the measures of ethnic heterogeneity and social cohesion used, for some of the links through which ethnic and national identity could mediate the relationship between ethnic heterogeneity and social cohesion. That said, in general we have to conclude that the overall evidence on the question whether the strength of ethnic and national identification can partly explain this relationship is weak. This at least seems to hold as far as the English context is concerned. Importantly, most of the indirect effects of ethnic heterogeneity on social cohesion via ethnic and national identity are statistically insignificant, regardless of the specific measure of ethnic heterogeneity and social cohesion used. An exception is the indirect effect of ethnic out-group density on generalized trust via ethnic identity, which is negative and in line with our hypotheses, but this indirect effect is only significant at the 10 percent level. We do find some more support for the role of ethnic and national identity as mediators in our analyses distinguishing ethnic majority from minority groups. Therefore, while an extensive analysis of such sub-population-specific patterns is beyond the scope of the present study, we stress that future research should delve further into this issue. In any case, our analysis shows that if we pool together the different ethnic sub-populations, the answer to the question as to what extent ethnic identity and national identity mediate the relationship between ethnic heterogeneity and social cohesion is "not a great extent at all."

There remain a number of caveats to this study. First, as with almost all studies on the relationship between ethnic heterogeneity and social cohesion, there is the issue of causality and selection, as already touched upon in Chapter 1 and elsewhere in this volume. In the absence of the ability to randomly allocate people to neighborhoods or local authorities with different ethnic composition, it remains a challenge to make solid causal claims on the relationship between these concepts, and our study is no exception to this rule, given that we only have observational data at our disposal. As Laurence (2013) notes, and as has also been pointed out in Chapter 1, it is virtually impossible under such circumstances to rule out the possibility that any relationships that we observe between ethnic heterogeneity and social cohesion (as well as ethnic and national identity, for that matter) originate from selection biases due to, for example, selective residential mobility rather than from true causal mechanisms. It is equally hard to attach any causal direction to the association between identity and social cohesion. Causality is very likely to run two ways between these concepts, and one could even go as far as to make the argument that the strength of national identification can be regarded as a dimension of social cohesion.

As mentioned in our results section, most theoretical assertions concerning the relationship between ethnic heterogeneity and social cohesion have a dynamic character, arguing how *changes* in the degree of ethnic heterogeneity lead to *changes* in social cohesion. An optimal test of these claims should, therefore, also have a dynamic character. Notwithstanding a few exceptions (e.g., Chapter 3 and Chapter 4 of this volume; Dinesen and Sønderskov, 2012; Kesler and Bloemraad, 2010), however, most studies in this area have a cross-sectional design. Although we only have measures of social cohesion and identity available for one point in time in this study, we have looked at the influence of changes in ethnic heterogeneity over time, thus making a modest step in the right direction. These analyses illustrate that *changes* in ethnic heterogeneity do not necessarily yield the same results as *levels* of ethnic heterogeneity. In fact, when concentrating on changes in ethnic heterogeneity, our results are even more dismissive of the idea that identity (partially) mediates the relationship between ethnic heterogeneity and social cohesion.

Another caveat concerns our inability to distinguish between in-group and out-group directed measures of social cohesion in the Citizenship Survey. Many theoretical arguments suggest that the effects of ethnic heterogeneity on social cohesion may differ depending on whether one looks at "bonding" or "bridging" forms of social cohesion, and such arguments can easily be extended to incorporate the mediation effects of national and particularly ethnic identity as well. Even though empirical studies are yet to convincingly show that the effects of ethnic heterogeneity do indeed differ conditionally on whether one looks at in-group or out-group forms of social cohesion (Van der Meer and Tolsma, 2014), it is very likely that potentially differing impacts of ethnic identity on in-group and out-group social cohesion are concealed in our analysis as a consequence of our inability to distinguish between such concepts. For example, it remains unclear whether our finding that stronger ethnic identification is associated with lower levels of generalized trust would require further investigation if we were to distinguish between the effects of ethnic identity on trust towards ethnic in-groups and out-groups.

A final note of caution regards the magnitude of the effects that we find. In this respect, our study echoes the findings from previous studies on the UK, which emphasize the limited substantive significance of ethnic heterogeneity in terms of explaining variation in the outcome of interest (e.g., Letki, 2008; Sturgis *et al.*, 2011; Twigg *et al.*, 2010). For example, when we compare an individual from a local authority with an ethnic out-group density of practically 0 to an individual from a local authority with an ethnic out-group density of almost 1 (i.e., the two most extreme scores on the ethnic out-group density scale), we find that the second individual only has a 10 percentage points higher predicted probability of reporting that their ethnic or racial background is very important to them, despite the strong positive coefficient estimate that we find for the effect of ethnic out-group density on ethnic identity strength. Once again, this underscores the point that the role of ethnic and national identity as mediator of the relationship between ethnic heterogeneity and social cohesion seems limited in England. Nevertheless, it remains a task for future research to replicate this study for other countries, to examine more carefully how the explanatory power of the identity mechanism varies across ethnic subpopulations, and to explicitly address how the influence of ethnic and national identity relates to the influence of other possible mechanisms underlying the relationship between ethnic heterogeneity and social cohesion.

Notes

1 This restriction is based on the following survey question: "What do you consider your national identity to be? Please choose as many or as few as apply." The answer options are

English, Scottish, Welsh, Irish, British, and other. Among the 14,322 respondents living in England, 84.6 percent report to have a British or English national identity, with 9.5 percent declaring to have both. Including those respondents who do not consider their national identity to be British or English in our analyses does not substantially alter our results. Notice also that the survey question from which we derive our indicator for the *strength* of national identification refers back to the survey question quoted above (see footnote 4).

2 We follow the bulk of the literature in this field by assuming linear effects of these heterogeneity measures in our analyses. We acknowledge that it is possible that ethnic heterogeneity has a non-linear impact, exhibiting threshold effects for instance (see also Chapter 3), but a detailed analysis of such non-linearities is beyond the scope of this chapter.

3 The census measures of ethnicity represent self-reported ethnic identity rather than ethnicity derived from country of birth and, as such, are relatively more subjective measures (respondents are also limited in the response options on the survey; although write-in response options are available, these are harder to access and difficult to use).

4 The importance of ethnic/racial identity refers to the following question asked earlier in the questionnaire "Please could you look at this card and tell me which of these best describes your ethnic group? (1) white—British, (2) white—Irish, (3) any other white background, (4) mixed white and black Caribbean, (5) mixed white and black African, (6) mixed white and Asian, (7) any other mixed background, (8) Asian or Asian British—Indian, (9) Asian or Asian British—Pakistani, (10) Asian or Asian British—Bangladeshi, (11) any other Asian/Asian British background, (12) black or black British—Caribbean, (13) black or black British—African, (14) Any other black/black British background, (15) Chinese, (16) any other ethnic group." The importance of national identity refers to the survey question that we also use for selecting our sample of analysis; see footnote 1.

5 In fact, the coefficient estimates we find for the direct effects of ethnic heterogeneity on all of our cohesion measures are virtually the same as when we omit the identity-based mediation channels from our models (results available upon request).

6 If we instead look at *changes* in ethnic heterogeneity, we observe that for white British respondents increases in both ethnic out-group density and ethnic diversity are weakly associated with *stronger* national identities but are not related to the strength of ethnic identification. For the ethnic minority subpopulation changes in ethnic out-group density are neither associated with the strength of ethnic identity nor with the strength of national identity, while increases in ethnic diversity are related to *stronger* ethnic and *stronger* national identification.

References

Ashmore, R. D., Deaux, K., and McLaughlin-Volpe, T. (2004) An organizing framework for collective identity: articulation and significance of multidimensionality. *Psychological Bulletin*, 130(1): 80–114.

Blalock, H. M. (1967) *Toward a Theory of Minority-Group Relations*. New York: Wiley.

Blumer, H. (1958) Race prejudice as a sense of group position. *Pacific Sociological Review*, 1(1): 3–7.

Brewer, M. B. (1979) Ingroup bias in the minimal intergroup situation: a cognitive motivational analysis. *Psychological Bulletin*, 86: 307–324.

Dinesen, P. T. and Sønderskov, K. M. (2012) Trust in a time of increasing diversity: on the relationship between ethnic heterogeneity and social trust in Denmark from 1979 until today. *Scandinavian Political Studies*, 35(4): 273–94.

Gaertner, S. L., Dovidio, J. F., Anastasio, P. A., Bachman, B. A., and Rust, M. C. (1993) The common ingroup identity model: recategorization and the reduction of intergroup bias. *European Review of Social Psychology*, 4(4): 1–26.

Goodhart, D. (2013) *The British Dream: Successes and Failures of Post-War Immigration.* London: Atlantic Books.

Hewstone, M., Rubin, M., and Willis, H. (2002) Intergroup bias. *Annual Review of Psychology,* 53: 575–604.

Hopkins, D. J. (2009) The diversity discount: when increasing ethnic and racial diversity prevents tax increases. *Journal of Politics,* 71(1): 160–177.

Kesler, C. and Bloemraad, I. (2010) Does immigration erode social capital? The conditional effects of immigration-generated diversity on trust, membership, and participation across 19 countries, 1981–2000. *Canadian Journal of Political Science,* 43(2): 319–347.

Koopmans, R. and Schaeffer, M. (2013) De-composing diversity: in-group size and out-group entropy and their relationship to neighbourhood cohesion. *WZB Discussion Paper SP VI 2013-104.*

Laurence, J. (2011) The effect of ethnic diversity and community disadvantage on social cohesion: a multi-level analysis of social capital and interethnic relations in UK communities. *European Sociological Review,* 27(1): 70–89.

——— (2013) "Hunkering down or hunkering away?" The effect of community ethnic diversity on residents' social networks. *Journal of Elections, Public Opinion & Parties,* 23(3): 255–278.

Letki, N. (2008) Does diversity erode social cohesion? Social capital and race in British neighbourhoods. *Political Studies,* 56(1): 99–126.

Miller, D. (1995) *On Nationality.* New York: Oxford University Press.

Muthén, L. K. and Muthén, B. O. (1998–2012) *Mplus User's Guide.* Los Angeles, CA: Muthén & Muthén.

Putnam, R. D. (2007) *E pluribus unum*: diversity and community in the twenty-first century. *Scandinavian Political Studies,* 30(2): 137–174.

Reeskens, T. and Wright, M. (2013) Nationalism and the cohesive society: a multilevel analysis of the interplay among diversity, national identity, and social capital across 27 European societies. *Comparative Political Studies,* 46(2): 153–181.

Savelkoul, M., Scheepers, P., Tolsma, J., and Hagendoorn, L. (2011) Anti-Muslim attitudes in the Netherlands: Tests of contradictory hypotheses derived from ethnic competition theory and intergroup contact theory. *European Sociological Review,* 27(6): 741–758.

Scheffer, P. and Waters, L. (2011) *Immigrant Nations.* Cambridge: Polity.

Smith, H. P. and Bohm, R. M. (2008) Beyond anomie: alienation and crime. *Critical Criminology,* 16(1): 1–15.

Sturgis, P., Brunton-Smith, I., Read, S., and Allum, N. (2011) Does ethnic diversity erode trust? Putnam's 'hunkering down' thesis reconsidered. *British Journal of Political Science,* 41: 57–82.

Tajfel, H. (1978) *Differentiation Between Social Groups: Studies in the Social Psychology of Intergroup Relations.* London and New York: Published in cooperation with European Association of Experimental Social Psychology by Academic Press.

Tajfel, H. and Turner, J. C. (1979) An integrative theory of intergroup conflict. In W. G. Austin and S. Worche (eds) *The Social Psychology of Intergroup Relations.* New York: Praeger, pp. 33–47.

Twigg, L., Taylor, J., and Mohan, J. (2010) Diversity or disadvantage? Putnam, Goodhart, ethnic heterogeneity, and collective efficacy. *Environment and Planning A,* 42(6): 1421–1438.

Van der Meer, T. and Tolsma, J. (2014) Ethnic diversity and its effects on social cohesion. *Annual Review of Sociology,* 40: 459–478.

8 Diversity, trust, and intergroup attitudes

Underlying processes and mechanisms*

Katharina Schmid, Miles Hewstone, and Ananthi Al Ramiah

Introduction

Many of us now live in ethnically, racially, or otherwise diverse neighborhoods or cities (see, e.g., Vertovec, 2007), and Western societies continue to grow ever more diverse (see Cornelius and Rosenblum, 2005). This diversity has raised the question of the potential consequences of such diversity for outcomes related to social capital, an issue that remains contentious in both academic and public policy domains alike. As a result there now exists a wealth of studies in many different contexts and countries examining the effects of living in diverse neighborhoods or cities on the growth and distribution of social capital. Despite this research, relatively little is as yet known about the processes and mechanisms that explain *how* diversity may, or may not, affect social capital.

This chapter thus seeks to shed light on three mediators that help explain the processes through which diversity may exert effects on outcomes related to social capital: intergroup contact, perceived threat, and social identity complexity. We focus specifically on two potential consequences: trust (especially out-group, in-group, and neighborhood trust) and intergroup attitudes. By summarizing some of our recent empirical work that explicitly considered the role of intergroup contact, perceived threat and social identity complexity as mediators, this chapter highlights the centrality of considering not only direct but also indirect effects of diversity on trust and attitudes.

The chapter is organized into three main sections. Part one begins with a brief overview of the main theoretical approaches of relevance to understanding the link between diversity and trust: conflict/constrict and contact theories. We focus especially on intergroup contact theory and summarize current thinking in this field based on recent social-psychological work, to explain why we consider intergroup contact a central mediator of the relationship between diversity and trust. We further discuss the role of perceived threat as an additional mediator in this relationship. This is followed by a summary of our recent empirical work, which

* We gratefully acknowledge funding from the Leverhulme Trust, as well as the Max-Planck Institute for the Study of Religious and Ethnic Diversity, Germany, which facilitated the writing of this chapter.

tested not only direct but also indirect effects of diversity on trust via the mediators intergroup contact and perceived threat (Schmid *et al.*, 2014).

Part two of this chapter then introduces a further social psychological mediator: social identity complexity (see Roccas and Brewer, 2002; Schmid and Hewstone, 2011). We begin by defining social identity complexity, as a concept that reflects the extent to which individuals perceive the multiple social groups they belong to (e.g., ethnic, national and religious groups) in more complex, differentiated and inclusive terms. We summarize research that shows that individuals with higher social identity complexity tend to hold more positive intergroup attitudes, and argue that social identity complexity can be considered a key mediator in the relationship between diversity and intergroup attitudes. Specifically, we argue that diversity can prompt individuals to perceive their multiple social groups in more complex terms (i.e., show increased social identity complexity), with positive consequences for intergroup relations. This part of the chapter further includes a detailed review of our recent empirical work that has considered social identity complexity as a process explaining the link between diversity and intergroup attitudes (Schmid *et al.*, 2013).

We conclude our chapter, in part three, with a discussion of the wider implications of our recent empirical work, highlighting the need for future research to consider the three mediators discussed in this chapter in seeking to provide a more complete understanding of the consequences of diversity on outcomes related to social capital, and the underlying processes involved. We especially emphasize the need for future research to take full account of intergroup contact experiences, including not only positive but also negative contact experiences. We further discuss some of the limitations of prior work, and end by making recommendations for future research on diversity and social capital.

Diversity and trust: mediation via intergroup contact and perceived threat

There has been considerable debate over whether neighborhood diversity, as a macro-level phenomenon characterizing a given spatial unit (i.e., the aggregate-level proportional representation of different subpopulations in a given spatial unit such as neighborhoods or cities), has negative consequences for trust. Much of this debate has been fuelled by a controversial view on the potential consequences of diversity (Putnam, 2007), suggesting that diversity may have negative consequences for individuals, groups and indeed societies at large. The introduction to this book (Chapter 1) provides a detailed summary of this debate, and the research evidence that has been amassed since Putnam's paper, seeking to validate or refute this claim. We therefore merely summarize briefly the key theoretical viewpoints, that, on the one hand, predict negative consequences of diversity on trust (conflict and constrict theories) and, on the other hand, predict positive consequences of diversity on trust (contact theory). This then forms the basis of our discussion of two key mediators central to understanding how diversity may affect trust, intergroup contact and perceived threat.

Negative consequences of diversity: conflict and constrict theory

Both "conflict theory" (also commonly referred to as "group threat theory"; e.g., Blalock, 1967; Blumer, 1958; Bobo, 1999) and the very loosely defined "constrict theory" (Putnam, 2007) predict negative consequences of diversity. Conflict theory focuses mainly on explaining majority group members' prejudice towards minority out-groups, arguing that environments characterized by greater proportions of (minority) out-group members inevitably invoke perceptions of competitive threat to the (majority) in-group's position, which then fuels intergroup tensions and negatively impacts intergroup attitudes (e.g., Fosset and Kiecolt, 1989; Quillian, 1995). Putnam's constrict theory extends conflict theory's predictions to other outcomes beyond prejudice, such as trust, and considers the impact of diversity on outcome measures relating to the in-group as well as the out-group.

To give a brief definition, trust can be seen broadly as a positive bias towards others in the processing of imperfect information (Yamagishi and Yamagishi, 1994) and making benign assumptions about other people's behavior (Kollock, 1994), thereby allowing individuals to overcome uncertain social situations (see Kollock, 1994). Trust thus places individuals in a state of vulnerability (Kramer, 1999), since extending trust to others despite one's uncertainty over their motives, intentions, and behavior involves relinquishing control and granting power to others, in the expectation that they will not exploit one's vulnerability (Tanis and Postmes, 2005).

Moreover, trust is commonly regarded as part of the "social glue" that holds communities together (see e.g., Uslaner, 2011), and people high in generalized trust are typically more tolerant of minority groups and supportive of affirmative action (see Uslaner, 2011). Trust thus appears to have positive outcomes for society, making it imperative to understand whether and how diversity affects trust.

In the context of the debate on diversity, considerable attention is placed on forms of interpersonal trust, such as generalized trust (i.e., trust in people in general; see e.g., Hooghe *et al.*, 2009) or neighborhood trust (i.e., trust of one's neighbors; see e.g., Lancee and Dronkers, 2011). However, trust may also be group-based, such that trust may be extended to or withheld from others based on their social group memberships and whether they are perceived to belong to one's in-group or out-groups (see e.g., Foddy *et al.*, 2009; Tam *et al.*, 2009). Indeed Putnam (2007) found that diversity lowered not only generalized and neighborhood trust, but also out-group trust (i.e., trust of ethnic out-groups), and even in-group trust (i.e., trust of one's ethnic in-group).

A number of studies, albeit focusing only on generalized or neighborhood trust, have revealed negative findings of diversity on trust similar to those reported by Putnam (see e.g., Alesina and La Ferrara, 2002; Hero, 2003). However, there also exists a sizable body of counterevidence that appears to refute Putnam's findings (see e.g., Gesthuizen *et al.*, 2009; Hooghe *et al.*, 2009; Lancee and Dronkers, 2011; see Van der Meer and Tolsma, 2014, for a meta-analytic review). A defining feature of all these empirical studies, however, is that they only considered direct effects of diversity, without seeking to study *how* diversity may affect trust. By primarily testing direct relationships between diversity measures and outcomes of trust (albeit typically controlling for a range of socio-demographic variables), prior research has thus largely ignored a number of key potential mediating processes that are crucial to understanding the link between diversity and trust. Two such processes that we focus on in the following section are intergroup contact and perceived threat.

Positive consequences of diversity: contact theory

Conflict and constrict theories stipulate direct negative consequences of diversity on intergroup attitudes and trust, respectively. Yet many empirical tests of these theories have ignored some of the processes and mechanisms that explain how diversity is subjectively perceived and encountered. Crucially we argue that diversity may not only be experienced and encountered negatively. On the contrary, diverse contexts also offer opportunities for positive intergroup contact, i.e., for having positive face-to-face interactions with those diverse others who make up one's environment. Thus, individuals living in geographical units with greater proportional shares of out-group residents tend to have more positive contact (see, e.g., Pettigrew *et al.*, 2010; Schlueter and Wagner, 2008; Stein *et al.*, 2000; Wagner *et al.*, 2006). Similarly, individuals perceiving greater opportunities for intergroup contact (i.e., greater perceived diversity) also report having more contact, a relationship observed among majority (see, e.g., Wagner *et al.*, 1989) as well as ethnic minority (see e.g., Vervoort *et al.*, 2010) populations. Importantly, then, we know that intergroup contact tends to exert positive effects on intergroup attitudes and trust, as is stipulated in "intergroup contact theory" (see Allport, 1954).

Contact theory thus offers a sharply contrasting, and more optimistic, view of the consequences of diversity for trust and intergroup attitudes, compared to conflict or constrict theory. Contact theory essentially postulates that engaging in positive contact with individuals from different groups promotes positive intergroup attitudes via processes of generalization of positive attitudes from the encountered individual to the wider out-group (see Brown and Hewstone, 2005; Hewstone, 2009). Although such positive effects are maximized if the contact between group members is cooperative, if group members meet under equal status conditions, if there is some pursuit of common goals, and if the contact is in some form institutionally supported (see Allport, 1954), we know now that contact can often be effective even if these conditions are not met (see Pettigrew and Tropp, 2006).

Since the inception of Allport's (1954) contact hypothesis, researchers have accumulated widespread empirical support for the effects of contact in many different contexts and under many different conditions, showing that contact is consistently associated with more positive attitudes (see Pettigrew and Tropp, 2006, for meta-analytic support) and trust (see, e.g., Tam *et al.*, 2009). Moreover, contact researchers have furthered a more in-depth understanding of the different *types* of contact, and *when* and *how* contact works (for a detailed review see, e.g., Brown and Hewstone, 2005). It is thus now well established that not only the frequency (or quantity) of contact, but importantly, the *quality* of contact determines the extent to which contact positively affects out-group attitudes. Hence it is positive contact that is most important for improving intergroup attitudes and trust.

Moreover, considerable strides have been made in understanding the mediating processes that help explain how contact positively affects intergroup relations. We thus know, for example, that contact works by reducing intergroup anxiety or increasing empathy and perspective taking (see, e.g., Pettigrew and Tropp, 2008). Of most importance to this chapter, intergroup contact also tends to be associated with reduced intergroup threat perceptions (e.g., Tausch *et al.*, 2007). Perceived intergroup threat is conceptualized as the belief that the out-group is in some way detrimental to the in-group, and although perceived threat often concerns "realistic" issues, such as competition over resources, territory or status, it may also be more intangible and "symbolic" in nature (see e.g., Riek *et al.*, 2006, for a review). Indeed, perceived intergroup threat has been found to mediate the effects of intergroup contact on intergroup attitudes and also out-group trust (e.g., Tausch *et al.*, 2007).

Toward an integration of conflict/constrict and contact theories

To date, the majority of research testing the predictions of conflict and constrict theories has solely considered direct relationships between diversity at the context-level and outcomes of attitudes and trust without considering additional individual-level mediators (such as contact or threat) that help explain how such diversity may affect these outcomes. Conversely, the majority of research on intergroup contact has focused only on individual-level consequences thereof, thereby largely ignoring its interplay with wider contextual and societal phenomena, such as the diversity of individuals' immediate social contexts. Yet as mentioned above, it is increasingly being recognized that diversity at the context-level offers important opportunities for contact, and that individuals in diverse contexts do in fact have more contact, which tends to be related with reduced threat perceptions and positive outcomes for intergroup attitudes (e.g., Pettigrew *et al.*, 2010; Schlueter and Wagner, 2008). There is thus growing recognition among researchers interested in the consequences of contact of the importance of considering wider contextual phenomena and their interplay with individual-level outcomes (see, e.g., Christ and Wagner, 2012; Pettigrew and Tropp, 2011).

In order to move towards a synthesis of these seemingly opposing theoretical viewpoints (conflict/constrict theory versus contact theory) one can argue that a more fruitful approach to the question of the potential consequences of diversity is not to consider these theories as oppositional, but rather as complementary, that is, to move towards an integration of the theories when empirically examining the consequences of diversity. Based on the assumption that diverse social contexts offer opportunities for intergroup contact, one can predict that greater diversity will be associated with more neighborhood contact, which in turn should be associated with reduced intergroup threat perceptions. Consequently, diversity may not only exert *direct negative* effects on attitudes and trust (as postulated by conflict/constrict theories) but can also exert *positive indirect* effects via increased positive intergroup contact and reduced intergroup threat. Considering processes of intergroup contact and perceived intergroup threat is thus crucial to fully understanding, and testing in a theory-driven manner, the relationship between diversity and trust.

Previous research has tested some of these predictions, either in full or in part, yet primarily in relation to intergroup attitudes and prejudice (a few studies have also tested these predictions in relation to social ties, see, e.g., Savelkoul *et al.*, 2011). Research has thus shown that diversity can exert indirect effects on prejudice, via its positive effects on intergroup contact (e.g., Schlueter and Scheepers, 2010; Schlueter and Wagner, 2008; Wagner *et al.*, 2006; Pettigrew *et al.*, 2010). For example, Wagner *et al.* (2006) found that respondents living in diverse districts in Germany held more positive out-group attitudes, an effect mediated by contact. Similarly, Pettigrew *et al.* (2010) have shown diversity to be associated with greater intergroup contact, which was associated with lower threat perceptions and, consequently, less prejudice. Research has also shown diversity of different European regions to be associated with less prejudice towards immigrants, via greater contact and reduced threat (Schlueter and Wagner, 2008). Similar results were obtained in a study in the Netherlands (Schlueter and Scheepers, 2010). Yet Schlueter and Wagner (2008) were only able to use the share of the non-national workforce in a given region as a proxy for diversity, while Schlueter and Scheepers (2010) only measured perceived, rather than actual, neighborhood diversity.

Importantly, however, although this handful of studies highlights the importance of considering intergroup contact as a key process in examining potential consequences of diversity, none of these studies allows us to draw any conclusions about the indirect effects of diversity on trust. A study that tentatively points to the critical role of contact in understanding the effects of diversity on trust is that of Stolle *et al.* (2008), who found that, although diversity exerted negative effects on generalized trust in the US and Canada, these effects were reduced when controlling for the extent to which individuals tended to engage in social interaction with neighbors. This study did not, however, probe for indirect effects of diversity on various types of trust via positive intergroup contact.

An empirical examination of the diversity-trust relationship via contact and threat

In order to provide the first empirical test of the aforementioned integrative predictions on the consequences of diversity for trust, we conducted a purposely designed study in England (Schmid *et al.*, 2014). Our aim in this study was to examine the relationship between neighborhood ethnic diversity and three different types of trust: out-group, in-group, and neighborhood trust, as well as intergroup attitudes. We tested these relationships while accounting for intergroup contact and perceived intergroup threat, thereby examining potential indirect effects of diversity on trust and attitudes via these two mediators. In so doing, our research constitutes a theoretically driven empirical investigation of Putnam's diversity-distrust hypothesis that simultaneously tested, and in an integrated manner, the predictions of conflict, constrict, and contact theories.

Our study involved a sample of the general population of England, derived from neighborhoods varying in their proportion of ethnic minority residents (based on middle layer super output areas, which are small geographical units derived by the Office for National Statistics in the UK with a minimum population of n = 5,000 residents and a mean of n = 7,200 residents). Focusing on smaller geographical units such as neighborhoods is more meaningful than using larger areas since it is in such smaller community contexts that individuals negotiate their everyday relations (see also Eric Oliver and Wong, 2003).

We sampled 868 white British majority respondents from 218 different neighborhoods, and 798 ethnic minority respondents from 196 neighborhoods, which allowed us to test our predictions separately among white British majority and ethnic minority respondents. Specifically, we examined for the white British majority, the consequences of living in neighborhoods of varying proportions of ethnic minority residents, and for the ethnic minority sample, the consequences of living in neighborhoods of varying proportions of white British majority residents. For the white British respondents, our indicators of diversity at the neighborhood level (based on objective population statistics) consisted of the ethnic fractionalization (EF) index (which ranges from low (0) to high (1), with higher scores reflecting higher probability of encountering someone from a non-white British background in the neighborhood; see, e.g., Montalvo and Reynal-Querol, 2005). For the ethnic minority respondents, we used as an indicator of diversity the Herfindahl index (which is the inverse of the EF index, with scores varying from 0 to 1, such that higher scores reflect a higher probability of encountering a white British person in the neighborhood; see Hirschman, 1964). Although we subsequently refer to both indexes in broad summary fashion as "diversity" measures, in drawing conclusions based on these findings, we ask the reader to keep in mind that our measures of diversity refer, in basic terms, to the relative size of the respective out-groups in individuals' neighborhoods.

Data for our study was collected by means of a survey, subcontracted to a professional survey company who conducted face-to-face interviews in respondents' own homes (for full details on design and methodology see Schmid *et al.*, 2014). The survey asked respondents questions about their perceptions of and experiences with the out-group (i.e., ethnic minority members for the white British respondents, and white British majority members for the ethnic minority respondents) and the in-group (i.e., members of one's own ethnic group). We measured respondents' positive contact with out-group members in their neighborhood, by asking them how often they mixed socially and had brief encounters with the out-group (for example, when buying a newspaper in local shops). Respondents were also asked about perceived intergroup threat from the out-group, by asking, for example, whether they felt the out-group threatened their own group's way of life, or whether they thought the out-group committed crimes that negatively affect the in-group or perceived the out-groups as taking away jobs from in-groups. We then asked respondents to rate their levels of trust of the out-group, the in-group, and their neighbors. In addition we measured respondents' out-group attitudes, by asking how warm or cold they felt towards the out-group on a feeling thermometer

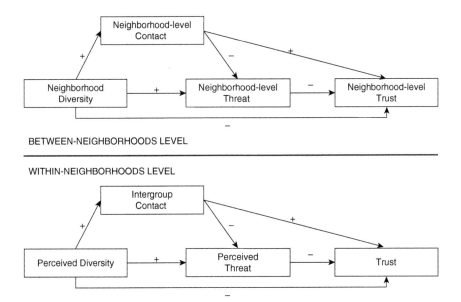

Figure 8.1 Theoretical model showing hypothesized relationships between diversity, intergroup contact, perceived threat, and trust.

(a common measurement tool for assessing intergroup attitudes; see Lolliot *et al.*, forthcoming).

We also measured perceived diversity, by asking respondents to rate the perceived proportion of out-group residents in their neighborhood. This allowed us to test the effects of both conceptualizations of diversity, objective and subjective, on trust and attitudes, i.e., the neighborhood-level effects of actual diversity (based on the ethnic fractionalization and the Herfindahl index), and the individual-level effects of perceived diversity (based on subjective ratings), respectively. Finally, we controlled for demographic variables (age, gender, education, and income), as well as an additional macro-level variable, neighborhood deprivation (a variable which typically yields significant negative effects on trust and social capital; see, e.g., Letki, 2008). Controlling for neighborhood deprivation was thus essential, since it allowed us to ensure that any effects of diversity did not simply occur due to co-variation between diversity and deprivation.

Figure 8.1 provides a graphical illustration of our predictions, at both the between-neighborhoods level (where we examined the effects of objective diversity measures on trust) and the within-neighborhoods level (where we examined the effects of perceived diversity on trust). At both the between-neighborhoods and within-neighborhoods levels, we expected diversity to exert direct negative effects on perceived threat and trust, yet at the same time to also exert positive direct effects on intergroup contact. We then further predicted that intergroup contact would be associated with reduced intergroup threat perceptions, and thus positively affect trust. As a consequence of these predicted effects, we also predicted that diversity, both actual and perceived, would be indirectly positively associated with increased trust, and that this would impact the total effects of diversity, such that the negative direct effects of diversity on trust would be reduced.

In analyzing our data, we calculated direct, indirect, and total effects of both actual and perceived diversity on in-group, out-group, and neighborhood trust, and intergroup attitudes, separately for the white British majority and the ethnic minority samples. Direct effects simply involve the estimation of direct relationships between diversity and the various outcome variables (as have typically been considered in prior work; see Chapter 1 in this volume). Indirect effects refer to the mediated effects of diversity on the outcome variables, such that one is able to assert indirect relationships between diversity and trust and attitudes, via intergroup contact and perceived threat. Total effects refer, then, to the sum of the direct and indirect effects for each of the outcome variables, which allow us to gauge the overall, or net, effect of diversity on each outcome once the mediators were accounted for. Tables 8.1 and 8.2 summarize the results of these findings for the white British majority and the ethnic minority samples, respectively (for the full set of results see Schmid *et al.*, 2014).

We start by summarizing our findings for the white British sample. Considering first the effects of actual diversity (measured by ethnic fractionalization, i.e., higher probability of encountering someone from an ethnic minority background in one's neighborhood), our study showed that diversity was directly associated with lower out-group and neighborhood trust, similar to effects reported by Putnam (2007) and others. Yet unlike Putnam's (2007) findings, we did not observe a significant effect of diversity on in-group trust, nor on out-group attitudes. Moreover, greater diversity was associated with increased contact with ethnic minorities in the neighborhood, which in turn was associated with reduced intergroup threat perceptions. Consequently, all indirect effects of diversity via the mediators of contact and threat were positive, for all types of trust, and out-group attitudes. Importantly, when we estimated the total effects of diversity on trust and attitudes, these were all non-significant for trust and were, in fact, positive for out-group attitudes. These findings show that any direct negative effects of actual diversity in the neighborhood were canceled out once the indirect effects via intergroup contact were accounted for.

When considering the effects of perceived diversity, again we obtained direct negative effects on trust (out-group, in-group, and neighborhood trust), but not on attitudes. However, all indirect effects via contact and threat for all trust and attitudes outcomes were positive, such that greater perceived diversity was associated with more contact, and consequently less threat, which then led to positive indirect effects. Consideration of the total effects of perceived diversity revealed non-significant effects for out-group trust and attitudes, yet for in-group and neighborhood trust the total effects were negative (accounting for individuals' levels of contact thus did not cancel out these negative effects of perceived diversity on in-group and neighborhood trust).

Table 8.1 Summary of direct, indirect, and total effects of diversity on outcome variables for white British sample.

	Direct, indirect, and total effects of diversity			
	Out-group trust	In-group trust	Neighborhood trust	Out-group attitudes
BETWEEN-NEIGHBORHOODS LEVEL				
Direct effect	–*	–	–*	–
Indirect effect via contact and threat	+*	+*	+*	+*
Total effect	+	+	–	+*
WITHIN-NEIGBORHOODS LEVEL				
Direct effect	–*	–*	–*	–
Indirect effect via contact and threat	+*	+*	+*	+*
Total effect	–	–*	–*	+

Note: + denotes positive effect; – denotes negative effect; * denotes statistically significant effect. At the between-neighborhoods level, the measure of diversity is ethnic fractionalization. At the within-neighborhoods level, the measure of diversity is perceived diversity. See Schmid *et al.* (2014) for a full description of results.

Table 8.2 Summary of direct, indirect, and total effects of diversity on outcome variables for ethnic minority sample.

	Direct, indirect, and total effects of diversity			
	Out-group trust	In-group trust	Neighborhood trust	Out-group attitudes
BETWEEN-NEIGHBORHOODS LEVEL				
Direct effect	–	–	–	+
Indirect effect via contact and threat	+*	+*	+*	+*
Total effect	+	–	+	+
WITHIN-NEIGHBORHOODS LEVEL				
Direct effect	+	+*	+	+
Indirect effect via contact and threat	+*	+*	+*	+*
Total effect	+*	+*	+*	+

Note: + denotes positive effect; – denotes negative effect; * denotes statistically significant effect. At the between-neighborhoods level, the measure of diversity is Herfindahl. At the within-neighborhoods level, the measure of diversity is perceived diversity. See Schmid *et al.* (2014) for a full description of results.

Results for the ethnic minority sample did not mirror those obtained for the white British majority. When we considered the effects of actual diversity (as measured by Herfindahl, i.e., higher probability of encountering a white British person in the neighborhood) we thus did not observe any direct negative effects on trust or attitudes. Conversely, all indirect effects of actual diversity, via contact and threat were positive, yet no significant total effects emerged such that diversity did not exert significant total effects on any of the outcome variables.

Similar findings were obtained for perceived diversity, where no direct effects emerged, with the exception of in-group trust for which we actually observed a positive direct effect. As before, all indirect effects via contact and threat were positive. Moreover, total effects on trust were positive, yet no total effect on attitudes emerged.

In sum, these findings revealed a somewhat different pattern for the white British majority and the ethnic minority samples. While for the white British majority we did observe some negative effects (similar to those reported by Putnam, 2007, and others), especially for neighborhood trust and in-group trust, for the ethnic minority sample, living in neighborhoods with greater numbers of majority group members did not adversely affect trust and intergroup attitudes. Importantly, for the white British majority we saw that intergroup contact played a crucial role: living in neighborhoods co-inhabited by greater proportions of ethnic minority members was associated with greater frequency of positive intergroup contact with ethnic minority members, such that most of the negative direct effects of diversity (both actual and perceived) were canceled out once these positive contact experiences were accounted for. The only negative total effects that remained significant were the effects of perceived (but not actual) diversity on in-group and neighborhood trust. This finding with regard to neighborhood trust confirms meta-analytic findings by Van der Meer and Tolsma (2014), who show that the most consistent negative effects of diversity were on neighborhood trust.

The fact that we observed negative total effects of perceived diversity on in-group and neighborhood trust, but *not* on out-group trust and out-group attitudes is somewhat surprising for another reason, and therefore particularly noteworthy. Predictions of conflict and constrict theory may lead one to expect the most pronounced negative effects for outcomes related to the out-group, in this case out-group trust and attitudes. Yet the fact that we instead observed only negative net effects on in-group and neighborhood trust may allow us to draw more measured conclusions on the negative impact of diversity on these outcomes. We thus argue that our findings, rather than reflecting negative consequences per se, may instead reflect processes akin to the psychological process of "deprovincialization" (see Pettigrew, 1997).

Deprovincialization refers to a process whereby individuals, as a consequence of intergroup contact, come to reappraise the importance of their own group's norms and values, and to recognize that their in-group's customs and way of life are not the only legitimate way to navigate the social world. Such in-group reappraisal (or deprovincialization) is then thought to have positive consequences for intergroup relations. In the context of our study, it is thus plausible that subjective perceptions of diversity evoke similar deprovincialization processes, involving perhaps a lowering of in-group trust *relative* to out-group trust rather than a reduction of trust per se. Indeed, such processes may be particularly applicable to dominant majority groups, which is why we may have only witnessed this pattern of effects for the white British majority. While this is an intriguing possibility, it remains for future research to explore this prediction further, and to consider additional mediators that may tap processes of deprovincialization. For example, it will be worthwhile to explore whether the effects of diversity on trust are mediated by changes in in-group identification or in-group norms. In our recent research we have already begun to explore the possibility that diversity may not only work by affecting inter-group contact and perceived threat, but may also lead to increased social identity complexity (i.e., the extent to which individuals perceive their multiple in-groups in more or less inclusive and differentiated terms). This work, which we review below, has shown that diversity was indirectly associated with more positive inter-group attitudes, via increased social identity complexity (Schmid *et al.*, 2013).

Diversity and intergroup attitudes: mediation via social identity complexity

While Putnam is often criticized for having placed undue emphasis on the negative implications of his findings concerning the consequences of diversity (especially those that may be observed in the short term), we acknowledge here that Putnam may also have been unjustly credited with making solely pessimistic predictions on the consequences of diversity. Indeed, he argues that diversity can also have positive consequences, which may, however, require more time to manifest themselves. He writes:

> In the medium to long run, on the other hand, successful immigrant soci-eties create new forms of social solidarity and dampen the negative effects of diversity by constructing new, more encompassing identities. Thus, the central challenge for modern, diversifying societies is to create a new, broader sense of "we."
>
> (Putnam, 2007: 138)

Putnam's reasoning here suggests that diversity may prompt individuals to reframe their in-group boundaries and embrace broader, more inclusive common in-group identities. Moreover, social psychological theorizing and research suggests that individuals who embrace more inclusive identities tend to hold more positive intergroup attitudes (see, e.g., Gaertner and Dovidio, 2000, for a detailed social psychological overview of the common in-group identity and the dual identity models; see also Schmid and Hewstone, 2010, for a review of the relationship between contact and multiple social categorization processes in diverse settings). For the remainder of this chapter, we focus on a related, but conceptually distinct social-psychological process concerning the extent to which individuals perceive their in-groups in more or less exclusive terms: social identity complexity.

Social identity complexity

Individuals typically belong to and identify with multiple different groups, identifying simultaneously, for example, with religious, national, ethnic, or racial groups, among many others (for an overview of social psychological theorizing on social identities see, e.g., Schmid *et al.*, 2011). The concept of social identity complexity (Roccas and Brewer, 2002) rests upon the notion that individuals differ in the extent to which they perceive the multiple in-groups they belong to in complex or non-complex ways (see Schmid and Hewstone, 2011, for a review). More specifically, individuals may differ in social identity complexity, such that individuals who perceive high interrelationships between the multiple groups they belong to reflect relatively lower social identity complexity, whereas individuals who are able to differentiate and perceive lower interrelationships between their multiple in-groups are relatively higher in social identity complexity. Individuals may thus perceive their multiple in-group identities as largely overlapping and similar in meaning, or as non-overlapping and different in meaning. Importantly then, being high in social identity complexity does not merely imply that one identifies highly with various different groups. Rather, the concept of social identity complexity captures the extent to which individuals perceive their multiple groups to be interrelated and convergent. In other words, social identity complexity captures whether individuals are aware of the fact that their various multiple in-groups actually constitute separate groups, and recognize that these separate groups do not necessarily overlap.

Take, for example, a white British Christian. This individual may perceive high overlap between these three identities (thus perceiving that most British people are white and Christian) and may also perceive high similarity in meaning surrounding these three identities (thus perceiving that being British means very much the same as being white and Christian). This individual may thus be regarded as low in social identity complexity since he perceives his various in-groups as highly overlapping and similar in meaning. Conversely, another white British Christian who does in fact recognize that not all British people are white or Christian, and who also does not ascribe the similar prototypical attributes to these three identities then reflects relatively higher social identity complexity. Individuals low in social identity complexity thus see little distinction between their multiple in-groups, believing that most British people are also white and Christian, and that the typical attributes of British people also apply to white people and Christians in general. Individuals high in social identity complexity on the other hand do recognize that not all fellow British people are white or Christian, and also do not apply the same characteristic and prototypical attributes of British people to white or Christian people also.

Crucially, research has shown that individuals with relatively higher social identity complexity tend to be higher in tolerance of out-groups and more supportive of affirmative action and multiculturalism policies. Support for this positive relationship between social identity complexity and intergroup attitudes comes from studies conducted, for example, in the US (Brewer and Pierce, 2005; Miller *et al.*, 2009), Israel (Roccas and Brewer, 2002), Northern Ireland (Schmid *et al.*, 2009), and the Netherlands (Verkuyten and Martinovic, 2012). An interesting question to ask therefore is whether social identity complexity acts as a mediator in the relationship between diversity and intergroup attitudes, i.e., whether diversity might prompt increased social identity complexity, with positive consequences

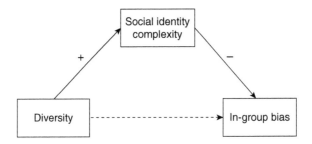

Figure 8.2 Theoretical model showing hypothesized relationships between diversity, social identity complexity, and intergroup attitudes.

for intergroup attitudes. Brewer and Pierce (2005) have argued that exposure to socially diverse environments should increase awareness of the multitude of different groups, and importantly, of the non-overlapping nature of these groups. Exposure to diverse contexts should thus provide the optimal basis for recognizing diversity surrounding individuals' multiple group memberships, and consequently also lead to more complex multiple in-group perceptions, i.e., increased social identity complexity. We tested these predictions, that diversity should be associated with increased social identity complexity, which would then positively mediate the effects on intergroup attitudes, in two studies (Schmid *et al.*, 2013). Figure 8.2 graphically illustrates these predictions.

An empirical test of the consequences of diversity on social identity complexity and intergroup attitudes

We conducted two studies, one in Germany (Study 1), and one in England (Study 2), to examine the consequences of living in more or less diverse neighborhoods on intergroup attitudes, and whether these effects were mediated by social identity complexity (Schmid *et al.*, 2013). Both studies involved majority respondents sampled from neighborhoods varying in their proportional share of foreigners (in Germany) and ethnic minorities (in England), and for both studies we operationalized our measure of neighborhood diversity in terms of the ethnic fractionalization index.

Study 1 involved a sample of 1,381 German nationals sampled from 50 different neighborhoods (*Wohnviertel*) in 16 different towns and cities in Germany. In order to measure individuals' social identity complexity we focused on two identities held by all respondents, German nationality and Christian religion (i.e., including only those respondents without an immigrant background and who adhered to Christian religion), and asked them questions concerning the perceived similarity between these categories (for exact details on methodology, see Schmid *et al.*, 2013). We measured social identity complexity by asking respondents whether they perceived that being German means the same as being Christian, and whether they thought the typical German person to be similar to the typical Christian person. Respondents rated their extent of agreement to these questions on a five-point scale, allowing us to compute an index of social identity complexity ranging from low to high.

We also measured respondents' intergroup attitudes in the form of in-group bias. This involved asking respondents to first rate their attitudes towards Germans (the in-group) on a feeling thermometer ranging from 0 (cold) to 100 (warm), and then subsequently to rate their attitudes towards two out-groups, individuals of Turkish and Russian background, on a similar feeling thermometer; we then obtained a bias score by subtracting out-group ratings from in-group ratings.

The results of this study revealed that diversity did not exert a direct effect on intergroup attitudes, but that diversity was associated positively with greater social identity complexity. Individuals living in more diverse neighborhoods in Germany thus perceived their two identities (nationality and religion) in more complex and differentiated terms. Moreover, we also found that higher social identity complexity was associated with lower in-group bias scores. Social identity complexity thus had a positive impact on intergroup attitudes. Crucially then, when we computed the indirect effect of diversity on in-group bias results revealed a significant mediated relationship, such that diversity was indirectly associated with reduced in-group bias via increased social identity complexity. Importantly, these results were obtained while controlling for demographic variables, such as education, income, age, and gender.

We sought to replicate these findings in a different context. Study 2 involved 580 white British Christian adults, sampled from 192 neighborhoods in England. We again measured social identity complexity, this time concerning three identities: ethnicity, nationality, and religion, with questions concerning the perceived similarity between these three identities. Similar to Study 1, we thus asked respondents to rate the perceived similarity between the typical British person and the typical white person, between the typical British and the typical Christian person, and between the typical white and the typical Christian person. We again measured intergroup attitudes surrounding ethnic minorities, using two different measures. Similar to Study 1, we again measured in-group bias, capturing whether individuals felt warmer towards the majority in-group than towards ethnic minorities. In addition we also measured social distance, which captured the extent to which respondents would be bothered by having someone in their family marry someone from an ethnic minority background, by having a doctor from an ethnic minority background, and by having neighbors from ethnic minority backgrounds in their street.

Results for this study largely mirrored those obtained for Study 1. Living in neighborhoods characterized by higher diversity (i.e., higher ethnic fractionalization) did not exert direct effects on in-group bias or social distance. Instead, our results showed that living in more diverse neighborhoods was associated with greater social identity complexity, such that individuals living in more diverse neighborhoods perceived less similarity between their various in-groups. As a consequence, higher levels of social identity complexity were then associated with lower in-group bias scores, as well as with lower social distance scores. Greater social identity complexity thus had positive consequences for outcomes related to intergroup relations, confirming prior research (e.g., Brewer and Pierce, 2005; Schmid et al., 2009). When we then probed for potential indirect effects, results showed that social identity complexity mediated the effects of diversity on intergroup attitudes. Diversity was indirectly associated with lower in-group bias and social distance, via its positive effects on social identity complexity. Again, these findings emerged while controlling for key demographic variables (education, income, age, and gender).

In sum, this research provided the first empirical evidence to suggest that social identity complexity is a key psychological process that can help explain how diversity may positively affect intergroup attitudes (whether such changes in social identity complexity also generalize to positive changes for various types of trust remains to be examined). By showing that diversity was associated with more complex and inclusive multiple in-group perceptions, which brought about positive effects for intergroup attitudes, this work suggests that diversity may not only affect how we perceive those diverse others who make up our diverse social contexts, but that we also come to re-evaluate how we perceive our own groups and our social selves. Our research thus suggests that diversity may not simply lead individuals to "hunker down" (as suggested by Putnam, 2007: 149), but that exposure to diverse settings may lead individuals to open up and expand their sense of self, with positive consequences for intergroup relations. This work has thus opened up important avenues for future research, to consider, for example, identity processes or in-group norms to test, as suggested above, the involvement of deprovincialization processes in the link between diversity and social capital.

Conclusions

This chapter has reviewed a recent line of research that has begun to study not only direct but also indirect effects of diversity on outcomes related to social capital, especially trust and intergroup attitudes. In so doing, we have highlighted how a consideration of underlying mechanisms and processes (especially intergroup contact, perceived intergroup threat, and social identity complexity) significantly enhances our understanding of the complex effects of diversity. We have thus shown that living in diverse neighborhoods provides important opportunities for intergroup contact, which are consistently related with actual uptake of contact. Indeed, accounting for the indirect relationship between diversity and trust (and attitudes) is crucial to fully understand the consequences of diversity for trust, since once we accounted for the indirect positive effects of contact, most of the negative direct effects of diversity on trust were canceled out. We do, however, wish to emphasize here that diversity does not equal contact, and even though we see that diversity offers important opportunities for contact (being consistently associated with contact) they are not to be conceptually conflated. In fact, there will always be people for whom diversity does not lead to contact, i.e., people who do not take up available opportunities for contact. Understanding the moderating conditions of the relationship between diversity and contact, i.e., the facilitating or hindering conditions and factors that explain when individuals will or will not take up opportunities for contact, remains an important task for future research in this area.

Moreover, just as diversity does not equal contact, we further wish to emphasize that not all forms of intergroup contact are identical. Indeed, we wish to point out explicitly that the research reviewed here, and underlying predictions on the role of intergroup contact considered *positive* forms of contact only. Yet of course, diverse contexts offer opportunities for all kinds of contact, both positive and negative, and it remains for future work to examine especially *negative* forms of contact when examining the relationship between diversity and trust (and other social capital related outcomes). Only by comparing both positive *and* negative contact will we be able to move towards a more complete understanding of the nature of the relationship between diversity and social capital related outcomes.

A study that has examined the consequences of living in segregated as opposed to mixed neighborhoods in Northern Ireland allows us to derive some tentative conclusions on the role of negative intergroup encounters (Schmid *et al.*, 2009). Since this study was conducted in a context of divisive intergroup relations, involving a longstanding ethno-religious conflict, we were particularly interested in whether living in ethno-religiously mixed neighborhoods would, on the one hand, lead to more positive intergroup contact, but on the other hand, also to greater exposure to intergroup violence (which may be considered a proxy for negative intergroup contact). Results confirmed these predictions, showing that individuals living in mixed neighborhoods were indeed more likely to report positive intergroup contact, which then positively mediated effects on intergroup attitudes (leading to a positive indirect effect of living in mixed neighborhoods). However, findings also revealed that individuals living in mixed neighborhoods reported greater experience of conflict, which then negatively mediated effects on intergroup attitudes. We wish to stress however that this study was set in a very specific context of intergroup relations and did not test the effects of diversity per se. This makes it imperative for future research to examine the involvement of not only positive but also negative forms of contact in other settings with varying levels of diversity. Moreover, it remains for future work to study more comprehensively the effects of segregation as opposed to diversity. Indeed, recent work suggests that it is segregation rather than diversity that drives down trust and other outcomes related to social capital (see Uslaner, Chapter 5, this volume, for a detailed discussion).

Our chapter also shed light on a previously unexplored psychological mechanism that can explain the link between diversity and intergroup attitudes: social identity complexity. In very general terms, our recent work shows that diversity may lead people to expand their sense of self and embrace more inclusive forms of self-definition. We focused explicitly on the social psychological concept of social identity complexity, showing that living in diverse contexts was associated with more complex and differentiated representations of multiple ingroup memberships, which were then positively related to intergroup attitudes. Future research may take this as a starting point to consider also the combined role of intergroup contact, threat, and social identity complexity in explaining diversity effects also for other outcomes not exclusively confined to attitudes, since prior research has found that contact and threat can also be conceived of as antecedents of social identity complexity (Schmid *et al.*, 2009). Our recent work also paves the way for considering additional mediators not previously examined. Van der Meer and Tolsma (2014) make important theoretical predictions concerning additional mediating processes that should explain how diversity affects social cohesion, such as anomie and social disorganization, which should be explicitly tested in future work (for a detailed discussion see Van der Meer and Tolsma, 2014). Additional mediators of the diversity-trust relationship that could be explored are changes in in-group identification or in-group norms, two potential mediating processes we already discussed above. Future research may also consider empathy and perspective taking, or intergroup anxiety as mediating processes. Since empathy/perspective taking and intergroup anxiety are considered key mediators of the relationship between contact and a range of outcomes (see Pettigrew and Tropp, 2008, for a meta-analytic review), it is plausible that they also reflect processes that explain how diversity affects trust indirectly. It remains for future research to test the involvement of these and other processes in seeking to provide a more comprehensive understanding on the processes that underlie the effects of diversity on key outcomes related to social capital.

In closing, we wish to mention a methodological caveat surrounding prior work that has considered the link between diversity and social capital. Most prior studies rely on cross-sectional data, hindering us from drawing clear and definite conclusions about causality. It is thus imperative that future work seeks to employ longitudinal methods, which will allow for the estimation of cross-lagged paths to test possible bidirectional relationships between diversity and trust, and indeed any mediating variables. Chapters 3 and 4 of this volume are promising steps in this direction. Further studies of this kind, employing longitudinal analyses, and testing both underlying mechanisms and moderating factors, will allow us to ascertain with greater confidence whether, how, and when diversity affects social capital. Nevertheless, important strides in elucidating the complex nature of the consequences of diversity on social capital have already been made and, indeed, this entire volume serves as testament to that.

References

Alesina, A. and La Ferrara, E. (2002) Who trusts others? *Journal of Public Economics*, 85: 207–234.

Allport, G. W. (1954) *The Nature of Prejudice*. Reading, MA: Addison-Wesley.

Blalock, H. M. (1967) Percent non-white and discrimination in the South. *American Sociological Review*, 22: 677–682.

Blumer, H. (1958) Racial prejudice as a sense of group position. *Pacific Sociological Review*, 23: 3–7.

Bobo, L. D. (1999) Prejudice as a sense of group position: microfoundations of a sociological approach to racism and race relations. *Journal of Social Issues*, 17: 445–472.

Brewer, M. B. and Pierce, K. P. (2005) Social identity complexity and outgroup tolerance. *Personality and Social Psychology Bulletin*, 31: 428–437.

Brown, R. J. and Hewstone, M. (2005) An integrative theory of intergroup contact. In M. Zanna (ed.) *Advances in Experimental Social Psychology, 37.* San Diego, CA: Academic Press, pp. 255–331.

Christ, O. and Wagner, U. (2012) Methodological issues in the study of intergroup contact: towards a new wave of research. In G. Hodson and M. Hewstone (eds) *Advances in Intergroup Contact.* London: Psychology Press, pp. 223–261.

Cornelius, W. and Rosenblum, M. (2005) Immigration and politics. *Annual Review of Political Science*, 8: 99–119.

Foddy, M., Platow, M. J., and Yamagishi, T. (2009) Group-based trust in strangers: the role of stereotypes and expectations. *Psychological Science*, 20: 419–422.

Fosset, M. A. and Kiecolt, K. J. (1989) The relative size of minority populations and white racial attitudes. *Social Science Quarterly*, 70: 820–835.

Gaertner, S. L. and Dovidio, J. F. (2000) Reducing intergroup bias: the common ingroup identity model. Philadelphia, PA: Psychology Press.

Gesthuizen, M., Van der Meer, T., and Scheepers, P. (2009) Ethnic diversity and social capital in Europe: tests of Putnam's thesis in European countries. *Scandinavian Political Studies*, 32: 121–142.

Hero, R. (2003) Social capital and racial inequality in America. *Perspectives on Politics*, 1: 113–122.

Hewstone, M. (2009) Living apart, living together? The role of intergroup contact in social integration. *Proceedings of the British Academy*, 162: 243–300.

Hirschman, A. O. (1964) The paternity of an index. *American Economic Review*, 54: 761–762.

Hooghe, M., Reeskens, T., Stolle, D., and Trappers, A. (2009) Ethnic diversity and generalized trust in Europe: a cross-national multilevel study. *Comparative Political Studies*, 42: 198–223.

Kollock, P. (1994) The emergence of exchange structures: an experimental study of uncertainty, commitment, and trust. *American Journal of Sociology*, 100: 313–345.

Kramer, R. M. (1999) Trust and distrust in organizations: emerging perspectives, enduring questions. *Annual Review of Psychology*, 50: 569–598.

Lancee, B. and Dronkers, J. (2011) Ethnic, religious and economic diversity in Dutch neighborhoods: explaining quality of contact with neighbors, trust in the neighborhood and interethnic trust. *Journal of Ethnic and Migration Studies*, 37: 597–618.

Letki, N. (2008) Does diversity erode social cohesion? Social capital and race in British neighborhoods. *Political Studies*, 56: 99–126.

Lolliot, S., Fell, B., Schmid, K., Wölfer, R., Swart, H., Voci, A., Christ, O., New, R., and Hewstone, M. (forthcoming) Measures of intergroup contact. In G. J. Boyle, D. H. Saklofske, and G. Matthews (eds) *Measures of Personality and Social Psychological Constructs.* London: Academic Press.

Miller, K. P., Brewer, M. B., and Arbuckle, N. L. (2009) Social identity complexity: its correlates and antecedents. *Group Processes & Intergroup Relations*, 12(1): 79–94.

Montalvo, J. G. and Reynal-Querol, M. (2005) Ethnic polarization, potential conflict and civil wars. *American Economic Review*, 95: 796–813.

Oliver, J. E. and Wong, J. (2003) Intergroup prejudice in multiethnic settings. *American Journal of Political Science*, 47: 567–582.

Pettigrew, T. F. (1997) Generalized intergroup contact effects on prejudice. *Personality and Social Psychology Bulletin*, 23: 173–185.

Pettigrew, T. F. and Tropp, L. R. (2006) A meta-analytic test of intergroup contact theory. *Journal of Personality and Social Psychology*, 90: 751–783.

—— (2008) How does intergroup contact reduce prejudice? Meta-analytic tests of three mediators. *European Journal of Social Psychology*, 38: 922–934.

—— (2011) *When Groups Meet: The Dynamics of Intergroup Contact*. Philadelphia, PA: Psychology Press.

Pettigrew, T. F., Wagner, U., and Christ, O. (2010) Population ratios and prejudice: Modelling both contact and threat effects. *Journal of Ethnic and Migration Studies*, 36: 635–650.

Putnam, R. (2007) *E pluribus unum*: diversity and community in the twenty-first century. *Scandinavian Political Studies*, 30(2): 137–174.

Quillian, L. (1995) Prejudice as a response to perceived group threat: population composition and anti-immigrant and racial prejudice in Europe. *American Sociological Review*, 60: 586–611.

Riek, B. M., Mania, E. W., and Gaertner, S. L. (2006) Intergroup threat and outgroup attitudes: a meta-analytic review. *Personality and Social Psychology Review*, 10: 336–353.

Roccas, S. and Brewer, M. B. (2002) Social identity complexity. *Personality and Social Psychology Review*, 6: 88–106.

Savelkoul, M., Gesthuizen, M., and Scheepers, P. (2011) Explaining relationships between ethnic diversity and informal social capital across European countries and regions: tests of constrict, conflict and contact theory. *Social Science Research*, 40(4): 1091–1107.

Schlueter, E. and Scheepers, P. (2010) The relationship between outgroup size and anti-outgroup attitudes: a theoretical synthesis and empirical test of group threat and intergroup contact theory. *Social Science Research*, 39(2): 285–295.

Schlueter, E. and Wagner, U. (2008) Regional differences matter: examining the dual influence of the immigrant population on derogation of immigrants in Europe. *International Journal of Comparative Sociology*, 49: 153–173.

Schmid, K. and Hewstone, M. (2010) Combined effects of intergroup contact and multiple categorization: consequences for intergroup attitudes in diverse social contexts. In R. Crisp (ed.) *The Psychology of Social and Cultural Diversity*. Chichester: Wiley-Blackwell, pp. 297–321.

—— (2011) Social identity complexity: theoretical implications for the social psychology of intergroup relations. In R. Kramer, G. Leonardelli, and R. Livingston (eds) *Social Cognition, Social Identity, and Intergroup Relations: A Festschrift in Honor of Marilynn Brewer*. Philadelphia, PA: Psychology Press, pp. 77–102.

Schmid, K., Hewstone, M., Tausch, N., Cairns, E., and Hughes, J. (2009) Antecedents and consequences of social identity complexity: Intergroup contact, distinctiveness threat and out-group attitudes. *Personality and Social Psychology Bulletin*, 35: 1085–1098.

Schmid, K., Hewstone, M., and Al Ramiah, A. (2011) Social identity: understanding the impact of group membership on individual behaviour. In D. Chadee (ed.) *Theories in Social Psychology*. Chichester: Wiley-Blackwell, pp. 211–231.

—— (2013) Neighborhood diversity and social identity complexity: Implications for intergroup relations. *Social Psychological and Personality Science*, 4: 135–142.

Schmid, K., Al Ramiah, A., and Hewstone, M. (2014) Neighborhood ethnic diversity and trust: The role of intergroup contact and perceived threat. *Psychological Science*.

Stein, R. M., Post, S. S., and Rinden, A. L. (2000) Reconciling context and contact effects on racial attitudes. *Political Research Quarterly*, 53: 285–303.

Stolle, D., Soroka, S., and Johnston, R. (2008) When does diversity erode trust? Neighborhood diversity, interpersonal trust and the mediating effect of social interactions. *Political Studies*, 56: 57–75.

Tam, T., Hewstone, M., Kenworthy, J., and Cairns, E. (2009) Intergroup trust in Northern Ireland. *Personality and Social Psychology Bulletin*, 35: 45–59.

Tanis, M. and Postmes, T. (2005) A social identity approach to trust: interpersonal perceptions, groups membership and trusting behavior. *European Journal of Social Psychology*, 35: 413–424.

Tausch, N., Tam, T., Hewstone, M., Kenworthy, J., and Cairns, E. (2007) Individual-level and group-level mediators of contact effects in Northern Ireland: the moderating role of social identification. *British Journal of Social Psychology*, 46: 541–556.

Uslaner, E. M. (2011) Trust, diversity and segregation in the United States and the United Kingdom. *Comparative Sociology*, 10: 221–247.

Van der Meer, T. and Tolsma, J. (2014) Ethnic diversity and its supposed detrimental effects on social cohesion. *Annual Review of Sociology*, 40.

Verkuyten, M. and Martinovic, B. (2012) Social identity complexity and immigrants attitudes toward the host nation: the intersection of ethnic and religious group identification. *Personality and Social Psychology Bulletin*, 38: 1165–1177.

Vertovec, S. (2007) Super-diversity and its implications. *Ethnic and Racial Studies*, 30: 1024–1054.

Vervoort, M., Flap, H., and Dagevos, J. (2010) The ethnic composition of the neighborhood and ethnic minorities' social contacts: three unresolved issues. *European Sociological Review*, 27: 586–605.

Wagner, U., Hewstone, M., and Machleit, U. (1989) Contact and prejudice between Germans and Turks: a correlational study. *Human Relations*, 42: 561–574.

Wagner, U., Christ, O., Pettigrew, T.F., Stellmacher, J., and Wolf, C. (2006) Prejudice and minority proportion: contact instead of threat effects. *Social Psychology Quarterly*, 69: 380–390.

Yamagishi, T. and Yamagishi, M. (1994) Trust and commitment in the United States. *Motivation and Emotion*, 18: 129–166.

Part III

Ethnic diversity in schools

9 Thinking about ethnic diversity

Experimental evidence on the causal role of ethnic diversity in German neighborhoods and schools

Susanne Veit

Introduction

Since most of the empirical studies on ethnic diversity and trust have cross-sectional designs, they only occasionally provide evidence on the causality of the observed relationship. Cross-sectional studies are susceptible to problems of reversed causality and unobserved heterogeneity. Most correlative studies assume that ethnic diversity impacts trust and not the other way around. However, the opposite may be true as well. People who exhibit high levels of trust may differ in comparison to those with low levels in their preferences for or in the importance they attach to the ethnic composition of their environment, resulting in the self-selection of individuals who are high and low in trust into different settings. At the same time, contextual characteristics that are correlated with ethnic diversity or minority group size—such as education levels, unemployment rates, poverty, and crime rates—may be what actually brings about the observed relationships. Although regression analyses control for the impact of related contextual characteristics, standard analyses of cross-sectional correlative data cannot completely rule out the possibility that the observed associations between diversity and social cohesion are spurious. Multicollinearity problems, the restricted availability of official statistics, and the uncertainty about important impact factors make cross-sectional studies susceptible to biases.

How can these problems be solved? Innovative approaches have been presented in the previous chapters of this book. Camille Hémet (Chapter 2), for example, studied diversity effects by drawing on the public housing policy in France that minimizes the effects of self-selection into neighborhoods (see also Algan *et al.*, 2012). In Chapter 4, Abigail Fisher Williamson presented the results of a natural experiment that rules out effects of self-selection and reversed causality. Finally, Bram Lancee and Merlin Schaeffer presented a study in Chapter 3 that applies a difference-in-difference design to show the causal effects of moving to ethnically diverse neighborhoods on attitudes towards immigration.

Relying on experimental designs, this chapter addresses the causality in the relationship between ethnic diversity and social trust in two different contexts, namely German neighborhoods and public primary schools. Because of the random allocation of participants to treatment conditions, experiments are well suited to investigate questions of causality. However, most laboratory experiments that have taken ethnicity into account investigate ethnic stereotypes and in-group biases rather than the effects of diversity on social trust and cohesion, because they are conducted with interethnic and co-ethnic pairs instead of groups that differ in their ethnic compositions (but see the experiments by Adida *et al.*, 2011; Alexander and Christia, 2011; Koopmans and Rebers, 2009). The few field-experiments on the topic have a higher external validity than laboratory experiments, but involve the same potential biases as correlative studies, because the settings' ethnic diversity is most often not experimentally varied (see e.g., Falk and Zehnder, 2013; Koopmans and Veit, 2014). An ideal experiment on the causal effect of diversity on social cohesion would randomly vary the ethnic composition of the setting while keeping all other social characteristics of the individuals that are nested within settings constant, which is impossible to realize.

How else can we study the causal impact of ethnic diversity on social cohesion? Social identity approach (Tajfel and Turner, 1986; Turner *et al.*, 1987) and theories on group threat and ethnic competition (Blalock, 1967; Blumer, 1958; Stephan and Stephan, 2000) suggest that salient categorizations into ethnic in- and out-groups trigger intergroup processes that lower trust and cooperation in ethnically diverse settings. A promising alternative starting point is therefore the question of whether and how ethnic diversity is perceived. Studies on innumeracy (Herda, 2010; Nadeau *et al.*, 1993; Wong, 2007) showed that most people overestimate minority group sizes as a result of demographic (e.g., education), cognitive (e.g., television exposure), and emotional (e.g., perceived threat) factors. Herda (2010) found that innumeracy increases with countries' social inequality rather than with the percentage of foreign born residents. In a similar vein, Wong (2007) showed that perceptions but not objective census measures of minority shares on the community level are correlated with innumeracy with regard to the racial composition of the USA. Finally, Nadeau *et al.* (1993) reported that the overestimation of minority group sizes is associated with feelings of group threat.

There are a number of studies that have explicitly addressed the question of how the perception of ethnic diversity by individuals and its salience impact social attitudes in ethnically diverse and homogeneous settings. The evidence their results provide, however, has been contradictory. Koopmans and Schaeffer (forthcoming), for example, show that perceived levels of diversity (e.g., perceptions of linguistic and value diversity) mediate negative effects of local diversity on trust, but at the same time negatively correlate with trust independently of actual diversity levels. Hopkins (2010) has claimed that both the salience and the framing of ethnic diversity matter. According to his "politicized places" hypothesis, immigrants quickly become the target of aversion and a source of group threat when sudden changes (rather than levels) of ethnic diversity on the local levels are accompanied by a national rhetoric on immigration that further raises the salience of immigration issues and, at the same time, frames immigration as a problem. Helbling *et al.* (2013) found that the salience of ethnic diversity (measured by countries' political discourse about immigration and diversity) is particularly detrimental to social trust in societies with high levels of ethnic diversity. In addition, however, they demonstrated that the mere discourse about immigration rather than the evaluative tone of the discourse matters for trust. Finally, Schlueter and Davidov (2013) found that immigration-related news is more strongly correlated with high levels of group threat and anti-immigrant attitudes in Spanish regions with *few* immigrants. They argued in line with contact hypothesis (Allport, 1954; Pettigrew and Tropp, 2006) that media coverage on immigration triggers feelings of group threat more strongly in homogeneous regions because their residents lack interethnic contacts and experience with ethnic diversity.

In sum, the results of previous research point to the importance of diversity perceptions and suggest that "thinking about diversity" impacts social attitudes, over and above the ethnic composition of contexts. This chapter, therefore, approaches the causality problem by focusing on the salience of ethno-cultural diversity in homogeneous and diverse settings. Instead of experimentally varying the ethnic composition of groups, I experimentally varied the salience of ethno-cultural diversity. In what follows I present the results of two priming experiments that were conducted in ethnically homogeneous and diverse neighborhoods and schools. The findings substantiate the empirical evidence on the diversity-trust link by showing that raising the salience of ethno-cultural diversity causally affects how individuals judge others' cooperativeness. Second, the results provide evidence on the robustness of the causal effect of diversity by presenting similar results from experiments in two different settings. At the same time, however, the findings highlight that the context matters. The effect of drawing individuals' attention to ethno-cultural diversity on social trust is stronger in ethnically diverse than in homogeneous schools but weaker in ethnically diverse than in homogeneous places of residence.

Method

Two highly similar survey experiments were conducted in different settings: one in a range of German regions and one in a range of Berlin schools. The two experiments were part of a project that was funded by the German Federal Ministry of Family Affairs, Senior Citizens, Women and Youth.[1] In both studies, survey respondents were unobtrusively primed with stimuli that drew their attention to either ethno-cultural diversity or other forms of hetcrogeneity, such as age or income. This experimental variation makes it possible to investigate the causal impact of the salience of groups' ethno-cultural diversity on perceived cooperativeness while simultaneously considering the actual diversity of the context examined. Before describing the experimental procedure and the measures in more detail, the next paragraphs briefly introduce the surveys in which the experiments were embedded.

The EDCA survey

Residents' trust in their neighbors was analyzed for 3,565 residents who participated in a survey experiment that was embedded in the Ethnic Diversity and Collective

Action Survey (EDCAS, see Schaeffer *et al.*, 2011 for details). The EDCAS is a telephone survey on trust and civic engagement that was conducted between October 2009 and May 2010 in 55 German cities and communities. The interviews were stratified by three sub-samples: 60 percent native Germans, 26 percent immigrant respondents, and 14 percent respondents of Turkish origin. About half of the respondents were randomly allocated to the survey experiment. The survey covered questions on socio-demographic characteristics, social networks, attitudes, and civic engagement. The experiment was placed at the very end of the interview to avoid spillover effects to measures other than the dependent variable.

The school survey

With regard to judgments of parental cooperation, the analyses draw on the responses of 656 parents (from 40 schools) who participated in a school survey (see Koopmans *et al.*, 2011 for details). The survey was conducted between November and December 2010 in public primary schools that are located in Berlin neighborhoods of former West Germany[2] (in the following referred to as West Berlin). In total, more than 12,000 questionnaires in German, Turkish and Arabic were sent to 121 randomly selected and five intentionally chosen[3] public primary schools in West Berlin in order to survey the parents of 4th graders. The survey contained questions on individual characteristics (of the child and the two parents) with regard to socio-demographic attributes, attitudes, and involvement in the school. The experiment was presented on the first page of the questionnaire.

Dependent variables

The dependent variable in the two studies is perceived cooperativeness. The dependent measures that were applied in the two studies are not identical, but they focus on the same concept, namely whether one can rely on others' cooperativeness.[4] Moreover, both questions are situational measures of experience-based judgments of cooperativeness.

In the neighborhood study, respondents were asked to indicate their trust in neighbors to return a lost wallet ("If you lost your wallet containing your address and some money at your place of residence, how likely is it that the wallet would be returned with nothing missing from it?"), which is a standard measure of trust. Answers could range from "not at all likely" (0) to "very likely" (10). The wallet question was chosen because it directs respondents' attention to their place of residence and avoids the moralistic tone of the generalized trust question (see e.g., Soroka *et al.*, 2007; Uslaner, 2002).

Unfortunately, the wallet question was not suitable in the school context. Schools are small units, in which people know each other. The wallet question would likely result in little variation in the dependent measure. I assume that virtually all parents would either give a lost wallet back to the parents who lost it or to a member of the school staff. Therefore, in the school study the parents were asked to judge the parental cooperation at school ("How well is parental participation and cooperation among parents at your child's school working?"). Answers could range from "very badly" (0) to "very well" (5).

Experimental treatments

In both studies, respondents were randomly assigned to experimental groups, which differed with regard to the introduction of the measures of perceived cooperativeness. In the neighborhood study, four different stimuli were presented (see the first rows in Table 9.1). In all four groups the introduction started with the same sentence. In the control group, no further reference to any particular kind of similarity or difference was made and the respondents were immediately asked the wallet question (see 1.1 in Table 9.1). In the three experimental groups (see 1.2–1.4), the introductory sentence continued with references to the different generations the residents belong to (age prime), different countries of origin (ethnic prime), or different religious beliefs (religious prime).

In the school study, respondents were randomly allocated to one out of eight experimental groups (see 2.1–2.3.6 in Table 9.1). In all groups the question was introduced with a sentence that referred to parents' impact on schools. In the control condition (see 2.1), no further reference was made.[5] In the seven treatment groups, the sentence was followed by a reference to the heterogeneity of the parents either with regard to financial means (see 2.2) or the parents' ethnic backgrounds (see 2.3.1–2.3.6). In the ethnic treatment groups, respondents were confronted either with the ethnic prime only (see 2.3.1 in Table 9.1), or with the ethnic prime and an additional reference to differences between the parents with regard to the languages they speak, religious norms and values, educational goals, the lack of contact between the parents, and the prevalence of prejudices (2.3.2–3.2.6). The different versions of the ethnic prime were introduced in order to investigate theoretical mechanisms (i.e., diverging preferences, ethnic biases, and coordination problems) that are said to affect trust and cooperation in ethnically diverse groups (see Chapter 1).

In both studies, respondents were randomly allocated to control groups, ethnocultural treatment groups, or a comparison group. The comparison groups served as a further control that allowed me to investigate whether emphasizing any kind of social diversity reduces trust, or whether there is a specific effect of ethno-cultural diversity. Nevertheless, there are some differences between the two studies. First, respondents in the control group of the neighborhood study were primed with neighbors' diversity, whereas in the control group of the school study no reference to parents' diversity was made. Second, respondents in the comparison groups of the neighborhood study were exposed to a stimulus that points to neighbors' differences in age. Parents in the school study's comparison group, by contrast, were primed with a statement drawing attention to different financial means. Finally, the ethno-cultural stimuli in the neighborhood study refer to different countries of origin and religious beliefs. In the school study, by contrast, all respondents in the ethno-cultural treatment group were primed with different countries of origin, but five times out of six their attention was drawn to specific

Table 9.1 Experimental treatments.

NEIGHBORHOOD STUDY (EDCAS)

"Places of residence are different. In some locations residents are very similar; in others they are very different from one another…"

1.1 **Control group**	"."
1.2 **Age prime**	"…because they belong to different generations—some are, for example, still very young, some are middle-aged, and others are already elderly."
1.3 **Ethnic prime**	"… because they come from different countries—some are, for example, of German origin, some originate in Turkey, and others are from Italy."
1.4 **Religious prime**	"… because they have different religious beliefs—some are, for example, Christians, some are Muslims, and others are atheists."

SCHOOL STUDY

"It's not just teacher and pupils who shape the school, but also parents."

2.1 **Control group**	"."

"In some schools the parents are very similar, in others they are very different from one another…"

2.2 **Financial prime**	"… because they have different financial means"
2.3 **Ethnic prime**	"… because they originate from different countries…"
2.3.1	"."
2.3.2	"… and speak different languages."
2.3.3	"… and follow different religious norms and values."
2.3.4	"… and have different educational goals for their children."
2.3.5	"… and have little contact with each other."
2.3.6	"… and are prejudiced against each other."

associated problems and challenges (e.g., lack of contact, prejudices, or different norms and goals), which added a negative overtone to the primes. In the neighborhood study, by contrast, diversity was always neutrally framed, avoiding any positive or negative evaluations.

Predictor and control variables on the individual level

In both the neighborhood (EDCAS) and the school studies, the following individual characteristics are taken into account: a dummy for immigrant background (i.e., first generation immigrants and people with at least one foreign-born parent)[6], age, gender, education (low, medium, or high), employment status (EDCAS: gainfully employed versus not economically active; school study: hours of work per week[7]), relationship status (married or cohabiting versus single or widowed), parenthood (EDCAS: having children versus childless; school study: number of children), and religious affiliation (Protestant, Catholic, Muslim, and other religious affiliation versus atheist). In addition, in the neighborhood study the years of residence in the current neighborhood are taken into account, since long-term residents are more likely to trust their neighbors than people who more recently moved into a neighborhood. In the school study, I also consider dummies for households that receive social welfare benefits and for school choice (assigned catchment area school versus individually chosen school).

Predictor and control variables on the context level

The context-level units of analyses in the neighborhood study are German regions (*Kreise*). *Kreise* are residential areas with 200,000 inhabitants on average. Some residential areas are single cities, but in rural areas they cover larger areas with several small towns or villages. In the school study, the context-level units of analyses are public primary schools that are situated in neighborhoods of former West Berlin.

Ethnic diversity is the central explanatory variable on the context-level. Ethnic diversity is measured by the ethnic fractionalization index (EF), which reflects the sum of the shares (si) of all nationalities i (i = 1, ..., n) in residential areas and schools subtracted from unity. The values of the index are given by:

$$EF = 1 - \sum_{i=1}^{k} s_i^2 \qquad (9.1)$$

s_i is the share of national group i (i = 1, ..., n)

The values of the ethnic fractionalization index (in the following referred to as ethnic diversity) vary between contextual units. They indicate the probability that two randomly drawn residents or pupils belong to different nationality groups.

In addition, I control for socio-economic differences between regions and schools (EDCAS: unemployment rate; school study: the percentage of pupils who receive public funding for school materials, such as school books or workbooks). This is important because several studies have shown that economic deprivation is a crucial predictor of trust (Delhey and Newton, 2005; Letki, 2008). In the neighborhood study, in addition population density (i.e., the number of inhabitants per square kilometer), a dummy for residential areas that are situated in the area of the formerly socialist East Germany, and localities' street crime rate (i.e., the registered number of street crimes such as mugging, pick-pocketing, theft from cars, and physical assault in the public sphere multiplied by 100,000 and divided by number of residents) are included. In the schools study, I also take into account the total number of pupils attending the school (school size).

Results

Before presenting the results of the multilevel regression analyses, we explore the question of how the ethnic diversity of neighborhoods and schools as well as the salience of ethno-cultural differences affect judgments of cooperativeness

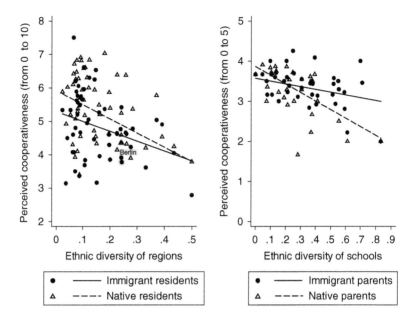

Figure 9.1 Perceived cooperativeness and ethnic diversity.

Note: The two charts plot average levels of perceived cooperativeness by the settings' ethnic diversity. On the left-hand side, the results of the neighborhood study are displayed, and on the right-hand side the results of the school study. Black dots show the results for immigrant residents and parents, whereas white triangles indicate the results for native respondents. Berlin, the city in which the schools study was conducted, is highlighted in the chart on the left-hand side.

by means of charts. Figure 9.1 plots separately, once for natives and once for immigrants, the average level of perceived cooperativeness by the ethnic diversity of residential areas and schools. Due to the younger age and the greater fertility of the immigrant population, but also because of residential and school segregation, the maximum ethnic diversity of schools is much higher than that of residential areas (see the left-hand side of Figure 9.1, which highlights the ethnic diversity of Berlin, the region where the school study was conducted).

The trends of the lines in Figure 9.1 suggest that respondents in ethnically diverse settings judge others' cooperativeness more negatively than respondents in homogeneous settings. This negative relationship holds in both studies for natives *and* immigrants, but the slopes steepen for natives. Native residents report on average more optimistic expectations regarding their neighbors' cooperativeness than immigrant residents, whereas native parents judge other parents' cooperativeness on average more negatively than immigrant parents.

In line with previous research, the results for both settings are supportive of the claim that ethnic diversity challenges social cohesion. Let us now turn to the effect of the priming of ethno-cultural diversity, and thereby to the causality question.

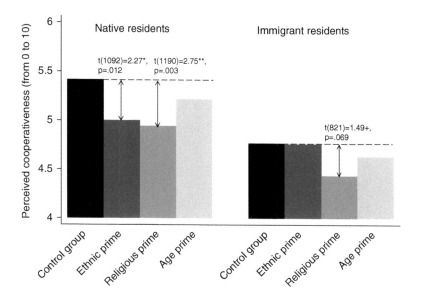

Figure 9.2 Treatment effects in the neighborhood study.
Note: The charts show the cooperativeness judgments of native and immigrant residents in the four experimental groups. Significant differences between treatments groups and the control group (see the dashed horizontal lines) are indicated by arrows and t-test results, which are shown above the bars.

Figure 9.2 shows, separately for the four experimental groups, the perceived likelihood that a lost wallet was returned by neighbors for native and immigrant residents. Compared to native respondents in the control group, native residents who were primed with ethnic or religious diversity trust their neighbors less (see the significant t-test results on the left-hand side of the chart). A similar pattern can be observed for immigrant residents who were primed with religious diversity, but not for the ethnic prime (see the t-test results on the right-hand side). The priming with age diversity, by contrast, does not significantly impact cooperativeness judgments.

Turning to the school study, Figure 9.3 shows the effect of the experimental treatments on judgments of parental cooperation. To make possible a comparison between the results of the school study and the neighborhood study, the treatment effects of parents' judgments are presented separately for natives and immigrants. However, the school study sample is relatively small, which strongly reduces the sample sizes for the experimental groups (for some groups it drops below 20 respondents). In order to have a robust treatment group, all six versions of the ethnic prime were merged into one "ethnic prime" indicator (see Figure 9.3).

The chart suggests that the salience of ethnic diversity decreases immigrant parents' trust in cooperation (see the significant t-test results). However, contrary to the predictions made above, the chart indicates similar levels of perceived

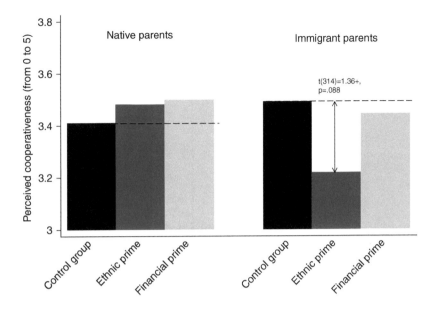

Figure 9.3 Treatment effects in the school study.

Note: The charts show the cooperativeness judgments of native and immigrant parents in the three experimental groups. Significant differences between treatments groups and the control group (see the dashed horizontal lines) are indicated by arrows and t-test results, which are shown above the bars.

cooperativeness for native parents in the control as well as the ethnic prime group. As expected, the priming of different financial means shows no effect in either of the two groups.

Regression results

The survey respondents in the two studies are nested within schools or neighborhoods. Empty multilevel regression models of perceived cooperativeness indicate that individual judgments systematically differ between context units (ICC = 0.06 for regions, and ICC = 0.08 for schools). Therefore, the relationships of the dependent measures with ethnic diversity and the experimental treatments are investigated by means of multilevel regressions (random intercept and slope models). Table 9.2 presents the results of regressions of cooperativeness judgments on the settings' ethnic diversity, the experimental treatments, and the full range of control variables. The first three models show the results for the full sample of residents in German neighborhoods, as well as separately for native and immigrant residents. Models four to six present the results for parents of children who visit public primary schools in West Berlin.

Table 9.2 Multilevel regressions of cooperativeness judgments of individuals who are nested in residential areas and schools.

	NEIGHBORHOODS			SCHOOLS		
	Model 1	*Model 2*	*Model 3*	*Model 4*	*Model 5*	*Model 6*
	all	natives	immigrants	all	natives	immigrants
INDIVIDUAL LEVEL						
Immigrants	-.246⁺ (.13)			-.134 (.11)	-.414* (.18)	.179 (.14)
Social welfare benefits				.046 (.11)		.172 (.14)
Education: low	*reference*	*reference*	*reference*	*reference*	*reference*	*reference*
medium	.226 (.20)	-.240 (.36)	.425⁺ (.25)	.197⁺ (.12)	.219 (.24)	.174 (.15)
high	.641** (.22)	.189 (.37)	.823** (.29)	.121 (.12)	.086 (.25)	-.019 (.16)
Relationship status	.283* (.12)	.250* (.14)	.331 (.21)	.059 (.11)	.020 (.13)	
Religion: atheist	*reference*	*reference*	*reference*	*reference*	*reference*	*reference*
Protestant	.360* (.15)	.308* (.16)	.565 (.36)	-.082 (.12)	-.070 (.13)	-.073 (.25)
Muslim	-.189 (.18)		-.158 (.21)	.383* (.16)		.318 (.21)
CONTEXT LEVEL						
Ethnic diversity / share of poor pupils	-3.161*** (.94)	-3.435** (1.19)	-2.344* (1.18)	-1.386*** (.34) / *-1.179*** (.22)*	-2.066*** (.49) / *-1.860*** (.36)*	-1.182** (.40) / *-1.091*** (.26)*
Street crime rate	.000* (.00)	.000* (.00)	.000* (.00)			
Unemployment rate	-.090** (.03)	-.090** (.03)	-.082⁺ (.04)			
East Germany	-.440* (.21)	-.564* (.25)	-.167 (.38)			
School size				.001 (.00)	.001* (.00)	.000 (.00)
Case study				.162 (.17)	.427* (.19)	.029 (.19)
EXPERIMENTAL TREATMENTS						
Control group	*reference*	*reference*	*reference*	*reference*	*reference*	*reference*
Ethnic prime	-.282* (.14)	-.373* (.17)	-.121 (.24)	-.151⁺ (.09)	.059 (.12)	-.303** (.12)
Religious prime	-.432** (.13)	-.475** (.17)	-.367⁺ (.22)			
Age or financial prime	-.115 (.15)	-.086 (.18)	-.129 (.27)	.004 (.15)	.127 (.21)	-.088 (.29)
CONSTANT	5.045*** (.32)	5.499*** (.48)	4.355*** (.48)	2.532*** (.34)	2.837*** (.53)	2.468*** (.50)
N individuals/contexts	3565 / 55	2153 / 55	1412 / 55	656 / 40	255 / 29	401 / 40
Rho	.003	.004	.000	.054	.014	.043

Note: The models are random intercept and slope models (STATA: xtmixed). All control variables are considered in the models, but only significant coefficients are displayed. Coefficients in italics refer to models in which ethnic diversity is substituted by the schools' share of pupils from families with little financial means. Levels of significance: *** p < .001, ** p < .01, * p < .05, ⁺ p<.10 (two-tailed).

Even though all aforementioned control variables are considered in the regression models, for the sake of clarity Table 9.2 only shows the coefficients of control variables that are significantly associated with the dependent variable in one of the regression models. In addition, the schools' socio-economic composition is omitted in the regressions of parents' perceived cooperativeness, because it correlates highly with the schools' ethnic composition (r = .83). Considering both variables simultaneously would result in multicollinearity. Therefore, I show the results of alternative models in which ethnic diversity is substituted by the schools' socio-economic composition in italics (see models 4 to 6 in Table 9.2).

With regard to the control variables, the results confirm previous research, i.e., higher levels of trust in neighbors for natives, for residents with high education, for people who are married or cohabiting, for Protestants, and for residents of West German regions as well as localities with low street crime and high employment rates (see the first column in Table 9.2). Satisfaction with parental cooperation is higher for Muslim than for non-religious parents. Among native parents without foreign roots, those who do not depend on social welfare benefits, who have purposefully chosen their child's primary school, and whose children attend large schools or one of the five case study schools more positively judge the parental cooperation at school.

In line with the expectations, the regression models confirm the statistical significance of the negative association between ethnic diversity for neighborhoods *and* schools. Moreover, they show that the negative relationship holds for natives *and* immigrants. Immigrant and native residents report lower levels of trust in their neighbors' cooperativeness the higher the ethnic diversity of their place of residence. Similarly, native and immigrant parents in ethnically diverse schools judge the parental cooperation at their schools more negatively than parents in ethnically homogeneous schools. Nevertheless, the results also confirm a significant negative association between the schools' share of pupils from families with little financial means and cooperativeness judgments. Unfortunately, virtually all schools that are high in ethnic diversity are at the same time characterized by high shares of pupils from families with little financial means, which makes it impossible to separate these effects. In the neighborhood study, however, ethnic diversity and the unemployment level are considered simultaneously. The results show that both negatively affect trust. We may therefore assume that in the school study both factors contribute to reducing expectations of cooperativeness as well.

With regard to the causality question, the results of both studies support the predicted negative effect of raising the salience of ethno-cultural diversity on perceived cooperativeness (see the first and fourth column in Table 9.2). This conclusion is strengthened by the fact that raising the salience of diversity in age or of different financial means shows no such effect. This finding rules out the possibility that referring to *any* specific dimension of diversity generates negative priming effects. Moreover, with regard to difficulties in separating the effects of the schools' ethnic compositions from that of their socio-economic compositions, the experimental results suggest that the perception of ethnic rather than socio-economic characteristics matters for cooperativeness judgments.

Separate analyses for natives and immigrants point to several differences between neighborhoods and schools (see the second, third, fifth, and sixth columns in Table 9.2). Whereas the negative effect of the ethnic prime fails to reach conventional significance levels for immigrant but not for native neighborhood residents, the opposite holds true for parents. Immigrant rather than native parents judge parental cooperation significantly more negatively after stimuli that directed their attention to ethnic diversity. Unfortunately, the small sample size of the school study makes it impossible to investigate this unexpected finding in more detail by estimating a regression of natives' judgments on the different versions of the ethnic prime. For the full sample of parents, however, the different versions of the ethnic prime do not differently impact perceived cooperativeness.

As a final step in the analysis, I now turn to the question of whether the causal effect of priming ethno-cultural diversity varies between settings with high and low levels of ethnic diversity. The two figures below show the effect of ethno-cultural primes on perceived cooperativeness for ethnically homogeneous and diverse neighborhoods and schools. The chart on the left-hand side of Figure 9.4 suggests that ethno-cultural primes reduce the trust of respondents who reside in ethnically homogeneous neighborhoods, whereas there is no negative priming effect for residents of heterogeneous localities. The opposite pattern emerges for parents (see Figure 9.5). Parents in ethnically diverse schools judge parental cooperation more negatively when the salience of schools' ethnic diversity was raised by experimental stimuli, whereas no such effect was observed for parents in homogeneous schools.

Table 9.3 shows the result of multilevel regressions of perceived cooperativeness on the control variables (not displayed), ethnic diversity, and the ethno-cultural primes, which include cross-level interaction terms between the settings' social composition and the ethno-cultural primes. In sum, the findings provide empirical evidence in favor of the "politicized places" hypothesis (Hopkins, 2010) *and* the contact hypothesis (see Schlueter and Davidov, 2013), but suggest that the relative importance of the two hypotheses depends on the context. Whereas raising the salience of religious diversity—but not ethnic diversity—more strongly decreases the trust in neighbors of people who live in ethnically more homogeneous regions (see the significant *positive* coefficient of the interaction term in the first column of Table 9.3), the priming of ethnic diversity more negatively impacts the cooperativeness judgments of parents in ethnically heterogeneous schools (see the significant *negative* coefficient of the interaction term in the second column). A similar moderation of the priming effect is observed for schools with high shares of pupils from families with little financial means (see in italics), but the moderation is only marginally significant. Most likely, the moderation of the priming effect by the schools' socio-economic composition is caused by the high correlation between ethnic and socio-economic school characteristics.

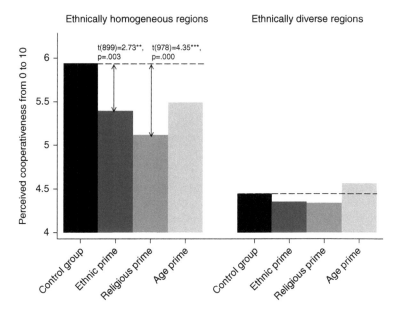

Figure 9.4 Interaction between experimental treatments and the ethnic diversity of regions.

Note: The charts show the cooperativeness judgments of people who reside in ethnically homogeneous (EF < .19) or diverse (EF > .19) German regions. Significant differences between treatments groups and the control group (see the dashed horizontal lines) are indicated by arrows and t-test results, which are shown above the bars.

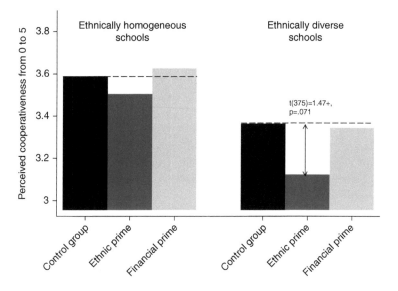

Figure 9.5 Interaction between treatments and schools' ethnic diversity.

Note: The charts show the cooperativeness judgments of parents in ethnically homogeneous (EF < .25) and diverse (EF > .25) West Berlin elementary schools. Significant differences between treatments groups and the control group (see the dashed horizontal lines) are indicated by arrows and t-test results, which are shown above the bars.

Table 9.3 Interaction between ethnic diversity and the ethno-cultural treatments.

	NEIGHBORHOODS	*SCHOOLS*
	Model 1 *all*	*Model 2* *all*
CONTEXT LEVEL		
Ethnic diversity/*share of poor pupils*	−4.439*** (1.17)	−.636 (.46) / −.788*** (.29)
EXPERIMENTAL TREATMENTS		
Control group	*reference*	*reference*
Ethnic prime	−.346* (.16)	−.146 (.09) / −.153+ (.09)
Religious prime	−.544*** (.14)	
Age or financial prime	−.156 (.16)	.014 (.15) / .022 (.15)
INTERACTION		
Ethnic diversity (or *share of poor pupils*) * ethnic prime	.787 (1.29)	−1.034* (.51) / −.645+ (.33)
Ethnic diversity (or *share of poor pupils*) * religious prime	2.286* (1.07)	
Ethnic diversity (or *share of poor pupils*) * age / financial prime	1.045 (1.22)	−1.135 (.87) / −.303 (.55)
CONSTANT	5.088*** (.32)	2.403*** (.38)
N individuals/contexts	3565 / 55	656 /40
Rho	.030	.061

Note: The models are random intercept and slope models and include cross-level interaction terms (STATA: xtmixed). All control variables are considered in the models, but only significant coefficients are displayed. Coefficients in italics refer to models in which ethnic diversity was substituted by the schools' share of pupils from families with little financial means. Levels of significance: *** $p < .001$, ** $p < .01$, * $p < .05$, + $p < .10$ (two-tailed).

Summary and discussion

This chapter presents the results of two experiments that analyse the causal effect of the salience of ethnic diversity on perceived cooperativeness. The two experiments were conducted in different settings—with residents of German neighborhoods and parents in Berlin primary schools—but applied a similar design. In both studies, the respondents were randomly assigned to experimental groups: either to a control group, to an experimental treatment group, or to a comparison group. All respondents were asked to judge others' cooperativeness, but the questions were introduced by slightly different sentences. In the experimental treatment groups, the introductory sentence referred to ethnic or religious differences between neighbors or parents. In the comparison group, differences in age or financial means were mentioned. Finally, in the control group, the introductory sentences referred to no specific dimension of difference.

The results of the two survey experiments complement the empirical research on consequences of ethnic diversity on trust and cohesion by providing *causal* evidence on negative consequences of the salience of ethno-cultural diversity on cooperativeness judgments. First, ethnic diversity and perceptions of cooperativeness are negatively associated. More importantly, however, "thinking about diversity" impacts perceived cooperativeness over and above the settings actual ethnic diversity. Raising the salience of ethnic or religious differences—but not of difference in financial affluence or diversity in age—deteriorates perceptions of cooperativeness. In addition, the causal link between perceived cooperativeness and the salience of ethno-cultural diversity is confirmed in two different settings—namely, residential areas and schools—which underlines the robustness of these findings.

At the same time, however, the results point to several differences between neighborhoods and schools. First, the relative susceptibility of native and immigrant respondents to experimental primes that raise the salience of ethno-cultural diversity differs between the two contexts. Whereas the salience of ethnic diversity affects native rather than immigrant residents' trust in their neighbors, the opposite holds true for parents. Immigrant rather than native parents judge parents' cooperativeness more negatively when their attention is drawn to ethnic diversity. The weak effect of the experimentally raised salience of ethnic diversity on immigrants' trust in their neighbors is little surprising, since the ethnic prime may make immigrants think about co-ethnic neighbors. By contrast, the results of the school study suggest that immigrant rather than native parents are susceptible to the priming of ethnic diversity. The reason for this unexpected finding remains open to question, since there is no theory that I am aware of that explains this result. One potential explanation, however, concerns ethnic school segregation and the differences in choice of school between native and immigrant parents. Native parents often avoid certain catchment area schools by applying for another public school, choosing private schools, or moving to another neighborhood, whereas immigrant parents often lack information about the educational system and the opportunities they have with regard to school choice (Kristen, 2005; Noreisch, 2007). In comparison to immigrant parents from the same schools, native parents may accordingly have been better informed about the ethnic composition of their school in the first place, which may weaken their susceptibility to experimental stimuli that raise the salience of ethno-cultural differences.

A second difference between the two studies concerns the effect of the interaction between primes that raise the salience of ethno-cultural diversity and settings' actual ethnic composition. The results of both studies show that respondents' susceptibility to external manipulations regarding the salience of ethno-cultural differences varies with the ethnic diversity of the context. However, whereas residents of ethnically homogeneous regions are more susceptible to the priming of religious differences than residents of ethnically diverse localities, the ethnic diversity of schools strengthens the negative effect of raising the salience of ethnic differences between parents. Both findings are supported by previous research. Schlueter and Davidov (2013) showed that the impact of immigration-related news on perceived group threat was strongest in Spanish regions with few immigrants. In line with this finding, the results of the neighborhood study suggest that residents of ethnically heterogeneous localities are immune to external manipulations of the salience of cultural diversity, probably because for them ethno-cultural differences are a neighborhood characteristic that is salient either way and an established factor in how they view and evaluate their neighborhood.

Parents in ethnically diverse schools, by contrast, judge parental cooperation more negatively if their attention is drawn to ethnic differences compared to parents in more homogeneous schools. Similarly, Helbling *et al.* (2013) found that intense political discourse on cultural diversity issues, which may increase the salience of ethnic diversity, was particularly detrimental to social trust in ethnically diverse societies. This finding fits the 'politicized places' hypothesis by Hopkins (2010), which emphasizes the conditions that lead immigrants to be perceived as threatening (e.g., sudden demographic change and media coverage that politicizes immigration). Drawing on this hypothesis, raising the salience of ethno-cultural differences more negatively affects cooperativeness judgments in ethnically diverse schools as a combined effect of ethnic school segregation (i.e., the shares of minorities in school populations often exceeds the neighborhoods' share of immigrant residents) and the public discourse about so-called "*Problemschulen*" (i.e., schools with disadvantageous social compositions and high shares of immigrant pupils). A related potential explanation regards the size of the setting and the density of networks, which is supposedly higher between the parents of classmates than between residents of German regions. Although dense networks are predicted to increase trust and cooperation, they simultaneously raise individuals' awareness of and knowledge about the ethnic composition of a setting. The experimental primes that raised the salience of the schools' ethnic diversity may for this reason have failed to show any effects in ethnically homogeneous schools, but not in homogeneous residential areas, where people overestimate the share of immigrants.

One might criticize that this study measures perceptions of cooperativeness— which are prone to biases as a result of social desirability concerns—instead of trusting behavior or cooperation. Laboratory experiments facilitate behavioral measures, but they are often criticized for their artificiality and the high complexity of experimental tasks. Therefore, I conducted survey-experiments, which combine the advantages of experiments (i.e., to investigate causality issues) with those of survey studies (e.g., external validity). This design makes it possible to simultaneously investigate the effects of contextual ethnic diversity and the salience of ethnic differences.

The results of this study point to the importance of ethnic diversity and to the causal effect of the salience of ethno-cultural differences, as well as to differences between settings. This study addressed two settings, neighborhoods and schools. Nevertheless, more studies in different contexts are necessary in order to better understand the specific characteristics of settings that determine how the salience of ethnic diversity and actual levels of ethnic diversity affect natives' and immigrants' social trust. The research on the role of the salience of ethno-cultural diversity would also benefit from laboratory experiments on the issue, because the cognitive and emotional processes that are triggered by experimental stimuli that raise the salience of ethnic and cultural differences deserve further attention. Investigating these processes will help to understand under which circumstances the salience of the ethnic composition of actually diverse groups erodes mutual trust and cooperation, and under which circumstances negative salience effects are instead mitigated by individual experience with ethnic diversity.

Notes

1 The funding source was neither involved in the study design, the analyses and interpretation of the data, nor in writing or submitting this article for publication.
2 Prior research has demonstrated that residents from former East Germany show lower levels of cooperation (e.g., Brosig-Koch *et al.*, 2011; Koopmans and Veit, 2014). Since our financial means were limited, schools at the territory of former East Berlin were excluded from the study.
3 The five schools were carefully selected by our colleague Anna Dunkel in order to conduct qualitative case studies.
4 In the EDCA-survey, perceived cooperativeness is measured by the wallet question. The responses to the wallet question are probably influenced by disorder and crime rates (the latter is considered in the regression analyses). In addition, the likelihood that a lost wallet is returned depends on the behavior of individual people who notice the wallet and take action. The action, however, can be either a cooperative one (returning the wallet or forwarding it to the lost property office), or a selfish one (stealing the wallet or money from it). The cooperativeness question in the school study, by contrast, measures satisfaction with cooperation rather than expectations. In addition, parental cooperation depends much stronger on whether there are sufficient parents who cooperate and engage for the school rather than on the behavior of individual parents.
5 The control condition had a three times higher chance of being randomly chosen than any of the other conditions.
6 Since the school survey was addressed to the parents of 4th graders, some parents may jointly have filled in the questionnaire. In the school study, therefore, the dummy indicates the background of the respondent *and* the other parent. When referring to immigrant or native parents, I focus on the background of the pair instead of that of the respondent. However, similar results emerge when instead considering a dummy that only indicates the respondents' ethnic background.
7 The indicator for hours of work per week could range between none to more than 40 hours (in steps of ten hours).
8 All statistics on the regional level refer to the year 2009. They were provided by the Federal Statistical Office and the statistical offices of the 16 German states (www.destatis.de), the German Federal Office for Migration and Refugees (www.bamf.de), and the German Federal Office of Criminal Investigation (www.bka.de). The school statistics were provided by the Berlin Senate Administration for Education, Science and Research (www.berlin.de/sen/bjw). They refer to the school year 2010-2011.

References

Adida, C. L., Laitin, D., and Valfort, M.-A. (2011) "One Muslim is enough!" – evidence from a field experiment in France. *IZA Discussion Paper, No.: 6122*. http://papers.ssrn.com/sol3/papers.cfm?abstract_id=1965139.

Alexander, M. and Christia, F. (2011) Context modularity of human altruism. *Science*, 334(6061): 1392–1394.

Algan, Y., Hémet, C., and Laitin, D. D. (2012) Diversity and local public goods: a natural experiment with exogenous residential allocation. *IZA Discussion Paper, No. 6053*. http://nbn-resolving.de/urn:nbn:de:101:1-201111029392.

Allport, G. W. (1954) *The Nature of Prejudice*. Cambridge: Addison-Wesley.

Blalock, H. M. (1967) *Toward a Theory of Minority-Group Relations*. New York: John Wiley & Sons.

Blumer, H. (1958) Race prejudice as a sense of group position. *Pacific Sociological Review*, 1(1): 3–7.

Brosig-Koch, J., Helbach, C., Ockenfels, A., and Weimann, J. (2011) Still different after all these years: solidarity behavior in East and West Germany. *Journal of Public Economics*, 95(11): 1373–1376.

Delhey, J. and Newton, K. (2005) Predicting cross-national levels of social trust: global pattern or Nordic exceptionalism? *European Sociological Review*, 21(4): 311–327.

Falk, A. and Zehnder, C. (2013) A city-wide experiment on trust discrimination. *Journal of Public Economics*, 100: 15–27.

Helbling, M., Reeskens, T., and Stolle, D. (2013) Political mobilization, ethnic diversity and social cohesion: the conditional effect of political parties. *Political Studies*.

Herda, D. (2010) How many immigrants? Foreign-born population innumeracy in Europe. *Public Opinion Quarterly*, 74(4): 674–695.

Hopkins, D. J. (2010) Politicized places: explaining where and when immigrants provoke local opposition. *American Political Science Review*, 104(1): 40–60.

Koopmans, R. and Rebers, S. (2009) Collective action in culturally similar and dissimilar groups: an experiment on parochialism, conditional cooperation, and their linkages. *Evolution and Human Behavior*, 30(3): 201–211.

Koopmans, R. and Schaeffer, M. (forthcoming) Statistical and Perceived Diversity and Their Impacts on Neighborhood Social Cohesion in Germany, France and the Netherlands. Manuscript submitted for publication.

Koopmans, R. and Veit, S. (2014) Cooperation in ethnically diverse neighborhoods: a lost-letter experiment. *Political Psychology*, 35(3): 379–400.

Koopmans, R., Dunkel, A., Schaeffer, M., and Veit, S. (2011) *Ethnische Diversität, soziales Vertrauen und Zivilengagement: Projektbericht*. Discussion papers, Wissenschaftszentrum Berlin für Sozialforschung (WZB). www.econstor.eu/handle/10419/57764.

Kristen, C. (2005) *School Choice and Ethnic School Segregation: Primary School Selection in Germany*. Münster: Waxmann.

Letki, N. (2008) Does diversity erode social cohesion? Social capital and race in British neighbourhoods. *Political Studies*, 56(1): 99–126.

Nadeau, R., Niemi, R. G., and Levine, J. (1993) Innumeracy about minority populations. *Public Opinion Quarterly*, 57(3): 332–347.

Noreisch, K. (2007) School catchment area evasion: the case of Berlin, Germany. *Journal of Education Policy*, 22(1): 69–90.

Pettigrew, T. F. and Tropp, L. R. (2006) A meta-analytic test of intergroup contact theory. *Journal of Personality and Social Psychology*, 90(5): 751–783.

Schaeffer, M., Koopmans, R., Veit, S., Wagner, M., and Wiedner, J. (2011) The ethnic diversity and collective action survey (EDCAS). Technical report. *WZB Discussion Paper* SP IV 2011-701. Berlin: WZB.

Schlueter, E. and Davidov, E. (2013) Contextual sources of perceived group threat: negative immigration-related news reports, immigrant group size and their interaction, Spain 1996–2007. *European Sociological Review*, 29(2): 179–191.

Soroka, S. N., Helliwell, J. F., and Johnston, R. (2007) Measuring and modelling interpersonal trust. In F. Kay and R. Johnston (eds) *Diversity, Social Capital and the Welfare State*. Vancouver, BC: University of British Columbia Press, pp. 95–132.

Stephan, W. G. and Stephan, C. W. (2000) An integrated threat theory of prejudice. In S. Oskamp (ed.) *Reducing Prejudice and Discrimination*. New Jersey: Lawrence Erlbaum, pp. 23–45.

Tajfel, H., and Turner, J. C. (1986) The social identity theory of intergroup behavior. In L. W. Austin and S. Abele (eds) *Psychology of Intergroup Relations*. Chicago: Nelson-Hall, pp. 7–24.

Turner, J. C., Hogg, M. A., Oakes, P. J., Reicher, S. D., and Wetherell, M. S. (1987) *Rediscovering the Social Group: A Self-Categorization Theory*. Oxford: Blackwell.

Uslaner, E. M. (2002) *The Moral Foundations of Trust*. Cambridge: Cambridge University Press.

Wong, C. J. (2007) "Little" and "big" pictures in our heads: Race, local context, and innumeracy about racial groups in the United States. *Public Opinion Quarterly*, 71(3): 392–412.

10 Ethnic diversity, homophily, and network cohesion in European classrooms*

Frank Kalter and Hanno Kruse

Introduction

In the rapidly growing literature on the empirical effects of ethnic diversity different indicators of social cohesion have been applied. Various types of trust, civic engagement, and attitudes supportive of the welfare state are among the most frequently employed variables. More seldom, but appealingly straightforward, is an understanding of social cohesion in terms of the actual ties that might exist between the members of a community, i.e., in a stricter, network-analytical way. When, in accordance with the overarching aims of this book, in this chapter we consider the consequences of ethnic diversity, we shall highlight this narrower aspect of "network cohesion."

When dealing with a concept like cohesion it has proved to be very useful to differentiate between a relational component, that refers to the connections between the involved individuals, and other ideational components, that capture the more psychological and attitudinal aspects (Fararo and Doreian, 1998; White and Harary, 2001). Most importantly, we are convinced that the explicit distinction of network cohesion helps to identify the more precise mechanisms that can contribute to explaining the potential consequences of ethnic diversity, certainly one of the most urgent needs in this field of research (see Chapter 1).

Many authors studying the consequences of ethnic diversity rely on relational aspects of cohesion at least in parts of their reasoning. Most prominently, in the first lines of his extremely influential paper, Robert Putnam refers to social capital as his key concept, emphasizing that this means on the one hand the social relations themselves, and on the other hand, the value they deliver to the included individuals by their associated norms (Putnam, 2007). In later passages he relies on the distinction between "bonding" social capital, which in the context of the argumentation basically means ties to people of the same ethnicity, and "bridging" social capital, which refers to ties between people of different ethnicities. Putnam then presents two crucial arguments that are central to the impact of diversity on the cohesion of networks. First, referring to "conflict theory" he

* Financial support from NORFACE research program on Migration in Europe—Social, Economic, Cultural and Policy Dynamics is acknowledged.

argues that people, when confronted with ethnic diversity, tend to stick to their own kind, thus preferring bonding to bridging social capital (Putnam, 2007: 142 et seq). This line of reasoning is supported by the fact that homophily seems to be a very general tendency in social life (McPherson *et al.*, 2001). Second, he adds the so-called "constrict theory," which, put into relational terms, claims that ethnic diversity might even lead people to have fewer social ties in general, i.e., less bridging *and* bonding capital (Putnam, 2007: 144). With regard to the over-all network structure, the first, conflict- or homophily-based, argument implies that, holding the number of ties constant, the relational cohesion of a network is disrupted because it breaks up into non-connected clusters. The second, "constrict," argument implies that relational cohesion is lost because networks become sparser overall.

Even sharp critics of Putnam seem to accept many of these relational elements of his argument: "The discovery that immigration reduces cultural homogeneity and communitarianism is perfectly reasonable" (Portes and Vickstrom, 2011: 474). Instead their critique concentrates foremost on the ideational elements: "The alarm following that discovery is not [reasonable]" (Portes and Vickstrom, 2011: 474). They challenge the idea that relational cohesion is a necessary condition for the ideational aspects of cohesion and argue that modern societies can do very well without these more traditional forms of "mechanical" solidarity in the Durkheimian sense.

One could marshal some compelling theoretical arguments, however, why certain aspects of relational network cohesion are likely to be helpful to produce specific desirable ideational outcomes. Even in modern societies, economic transactions are dependent on some level of trust embedded in social relations (Granovetter, 1985). Game-theoretical models of reputation effects on efficiency in interactions have underlined the importance of third parties (Raub and Weesie, 1990), thus supporting the more general view on the comparative advantage of closely knit networks in social capital theory (Coleman, 1988). The importance of personal networks for the flow of specific kinds of information and resources is also often brought forward, and the fact that they connect or bridge people belonging to different clusters or sub-groups can be crucial for many outcomes (Granovetter, 1973; Burt, 1992). In this chapter, we do not deal with these kinds of questions and ideational aspects any further. Rather, we mention them to emphasize the importance of getting the relational part of the story right: does ethnic diversity indeed decrease network cohesion?

Systematic research on this question is sparse, and existing work seldom relies on direct measures of tie connectivity between actors. This is mainly due to the lack of adequate data, as the requirements are quite demanding. What is necessary is a sample of complete networks that are comparable to each other and vary conveniently in their ethnic diversity. In this chapter we can rely on a new dataset that fulfills these prerequisites and thus provides a novel, empirical perspective on the topic. The "Children of Immigrants Longitudinal Survey in Four European Countries" (CILS4EU) has collected information about friendship networks in more than 900 adolescent classrooms. Due to the general design of the study, in each of the countries the classrooms show a large variance with respect to their ethnic diversity, which makes the data especially adequate for analyzing the central question.

Although friendship networks in schools seem only remotely connected to recent debates around Putnam's claim on diversity and social cohesion, they might reveal some important, more general fundamental processes of network formation. In this respect they even bear a strategic advantage: Friendship choices in the school context are comparably well-researched. This has provided useful theoretical arguments and empirical tests of more general mechanisms underlying network formation. As we will show, these general mechanisms of network formation are also crucial to understanding the precise relationship between ethnic diversity and network cohesion.

We start with a review of the theoretical arguments that research on friendship formation has revealed and link this back to our central interest, i.e., the relation between ethnic diversity and network cohesion. We then describe our data and the variables used. We continue with the empirical analyses, which basically address four subsequent questions: 1) How is ethnic diversity related to network cohesion in terms of tie quantity, in other words, network density? 2) Do we find ethnic homophily in European classrooms and how is ethnic homophily related to ethnic diversity in the CILS4EU data? 3) Given this ethnic homophily, is ethnic diversity related to network cohesion in terms of tie distribution, in other words, network connectivity? 4) How do the findings with respect to questions 2 and 3 fit together? Finally, we conclude with a summary discussion.

Network formation in ethnically diverse classrooms

The notion of cohesion in social networks departs from the idea that members of a network are connected to each other via a certain number of ties. The total of all ties constitutes the network structure, which exhibits some emergent features, cohesion being one of them. Empirical measures have to specify the exact nature of these features, for example, how much more-cohesive structures differ from less-cohesive ones, so as to be able to compare the degree of cohesion in different networks. We will outline our concrete operationalization in more detail further on.

Whatever their precise definition, the emergent overall features of a network are the results of individual processes of tie-formation. In order to investigate the impact of ethnic diversity on cohesion in social networks, two questions therefore deserve closer attention: we have to ask what the basic processes underlying tie-formation in general and specifically, in adolescent classrooms, are. At the same time, we need to lay out how ethnic diversity might impact these tie-formation processes.

It is one of the most robust empirical findings in the social sciences that people are more likely to have contacts to those who are similar to themselves than to those who are dissimilar. This has proved to hold for very different characteristics, for very different kinds of relationships, and in very different social settings

(McPherson *et al.*, 2001). Ethnicity is among the most salient of these characteristics, and ethnic homogeneity with respect to friendship relations in schools is an especially well-documented phenomenon (e.g., Moody, 2001; Lubbers, 2003; Mouw and Entwisle, 2006; Wimmer and Lewis, 2010).

In order to explain the tendency to form ties to similar others, scholars have identified more general mechanisms underlying the processes of tie-formation in networks; basically one can distinguish three different principal starting points: opportunity structures, preferences, and (amplifying) balancing mechanisms.

An obvious necessary condition of friendship choice is the mere *opportunity for contact* (Blau, 1977; Verbrugge, 1977). In this respect, classroom networks provide a strategic setting, as the condition can be seen as fulfilled for any pair of students. The chances of forming ethnically homogeneous versus heterogeneous friendships, however, are heavily determined by the numerical distributions. Dependent on the relative sizes of the groups even a random pairing could lead to a large degree of observed ethnic homogeneity in friendship patterns; this aspect has been called "baseline homophily" (McPherson *et al.*, 2001: 419) or "availability" (Wimmer and Lewis, 2010: 590). While ethnic diversity logically tends to decrease baseline homophily, empirical research has shown that usually there is a large amount of homogeneity over and above the pure opportunity set, so-called "inbreeding homophily." In fact, analyses based on data from the National Longitudinal Study of Adolescent Health have revealed that in American schools inbreeding homophily even rises with ethnic diversity (Moody, 2001; Mouw and Entwisle, 2006).

But there is more to opportunity structure than pure availability and numbers of potential friends in the classroom. Even for a given context such as a classroom, there might be additional structural elements that can increase the chances to make friends (Mouw and Entwisle, 2006: 397): Students might be assigned to different tracks, thus spending more time with some classmates than with others; they might also engage in the same extracurricular activities, like sports, or not. Students living in the same neighborhood and thus sharing the route to school or sitting next to each other on the school bus, will be more likely to spend time together out of school. Generally speaking, meeting opportunities arise in many further organizational foci (Feld, 1981) that vary for the individuals even within a specified context. In distinction to the availability effect, some authors call these "propinquity" effects (Wimmer and Lewis, 2010: 589).

The other obvious starting point to explain ethnically homogeneous friendship choice is underlying *individual preferences*. If two people share an attribute then this might reduce the cognitive and physical costs of communicating, anticipating, and evaluating behavior, building mutual expectations, developing trust, etc. (Kossinets and Watts, 2009). Empirical psychological research contains ample support for the relatively higher attractiveness of people who are similar to oneself (e.g., Byrne, 1971; Huston and Levinger, 1978). Next to the creation of ties, psychological factors also seem particularly relevant for the costs of maintaining existing ties (Felmlee *et al.*, 1990). Some authors reserve the term "homophily" only for preference-driven homogeneity (Mouw and Entwisle, 2006: 397; Wimmer and

Lewis, 2010: 588). Like others, we speak of "choice homophily" (Kossinets and Watts, 2009: 407) in order to make the preference aspect clear.

The preference-based line of explanation confronts a non-trivial complication: competing characteristics on which a preference may be grounded are often considerably correlated, and what appears to be ethnic choice homophily might be spurious. For example, if ethnicity tends to be correlated with socio-economic class, as is often the case, status choice homophily can lead to ethnic homogeneity (McPherson *et al.*, 2001; Moody, 2001: 683). In the case of ethnicity, matters are especially complex, as it is a multifaceted concept encompassing not only regional origin, but also linguistic, religious, and other aspects; on closer inspection, ethnic choice homophily can thus be language choice homophily or religious choice homophily. Also, ethnicity is a nested concept (Wimmer, 2008), meaning that individuals might identify with different levels of belonging, such as being Bavarian, German, or European for example. Higher-level homophily might thus be spurious to lower-level homophily (Wimmer and Lewis, 2010: 597), and, conversely, what is a cross-ethnic friendship at a finer level (e.g., Ukrainian-Kazakh) would count as a homophilous tie at a rougher level (e.g., former Soviet Union).

Next to opportunity structure and preferences, there is a third important class of tie-formation mechanisms, namely *balancing mechanisms*, resulting from the desire for coherence in social relations. Actors seek to balance their friendships by bringing their own tie assessment into accordance with that of those surrounding them. Inconsistencies among actors about the nature of their relations would lead to strain and is therefore avoided (Heider, 1946). Friendship choices thus tend to be reciprocated, and asymmetric friendship dyads, i.e., one-sided nominations, tend to be less stable (Hallinan, 1978). Similarly, actors try to avoid discomforting constellations within triadic structures: they seek psychological balance by assessing friends' other friends as their own friends, a tendency oftentimes referred to as "triadic closure."

Balancing effects differ from the other mechanisms laid out in that they are endogenous to the network structure, meaning that an actor's assessment of a specific relation depends on other friendship choices made within the network. In consequence, balancing effects have the potential to amplify other tie-generating dynamics present in a network. As an example, let's assume a classroom in which students have a moderate preference for intraethnic friends; on average, friends thus tend to share the same ethnic background. If we now assume that students have the tendency to befriend their friends' friends, intraethnic friendships would become even more dominant, thus leading to a higher level of overall ethnic homogeneity within the classroom (Kossinets and Watts, 2009). From this perspective, it is crucial to account for the endogenous character of balancing effects, namely reciprocity and triadic closure, if we are interested in network structural concepts such as choice homophily or cohesion.

With these general mechanisms of tie-formation in mind we turn back to the central question of how ethnic diversity affects network cohesion. We should now be able to render more precisely possible tie-formation mechanisms underlying the "constrict" and "conflict" arguments outlined before. We begin with the claim that ethnic diversity leads to a decrease in both bridging and bonding capital, in other words, to a decrease in overall tie quantity (constrict argument). Why could actors' general friendship-seeking activity decrease in more ethnically diverse settings? While constrict theory misses a clear-cut argument, one could possibly derive this from a strong version of ethnic choice homophily. Such a strong version would assume that: 1) actors prefer in-group to out-group members; 2) given that there are no in-group members available in the setting, they would rather remain without a friend than choose an out-group member. This would then explain why ethnically more diverse settings might not be able to provide sufficient choice alternatives for the actors, which in consequence leads to sparser networks and lower network densities overall.

The conflict argument claims that the more ethnically diverse a setting is the more bonding and the less bridging capital will be present. The diversity effect on social cohesion is in this case not related to mere tie quantity like before. Rather it should be understood as an effect on the tie distribution across the network: those ties that would connect actors of different ethnic groups become more seldom, whereas ties within the ethnic groups become more frequent. In its most extreme version we would thus end up with a network consisting of ethnic cliques that are densely connected among members of their own group, but remain unconnected to other groups. Here, a weaker version of ethnic choice homophily would be sufficient to explain the outcome: given there is a choice, actors prefer in-group members to out-group members as friends. In consequence, ethnically diverse settings would lead to ethnically specific friendship clusters with low connectivity between groups.

Data, variables, and central measures

The data come from the first wave of the "Children of Immigrants Longitudinal Survey in Four European Countries" (CILS4EU), which is a comparative panel survey of adolescents with and without a migration background in England, Germany, the Netherlands, and Sweden (Kalter *et al.*, 2013). The first wave of CILS4EU was conducted between autumn 2010 and spring 2011. The starting sample comprises students enrolled in school grades where the majority of the children are aged 14. CILS4EU delivers a nationwide random sample of the target population in each country, which was achieved by means of a three-stage sample design: The first-stage sampling units were schools enrolling our relevant target grades. In each of the four countries, the sampling frame was a full list of all eligible schools, from which schools were drawn with probabilities proportional to size. The second-stage sampling units were classrooms within the sampled schools; as a rule, two classrooms were chosen randomly from within the relevant grades. The third-stage sampling units were students within the sampled classrooms; here, all students in a sampled classroom were included. To ensure a suitable number of children of immigrants the survey oversampled schools with higher ethnic density at the first sampling stage. More precisely, schools were classified into four explicit strata, according to the expected proportion of students with a migration background within the target grades.

Overall, the study comprises 480 schools, 958 classrooms, and 18,716 students in the four countries. Interviews with the students in the selected classrooms were conducted during two school lessons. They included a short sociometric module capturing different types of social ties between the classmates.

The classroom networks we will be studying in the following are based on the question "Who are your best friends in class?" The students could nominate up to five classmates. In the analyses we will use the data from all classrooms where this question could be successfully administered[1] and where at least 12 students participated.[2] This leaves us with 701 classrooms in total, 141 in England,[3] 184 in Germany, 183 in the Netherlands, and 193 in Sweden and involves 15,029 students (ENG: 3,037; GER: 3,968; NET: 3,959; SWE: 4,065).

For our analyses we allocate these students to 165 different ethnic groups (ENG: 110; GER: 105; NET: 100; SWE: 114). Ethnicity is thereby based on parents' country of birth: if at least one of the parents was born abroad then the student is categorized into the respective origin group. If parents come from different foreign countries, the mother's country is decisive. If both parents are native-born then the student is defined as a member of the majority group, i.e., the category England, Germany, the Netherlands, or Sweden.[4] Ethnic diversity within classrooms is measured by the common Herfindahl-based index.[5] Due to the principal design of the study, the ethnic diversity in the classrooms is very conveniently distributed for the purposes of our analyses in each of the four countries, as some of the figures further below illustrate (see Figures 10.1, 10.3, and 10.5).

The concept of social cohesion within classrooms will be measured by basic methods of network analysis. We will rely on two different measures to capture different aspects of network cohesion, namely density and reachability. As this is very central for the aims of this chapter and needs more detailed explanation, we prefer to introduce the measures step-by-step during the empirical analyses below.

Analytical strategy and findings

To address the overarching question, our empirical analyses will proceed in four major steps. First, we analyze whether ethnic diversity in the classrooms leads to sparser networks overall, i.e., to less cohesion in terms of the density of networks. We will find that there is no such effect. We then put to test whether ethnic diversity has an impact on network cohesion in terms of the distribution of bonding and bridging ties in a network. More concretely, we investigate whether ethnic diversity prevents the formation of interethnic ties in a network, as the argument of ethnic conflict would suggest. Therefore we first ask whether we can confirm the general tendency of ethnic homophily with our data, i.e., in the case of adolescent classroom networks in the four countries; we are particularly interested in how ethnic choice homophily is related to ethnic diversity, thus replicating earlier findings from the studies cited above. We then look at the central correlation between ethnic diversity and network cohesion in terms of reachability. We will find that in spite of a clear

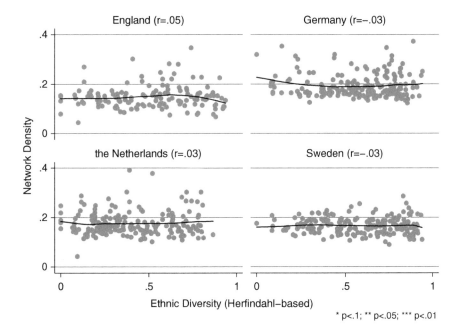

Figure 10.1 Ethnic diversity and network density in the classrooms of the four countries.

tendency towards ethnic homophily, even increasing with ethnic diversity, the reachability of ethnically diverse classroom networks is hardly smaller than of less diverse ones. To understand these seemingly contradictory findings, we finally add a kind of meta-analysis of the effects, showing that the potential negative impact of ethnic homophily on cohesion is covered by much stronger forces of network formation.

Ethnic diversity and network cohesion in terms of density

To study the relation between ethnic diversity and network cohesion, we treat the classrooms as our units of analysis. Each classroom has a quantifiable level of ethnic diversity, as laid out in section 3.

To assess the level of cohesion network analysis provides a rich repertoire of alternative measures, which start from different angles and emphasize different aspects.[6] The most prominent example is certainly the *density* of a network, which is defined as the number of observed ties divided by the number of possible ties; this measure emphasizes one aspect of cohesion in particular, namely tie quantity. This straightforwardly relates to Putnam's constrict argument that ties in general become sparser in more diverse settings. Figure 10.1 shows whether our data can confirm this tendency of "hunkering down," as it reports the relation between classroom diversity and network density in each of the four countries.

In all four countries we get the same impression: There is no systematic relation between ethnic diversity and network density. In none of the countries is the
correlation significantly different from zero.[7] One could argue that the size of the
classrooms potentially confounds the observed relation, as it correlates negatively
with density[8] and potentially also with the level of ethnic diversity in the classrooms. As it turns out, however, there is hardly any correlation between ethnic
diversity and classroom size. Controlling for the size of classrooms does not alter
our findings.

Concerning our first question we can conclude that ethnically more diverse
classroom networks are not any sparser than homogeneous ones; the data do not
confirm the constrict argument.

Ethnic diversity and ethnic homophily

Even though we cannot find an ethnic diversity effect on tie quantity this does
not imply that there is no effect on network cohesion at all. As laid out before,
there are different dimensions to the concept of network cohesion, with the overall
density of ties being only one. Another aspect of cohesion is that a network does
not fall apart into separated clusters. In this regard, ethnically diverse settings
could be especially at risk because people might turn towards their in-group rather
than towards their out-group. In other words, ethnic choice homophily is likely to
exist and might decrease the number of ties that cross group boundaries.

Therefore, our next empirical step is to explore whether there is a notable tendency towards ethnic choice homophily in European classrooms, and how this
tendency is related to ethnic diversity. We lay out our analytical strategy by looking
first at only one single exemplary classroom. Out of the total 701 classrooms in our
sample, we pick the one with ID number 2013100403, a classroom in Germany. It
consists of 23 students: nine girls and 14 boys. According to the definition sketched
above, its students belong to six different ethnic groups: eight Russians, six Turks,
five Germans, two Iraqis, one Lebanese, and one Croatian. Thus, we are dealing
with a classroom of relatively high ethnic diversity, its diversity index being .75.

Figure 10.2 shows the friendship network between these students, using the
very intuitive visualization of a *sociogram*, which is well-known since the pioneering
work of Moreno (1934). Speaking more generally and technically, a network, also
called a *graph*, is defined by a set of *nodes* (or *vertices*) and by a set of *edges* (or *arcs*) that
stand for the ties or relations between the nodes.[9] In our case a node represents a
student; squares indicating male students, circles females; different ethnic groups
are represented by country abbreviations (see legend in Figure 10.2). The edges
are in our case friendship nominations, displayed in the graph by arrows connecting the nodes. In this case we are dealing with directed relations, meaning that
the arrows start at a nominator (sending node) and point to a nominee (receiving
node); accordingly the graph is called a *directed graph* (or *digraph*).

The sociogram already provides some hints about network tendencies in this
classroom: we immediately see, for example, that friendships tend to be heavily
segregated by sex, which is a usual finding for friendship networks in this age

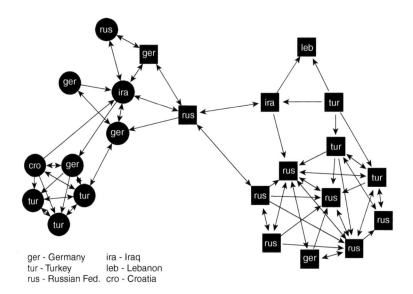

ger - Germany   ira - Iraq
tur - Turkey   leb - Lebanon
rus - Russian Fed. cro - Croatia

Figure 10.2 Friendship network of classroom 2013100402.

group. There also seems to be a notable degree of ethnic homophily: the Russian boys, for example, are strongly connected among themselves, and the same holds true for the three Turkish girls. We see, on the other hand, the above-discussed role of opportunity structures: the Lebanese boy and the Croatian girl simply have no chance to befriend someone of their own group, however strong their preference for co-ethnics might be.

Exponential random graph (ERG) models are a powerful tool to analyze ethnic homophily in networks more precisely (Robins *et al.*, 2007; Goodreau *et al.*, 2009; Lusher *et al.*, 2013). In simplified terms, one could say that they apply the logic underlying logistic regression analysis to network data by taking all possible dyads, consisting of a potential sending node and a potential receiving node, as cases and regarding the fact whether the respective tie is indeed observed (value is 1) or not observed (value is 0) as the dependent variable. Characteristics of the sending node, of the receiving node, or of the dyad as a whole can then be included as independent variables and the coefficients of ERG models represent their log-odds.

The most simple ERG model to analyze ethnic homophily would therefore include only one independent variable indicating whether the sender and the receiver have the same ethnic background ("same ethnic group"; 1 if yes, 0 if not). If we run such a model (see model 1 in Table 10.1) for the exemplary classroom 2013100402 the coefficient is .952, with a standard error of .267, thus being significantly different from zero. Taking the exponential of .952 yields about 2.6, thus the straightforward interpretation would be that the odds of observing a friendship choice when the receiver belongs to the same ethnic group as ego are 2.6 times higher than the odds when sender and receiver belong to different ethnic groups. In addition, the ERG

Table 10.1 ERG models for network 2013100402.

	Model 1	Model 2	Model 3
Same ethnic group	0.952 (0.267)***	0.894 (0.292)**	0.400 (0.214)*
Same sex	–	2.647 (0.409)***	1.268 (0.341)***
Reciprocity	–	–	2.736 (0.487)***
Triad closure (gwesp)	–	–	0.493 (0.145)**
Edges (constant)	−1.896 (0.147)***	−3.766 (0.395)***	−4.175 (0.319)***
AIC	437.2	367.4	311.5

* p < .1; ** p < .05; *** p < .01

model contains a constant, often referred to as "edges," which captures the baseline log-odds of making friendship choices in the classroom.

One of the most important advantages of ERG modeling is that, like the odds-ratio approach in general, it automatically and conveniently controls for marginal distributions and thus for the availability aspect of the opportunity structure given by the ethnic composition of the classrooms. Using the terminology as laid out in the theory section, the effect in model 1 is thus ethnic inbreeding homophily. The approach further proves to be extremely flexible and useful when it comes to disentangling the network formation processes underlying inbreeding ethnic homophily or interwoven with it. Take for example the relation to homophily with respect to other characteristics, in this case sex: the Iraqi girl and the Iraqi boy in Figure 10.2 are not befriended—here, the preference for the same sex seems to override a potential preference for the same ethnic group. In a similar vein, one might wonder how much of the mutual sympathy among the Russian boys is due to them being boys rather than Russian. ERG modeling allows us to consider a wide range of independent variables and thus to control for processes like this. When we include a variable for "same sex" in model 2, its coefficient is 2.647. This reflects the visual impression from Figure 10.2 that sex is a major dividing line in the network; the odds of choosing a friend of the same sex are more than 14 times as high ($\exp(2.647) \approx 14.112$). Nevertheless, ethnic homophily seems to be present even when controlling for sex homophily, which is indicated by the coefficient of .894 in model 2.

The theoretical discussion has further emphasized that there are crucial processes of network formation that could cover or catalyze existent tendencies towards ethnic choice homophily, most importantly reciprocity and triadic closure. Inspecting the network in Figure 10.2, we see that, indeed, a substantial number of relations are mutual friendship nominations, as indicated by arrows pointing in both directions. This holds even true within triadic structures, as many of them include all six possible friendship choices. Looking, for example, at the three Turkish girls in Figure 10.2 we could ask whether the girl in the lower middle nominated the girl on the upper left as a friend because both share the same ethnic background (ethnic choice homophily), as a reaction to friend-like behavior of the upper left girl (reciprocity), or maybe because the upper-left girl was a friend of her already

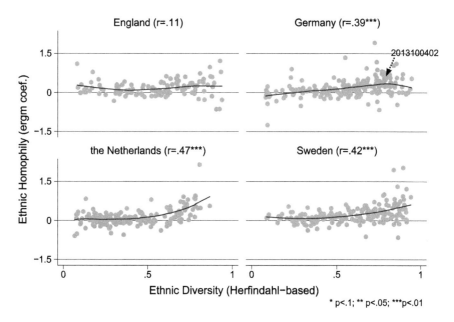

Figure 10.3 Ethnic diversity and ethnic homophily in the classrooms of the four countries.

existing friend on the upper right (triadic closure). Again, ERG models conveniently allow us to control for these network-structural processes.

In model 3 we include a reciprocity effect as well as a more sophisticated version of a transitivity effect to account for triadic closure (gwesp).[10] Model results confirm that reciprocity and triadic closure are of crucial importance in this classroom network, with both coefficients being significantly different from zero. Further, we see that the "same ethnic group" effect is notably reduced to about half of its former size. Thus, the seemingly strong tendency of ethnic homogeneity in our exemplary network is, to a considerable degree, due to the fact that an existing inclination to prefer co-ethnics as friends is amplified by more general processes of network formation. In other words, general balancing mechanisms reinforce a tendency towards ethnic choice homophily. A similar story holds, by the way, for sex homophily.

Note that ERG modeling provides many further options to come even closer to the detailed formation processes underlying the observed network in Figure 10.2. An obvious extension would be to allow for group-specific differences in ethnic homophily by including a separate "same ethnic group" variable for each ethnic group; in our case one result would be, for example, that the tendency among Turks and Russians is much higher than among Germans—which is in accordance with the impression gained from Figure 10.2. It would also be possible to take into account that groups might differ in their general nominating activity (Wimmer and Lewis, 2010) or might in general be more attractive as friends.[11] However, in the present analysis we do not go beyond the specification in model 3. To address the leading question we want to look not only at one but at all classrooms available in the sample and we have to make sure that we can estimate identical models for every single network included.

We now run model 3 for all 701 networks in the total sample. To make sure that our results are not influenced by outliers, we exclude all those classrooms whose estimates turn out to be extremely high or low.[12] From each individual ERG analysis we extract the coefficient for "same ethnic group" and plot it against the ethnic diversity of the respective classroom. The "same ethnic group" coefficient informs about the tendency in a classroom to choose in-group instead of out-group members as friends, controlling for the choices available and net of amplifying balancing dynamics.

Figure 10.3 shows the respective graphs, separate for each of the four countries; each dot represents a classroom in the total sample, our familiar classroom no. 2013100402 being one of the dots. The graphs reveal a clear and relatively consistent picture: ethnic homophily is widely present in European classrooms. The vast majority of homophily effects lie above 0; the mean values being .173 in England, .194 in Germany, .144 in the Netherlands, and .230 in Sweden. We also find that the effects of ethnic homophily even significantly increase with ethnic diversity, at least in three of the four countries. This result confirms important findings with other data from other contexts mentioned before.

Note again, however, that Figure 10.3 displays ethnic homophily estimates net of sex homophily, reciprocity, and triadic closure. It thus comes close to reflecting choice. It would be wrong, however, to assume that the estimates already represent students' pure preferences for intraethnic friends, i.e., ethnic choice homophily. As mentioned above, to take into account additional explanations one would have to control for further characteristics or structural processes tailored more narrowly to each idiosyncratic classroom case.

Ethnic diversity and social cohesion in terms of reachability

The previous analyses demonstrated that the cohesion of classroom networks is not systematically affected by ethnic diversity in terms of density and has revealed that there is a marked tendency for ethnic homophily in all of the four countries, even increasing with ethnic diversity. As we have argued in the theoretical section, this could endanger another aspect of cohesion, namely reachability. The seemingly obvious assumption is that, holding density constant, ethnic homophily might lead to ethnically closed sub-networks whose members share many ties among themselves (bonding ties), but either are not well or not at all connected to members of other subnetworks and cannot "reach" them (bridging ties). This feature of networks is usually called "closure" or "cliquishness." Given a fixed quantity of ties, there is thus a certain trade-off between cliquishness and reachability, and we will concentrate on the latter pole in the following. Roughly, our understanding of reachability as an important aspect of cohesion is thereby in accordance with the common intuition that the overall network cohesion is determined by the extent

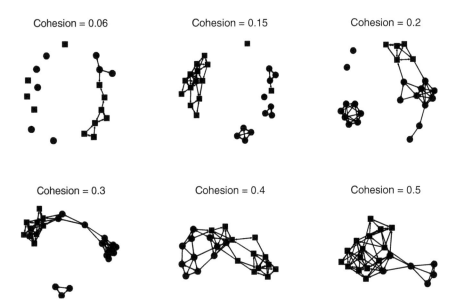

Figure 10.4 Classroom networks with varying social cohesion in terms of reachability.

of connectivity between the involved actors; those network structures that allow two randomly chosen actors to more easily reach each other are seen as being more cohesive (White and Harary, 2001; Moody and White, 2003).

Reachability is a central concept in network analysis (Wasserman and Faust, 1994: 132 et seq). A node n_j is reachable from node n_i if there is a path between n_i and n_j. A *path*, thereby, is defined as a sequence of (in our case: directed) connected edges, so that the ending node of a former edge is the starting node for the next, and no node is passed twice. In Figure 10.2, for example, the Lebanese boy is reachable from the Croatian girl, because there is a path from the Croatian girl—via the Iraqi girl, via one of the Russian boys, via the Iraqi boy—to the Lebanese boy. A simple measure of overall reachability in a network would thus be the proportion of (ordered) pairs of nodes that are reachable in this sense.

It is desirable, however, that the measure also account for how "easily" nodes are able to reach each other. This leads us to the concept of *(geodesic) distance*, which is defined as the length, in terms of the number of edges included, of the shortest path from one given node to another. The distance from the Croatian girl to the Lebanese boy in our example is thus 4, as the path described above consists of four friendship arrows and it is indeed the shortest of all possible paths (the connection from the Croatian girl could, e.g., also run via the Russian girl, to the German boy, to the Russian boy and then continue the former path—but this would include more steps in between). A more differentiated and preferable measure of reachability could thus build upon the average distance; and this is the lane we want to follow here. However, there is one last issue to solve: Some nodes might not be

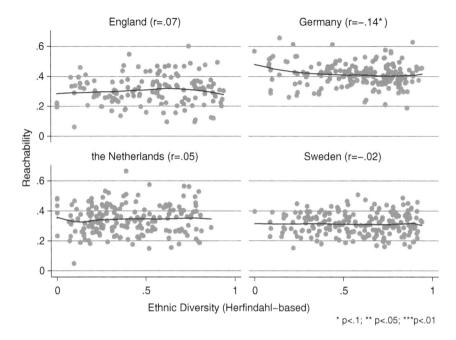

Figure 10.5 Ethnic diversity and reachability in the classrooms of the four countries.

reachable for another node at all, i.e., there might be no respective path. Note, that the reverse of our example above would be such a case: the Lebanese boy cannot reach the Croatian girl, as he has no outgoing tie at all. The question arises how to treat these cases when calculating average distances. An elegant solution is to set the path length between non-reachable actors equal to infinity and to take the reciprocal of the average of the reciprocal distances instead of the average distances (see Jackson, 2008: 33; following Newman, 2003). As the concept of cohesion is somewhat reciprocal to the idea of distance anyway, we suggest that the *average reciprocal distance* (setting distance to infinity in case of no reachability) is an adequate measure of network cohesion in terms of reachability.

If we calculate this measure for all classroom networks in our sample the values range from a minimum of .061 to a maximum of .666, the mean value being .348. Figure 10.4 gives some graphical examples of selected networks in our sample together with their value of reachability. It illustrates that the measure is well in line with what one would intuitively understand as an important aspect of cohesion within networks. The value for our exemplary classroom 2013100402 is .387. It is thus not only a classroom with relatively high ethnic diversity, but also one with a comparably high reachability.

This leads us back to the central question of this section and we are now prepared to answer it. Figure 10.5 illustrates the relation between ethnic diversity and social cohesion in terms of reachability for the whole sample of classrooms, again separated by country. And again, the results are surprisingly consistent: there is hardly any relation at all. We find a very weak negative correlation in Germany and a zero correlation in the other countries. There is little evidence that ethnic diversity is related to classroom network cohesion in terms of reachability at all.

Meta-analysis: what makes classroom networks cohesive?

The results from the last two subsections are somewhat puzzling: On the one hand, we find a pronounced tendency towards ethnic homophily in the European classrooms, net of other important network formation processes, and these effects even increase in size with growing ethnic diversity. On the other hand, there is no relation between ethnic diversity and reachability. This seems counterintuitive because one would expect ethnic homophily, given a fixed density, to lead to more ethnic clustering, and more bonding than bridging capital, thus increasing the length of pathways between network members in general or even separating them into subnetworks that are no longer connected to each other. So what is happening here?

To understand the findings we run a simple meta-analysis, regressing the reachability of a classroom on the results, i.e., on the parameters, of the classroom-specific ERG models (model 3). We report the standardized regression parameters of this meta-analysis in Table 10.2.

Table 10.2 indicates that ethnic homophily as expressed by the respective ERG model parameter has no significant negative impact on reachability in any of the countries. In general, ethnic homophily appears to be the weakest of all network formation influences. In contrast, sex homophily has a strong negative impact on reachability in all four countries. Moreover, the connectivity of networks is heavily determined by the general structural processes of reciprocity and, above all, by triadic closure. As the negative signs indicate, both of these processes undermine reachability, which intuitively makes sense given that networks with a fixed density can only be either well-connected overall or show strong local closure.[13]

If we now ask how these other tie-generating processes are related to ethnic diversity (Table 10.3), the puzzle comes close to being solved. In contrast to ethnic homophily they are not very systematically related to ethnic diversity. Sex homophily delivers a rather inconsistent picture over the countries. Reciprocity seems in general a little bit weaker in ethnically diverse networks, which is in principle good for reachability (controlling for the quantity aspect, which is captured by the constant of the ERG model). But the effects are relatively weak and should not be overinterpreted. Over and above, however, triadic closure, the most important obstacle to social cohesion, is not significantly correlated with ethnic diversity in most of the countries (the Netherlands being an exception, but the sign is negative here). This implies, in turn, that triadic closure is working, and undermining social cohesion with similar strength, in almost every classroom network—regardless of the ethnic diversity!

Table 10.2 Meta-analysis: regression of reachability on ERG model parameters (standardized regression coefficients).

Parameters from model 3	ENG	GER	NET	SWE
Same ethnic group	−0.072	−0.050	−0.017	−0.098
Same sex	−0.303***	−0.233***	−0.256***	−0.306***
Triadic closure	−0.335***	−0.395***	−0.415***	−0.374***
Reciprocity	−0.296***	−0.369***	−0.225***	−0.317***
Adj. R2	0.22	0.20	0.23	0.20
Number of classrooms	117	180	164	174

* p < .1; ** p < .05; *** p < .01

Table 10.3 Meta-analysis: bivariate correlations of ethnic diversity with…

Parameters from model 3	ENG	GER	NET	SWE
Same ethnic group	0.11	0.38***	0.47***	0.42***
Same sex	−0.14	0.19***	0.09	0.07
Triadic closure	−0.07	0.05	−0.17**	−0.07
Reciprocity	−0.08	−0.14**	−0.17**	−0.12

* p < .1; ** p < .05; *** p < .01

The meta-analysis thus reveals a very important point that oftentimes seems neglected in the discussion about the potential effects of ethnic diversity: there are more general processes undermining network cohesion (in terms of reachability), and these processes are effective and omnipresent—mostly irrespective of ethnic diversity. And they seem to be much stronger and to largely cover the weaker effects of ethnic homophily that tend to be accentuated in the ongoing debate.

Conclusion

Our analyses have shown that an explicit network-analytical approach to the topic of ethnic diversity and social cohesion can deliver novel insights into the underlying mechanisms. An explicit differentiation between a relational component of network cohesion and an ideational or behavioral aspect that might emerge from these networks seems promising to increase our general understanding of the consequences of ethnic diversity. Relying on a new and unique data set, the first wave of CILS4EU, we were able to show that there is hardly a clear correlation between ethnic diversity and cohesion when defining different dimensions of the latter concept in a stricter network-analytical sense. Overall network density is unrelated to ethnic diversity in the European classrooms. The same applies for cohesion in terms of reachability among students in the classrooms. This seems to be counterintuitive given the other important finding of our analyses: Confirming prior research in other contexts, ethnic homophily is an omnipresent phenomenon in European classrooms, and the tendency even increases with the level of ethnic diversity in the classroom. But despite the general tendency towards ethnic homophily, network cohesion does not decline with ethnic diversity. Basically, we find that common wisdom needs an important correction: arguments often seem to be based on the implicit assumption that less diverse networks show high levels of cohesion. This, however, seems not to be the case; other lines of segregation, most importantly sex, as well as basic processes of network formation set certain limits to cohesion in every network, mostly independent of its level of ethnic diversity. And these general forces tend to be much stronger for the resulting cohesion than the negative effects of ethnic homophily. The degree of network cohesion in ethnically less diverse networks thus tends to be overrated in current debates.

We have to emphasize that our contribution should be understood as a proof of existence, not as a carelessly generalizable result. We are not only dealing with the specific case of school classrooms at a specific age, we have also relied on very specific measures and operationalizations, and there would be many alternative ways of running the analyses. In general, an important next step would be to test the robustness of our results when going for other measures, definitions, and techniques. One example would be the measurement of ethnicity, which we based on the concept of country of birth, restricting the belonging to non-native categories to children of immigrants only. Another point for possible alternative specifications is the measurement of ties, which in our case is friendship allowing for five in-classroom nominations. One could certainly imagine some theoretical reasons why the findings could possibly differ when going for other empirical implementations.

While variants of ethnic diversity indices seem to correlate very highly empirically once the definition of ethnicity is given, thus not really making a large difference (Schaeffer, 2013), more uncertainty might be behind the stability of the results with respect to the specific measures of social cohesion. As mentioned in section 4.3, network analysis provides a wide range of different indices, and it would be important to study how they relate both logically and empirically, what specific dimension of cohesion they capture and how ethnic diversity relates to these separate dimensions of cohesion. Many additional empirical and theoretical contributions are necessary to reach a better understanding of the precise relation between ethnic diversity and cohesion, and we hope that our chapter has been able to stimulate further research along this road by taking a fruitful first step.

Notes

1 This entails all classrooms that comply with the following conditions: 1) at least 75 percent of all students in the classroom participated in the sociometric survey; 2) the proportion of invalid nominations does not exceed 10 percent; 3) no more than three students without any nominations and no more than three students that have never been nominated in any of the sociometric questions; 4) nominations possible within one's own classroom only.

2 The smallest gross classroom size is 12 students, the biggest 34, both from the English sample.

3 In England we have to exclude a relatively large share of the original sample of classrooms because the sociometric survey procedures differed for a substantial number of schools (allowing for cross-classroom nominations).

4 For n = 352 students there is no complete ethnic background information available.

5 The Herfindahl-based diversity index is computed as $D = 1 - \sum_{i=1}^{q} p_i^2$ with q being the number of groups and p_i being the proportion of individuals belonging to group i.

6 A comprehensive discussion of the relative advantages and disadvantages as well as the interrelations of all potential measures of cohesion in networks is far beyond the scope of this chapter. Some of the most obvious measures can be found in Chapter 2 of Jackson (2008).

7 Empirically, ethnically more diverse classrooms show slightly lower participation rates. Since non-participating students could in many classrooms not be nominated at all, participating students in these classrooms had on average a less complete list of class-mates to choose from. This could mean that ethnically diverse networks might be some-what sparser "by design." A negative correlation between ethnic diversity and network cohesion might therefore be overestimated, which would make the finding of a zero-correlation even more convincing.

8 The negative correlation comes about since there is an exponential relation between the number of actors in a network and the potential ties that can be formed. Also, the fact that students could only nominate up to a maximum of five classmates puts a strict boundary on the overall nomination possibilities.

9 For short general introductions to the basic descriptive concepts and terminology of network analysis see, for example, Chapter 4 in Knoke and Yang (2008: 45–91) or Chapter 2 in Jackson (2008: 20–53).

10 The geometrically weighted edgewise shared partner effect (gwesp) quantifies all nomi-nations in which ego and alter share a common friend. In contrast to other specifica-tions, the decaying weighting factor included in gwesp thereby accounts for the fact that few shared friends are empirically more common than many shared friends. This specification captures the idea of a positive but decreasing marginal utility of friend-ships and, at the same time, minimizes the risk of model degeneracy during the simula-tion process. In our models, we fixed the decay factor at .5. For more information, see Snijders *et al.* (2006) or Hunter (2007).

11 Most authors suggest that these sociality effects are crucial prerequisites to arrive at an unbiased estimate of group choice homophily (Stark, 2011). In multinetwork analyses, however, they can seldom be applied (for example, see Stark and Flache, 2012).

12 We exclude all results for those classrooms where at least one coefficient estimate has an absolute value > 8. When choosing this cutoff-point we made sure not to influence a substantive part of the estimates' distributions. In most cases the high coefficients result mainly from too little within-classroom variation in the attributes of interest.

13 When we include density, and thus a pure quantity aspect of cohesion, as an independ-ent variable in the meta-analyses, the effects of triadic closure are almost unchanged (there is only a slight reduction in the Netherlands). The effects of reciprocity, however, are considerably reduced. The same holds for the effects of sex homophily. The effects of ethnic homophily also hardly change and stay insignificant, the Netherlands again being an exception.

References

Blau, P. M. (1977) *Inequality and Heterogeneity: A Primitive Theory of Social Structure*. New York: The Free Press.

Burt, R. S. (1992) *Structural Holes: The Social Structure of Competition*. Cambridge, MA.: Harvard University Press.

Byrne, D. E. (1971) *The Attraction Paradigm*. New York: Academic Press.

Coleman, J. S. (1988) Social capital in the creation of human capital. *American Journal of Sociology*, 94: 95–120.

Fararo, T. J. and Doreian, P. (1998) The theory of solidarity: an agenda of problems. In P. Doreian and T. Fararo (eds) *The Problem of Solidarity: Theories and Models*. Amsterdam: Gordon & Breach, pp. 1–30.

Feld, S. L. (1981) The focused organization of social ties. *American Journal of Sociology*, 86(5): 1015–1035.

Felmlee, D:, Sprecher, S., and Bassin, E. (1990) The dissolution of intimate relationships: a hazard model. *Social Psychology Quarterly*, 53(1): 13–30.

Goodreau, S., Kitts, J., and Morris, M. (2009) Birds of a feather, or friend of a friend? Using exponential random graph models to investigate adolescent social networks. *Demography*, 46: 103–125.

Granovetter, M. S. (1973) The strength of weak ties. *American Journal of Sociology*, 78(6): 1360–1380.

—— (1985) Economic action and social structure: the problem of embeddedness. *American Journal of Sociology*, 91(3): 481–510.

Hallinan, M. T. (1978) The process of friendship formation. *Social Networks*, 1(2): 193–210.

Heider, F. (1946) Attitudes and cognitive organization. *The Journal of Psychology*, 21(1): 107–112.

Hunter, D. R. (2007) Curved exponential family models for social networks. *Social Networks*, 29(2): 216–230.

Huston, T. L. and Levinger, G. (1978) Interpersonal attraction and relationships. *Annual Review of Psychology*, 29(1): 115–156.

Jackson, M. O. (2008) *Social and Economic Networks*. Princeton, NJ: Princeton University Press.

Kalter, F., Heath, A. F., Hewstone, M., Jonsson, J. O., Kalmijn, M., Kogan, I., and van Tubergen, F. (2013) *Children of Immigrants Longitudinal Survey in Four European Countries* (CILS4EU). GESIS Data Archive, Cologne.

Knoke, D. and Yang, S. (2008) *Social Network Analysis*. Thousand Oaks, CA: Sage Publications.

Kossinets, G. and Watts, D. J. (2009) Origins of homophily in an evolving social network. *American Journal of Sociology*, 115(2): 405–450.

Lubbers, M. J. (2003) Group composition and network structure in school classes: A multilevel application of the p* model. *Social Networks*, 25(4), 309–332.

Lusher, D. ; Koskinen, J., and Robins, G. (2013) *Exponential Random Graph Models for Social Networks: Theory, Methods and Applications*. New York: Cambridge University Press.

McPherson, M., Smith-Lovin, L., and Cook, J. M. (2001) Birds of a feather: homophily in social networks. *Annual Review of Sociology*, 27: 415–444.

Moody, J. (2001) Race, school integration, and friendship segregation in America. *American Journal of Sociology*, 107(3): 679–716.

Moody, J. and White, D. R. (2003) Structural cohesion and embeddedness: a hierarchical concept of social groups. *American Sociological Review*, 68(1): 103–127.

Moreno, J. L. (1934) *Who Shall Survive? A New Approach to the Problem of Human Interrelations*. Washington, DC: Nervous and Mental Disease Publishing Company.

Mouw, T. and Entwisle, B. (2006) Residential segregation and interracial friendship in schools. *American Journal of Sociology*, 112(2): 394–441.

Newman, M. E. J. (2003) The structure and function of complex networks. *SIAM Review*, 45(2): 167–256.

Portes, A. and Vickstrom, E. (2011) Diversity, social capital, and cohesion. *Annual Review of Sociology*, 37: 461–479.

Putnam, R. D. (2007) *E pluribus unum*: diversity and community in the twenty-first century. *Scandinavian Political Studies*, 30(2): 137–174.

Raub, W. and Weesie, J. (1990) Reputation and efficiency in social interactions: an example of network effects. *American Journal of Sociology*, 96(3): 626–654.

Robins, G., Pattison, P., Kalish, Y., and Lusher, D. (2007) An introduction to exponential random graph (p*) models for social networks. *Social Networks*, 29(2): 173–191.

Schaeffer, M. (2013) Can competing diversity indices inform us about why ethnic diversity erodes social cohesion? A test of five diversity indices in Germany. *Social Science Research*, 42(3): 755–774.

Snijders, T. A. B., Pattison, P. E., Robins, G. L., and Handcock, M. S. (2006) New specifications for exponential random graph models. *Sociological Methodology*, 36(1): 99–153.

Stark, T. H. (2011) *Integration in Schools. A Process Perspective on Students' Interethnic Attitudes and Interpersonal Relationships*. Groningen: ICS Dissertation Series.

Stark, T. H. and Flache, A. (2012) The double edge of common interest: ethnic segregation as an unintended byproduct of opinion homophily. *Sociology of Education*, 85(2): 179–199.

Verbrugge, L. M. (1977) The structure of adult friendship choices. *Social Forces*, 56(2): 576–597.

Wasserman, S. and Faust, K. (1994) *Social Network Analysis: Methods and Applications*, Vol. VIII. Cambridge: Cambridge University Press.

White, D. R. and Harary, F. (2001) The cohesiveness of blocks in social networks: node connectivity and conditional density. *Sociological Methodology*, 31(1): 305–359.

Wimmer, A. (2008) The making and unmaking of ethnic boundaries: a multilevel process theory. *American Journal of Sociology*, 113(4): 970–1022.

Wimmer, A. and Lewis, K. (2010) Beyond and below racial homophily: ERG models of a friendship network documented on Facebook. *American Journal of Sociology*, 116(2): 583–642.

11 Diversity and intergroup contact in schools[*]

Miles Hewstone, Christina Floe, Ananthi Al Ramiah, Katharina Schmid, Esther Son, Ralf Wölfer, and Simon Lolliot

Introduction

Following Putnam's (2007) provocative claim—that ethnic diversity has negative consequences for trust—scholars in numerous disciplines (especially political science, sociology, and belatedly social psychology) have debated, and investigated, the potential consequences of living in diverse settings (see Chapter 1, this volume, for the background to the debate). The vast majority of this debate has, however, focused on ethnic neighborhoods or cities. In this chapter we review results from our own research program on the impact of diversity in secondary schools, i.e., the social environment in which adolescents spend most of their waking hours. Much of this research was conducted in English schools, but our approach is far from parochial. We also report evidence from our research in Northern Ireland and other Western European countries (Germany, the Netherlands, and Sweden).

The theoretical approach guiding our research is that of "intergroup contact theory" (Allport, 1954; Brown and Hewstone, 2005; Pettigrew and Tropp, 2011), which argues that positive face-to-face contact between members of different groups, rather than mere acquaintance, helps to reduce prejudice and improve intergroup relations. Intergroup contact theory emphasizes that it is the quality, rather than the mere quantity, of contact that especially promotes more positive out-group attitudes and behaviors. In this chapter we focus on four crucial characteristics of direct, face-to-face contact: quantity of contact (frequency of interaction with out-group members, e.g., "How often do you meet/talk to/etc. out-group members in school?"); positive quality of contact (nature of the interaction with out-group members, e.g., "How positive is the contact?"); negative contact (e.g., "Have you had any bad experiences with out-group members?");

[*] The research reviewed in this chapter was funded, in part, by a grant on "Ethno-religious diversity and trust in residential and educational settings" from the Leverhulme Trust; and by the NORFACE research programme on Migration in Europe—Social, Economic, Cultural and Policy Dynamics for the Children of Immigrants Longitudinal Survey in Four European Countries (CILS4EU) awarded to Frank Kalter, Anthony Heath, Miles Hewstone, Jan O. Jonsson, Matthijs Kalmijn, Irena Kogan, and Frank van Tubergen. We take this opportunity to also thank three people who gave us their unstinting support in conducting this research in educational settings: Jayne Clarke, Alun Francis, and Des Herlihy.

and cross-group friendship (being friends with out-group members, e.g., "How many close out-group friends do you have?"). Later in the chapter we will also explore more indirect forms of contact, including extended contact via family or friends (e.g., "How many of your family members/in-group friends have out-group friends?"), contact at the school level (i.e., "Are students affected by the level of contact in their school as a whole?"), and contact assessed via measures of social networks (for an overview of the studies, see Table 11.1).

We begin by studying the phenomenon of resegregation, where people fail to take up opportunities for mixing in diverse settings and, instead, resegregate themselves by their ethnic group memberships (e.g., sitting apart in a cafeteria). We review our research in British schools that first sought to observe this phenomenon, and then to explore its causes. Next, we report on our program of research in ethnically mixed and homogeneous schools in a city in the northwest of England, in which we have studied the impact of mixing on out-group attitudes in both cross-sectional and longitudinal studies, and among ethnic majority and minority students. In the following section we highlight the results, to date, of a "natural experiment," an evaluation of a social intervention, in which students from two ethnically distinct schools are merged, over time. The research reported in these first three sections demonstrates effects of positive contact with members of one out-group on attitudes towards that same out-group. The next section shows that contact has a wider impact than this, whereby contact with "primary" out-groups also generalizes to "secondary" out-groups, not involved in the contact setting. Notwithstanding this consistent support for the positive consequences of intergroup contact, most of this research has taken an interpersonal or dyadic approach to the issue of whether contact reduces prejudice; in the next section, however, we show that contact has a wider impact, operating both on a contextual level and via social networks. Finally, we draw some general conclusions about the impact of intergroup contact and diversity in schools and where future research is needed.

Resegregation: why don't people always mix when they could?

When academics or policy advisers recommend, and politicians implement, the provision of multiethnic schools, there is an assumption that these spaces will not only provide people with opportunities to come into contact with dissimilar others, but that students will also avail themselves of these opportunities. However, anecdotal and research evidence demonstrates that such cross-ethnic mixing in diverse classrooms or cafeterias is not always common (e.g., Fisher Williamson, Chapter 4, and Kalter and Kruse, Chapter 10, in this volume; Campbell *et al.*, 1966; Clack *et al.*, 2005; McCauley *et al.*, 2001); rather, people tend to stick with ethnically similar others.

This phenomenon is known as *ethnic resegregation*[1] (Schofield, 1997), and is based on the sociological concept of *homophily*, the principle that people tend to have more contact with similar than dissimilar others, including, but not restricted to, ethnically or racially similar others (Orr *et al.*, 2012; McPherson, Smith-Lovin, and Cook, 2001; see also Taylor and Moghaddam's, 1994, discussion of "illusory contact," or continued segregation within the context of mixed environments). Homophily, expressed in terms of seating distance, has even been reported in terms of superficial characteristics such as hair length, or whether or not people wear glasses, even after controlling for sex and race (MacKinnon *et al.*, 2011).

Despite the significant body of research that demonstrates the value of interethnic mixing, or contact, in improving intergroup relations (Pettigrew and Tropp, 2006, 2011), this value cannot be realized if opportunities for contact are not actually taken up (Schofield and Eurich-Fulcer, 2001). In the research we report in this chapter, we focus on visible minority and majority group membership in studying ethnicity. The first reason for this is that some of our research is observational, and thus we needed clear physiognomic markers of ethnic group membership in determining seating patterns. The second reason is that most of the intergroup contexts of the studies we report are ethnically dichotomous in nature, where there is a clear visible majority and minority, and very few, if any, members from other ethnic groups. We believe such an approach to be reasonable and practical for our purposes, but acknowledge that it may at times obscure the richer ethnic makeup of a particular setting and also does not account for differences in fluency in English, which may account for some patterns of resegregation (although the vast majority of ethnic minority students in our studies have been schooled entirely in the UK).

Our first piece of research (see Al Ramiah *et al.*, 2014, Study 1) was inspired by the title of Beverley Daniel Tatum's (2003) popular book: *Why Are All the Black Kids Sitting Together in the Cafeteria?* Our own exploration of this question considered the perspectives of both ethnic majority *and* minority group members, in order to ascertain the vital roles played by each in determining the intergroup climate and patterns of resegregation. We sought, first, to document the phenomenon of resegregation between ethnic groups, and, second, to explain why it occurs. We conducted this research in schools in a city in northwest England, which has a history of significant ethnic disturbances, socio-economic deprivation and both residential and educational segregation (especially at the elementary-school level, but with some mixing at the secondary level). We were motivated to investigate these questions in this challenging environment so that our work might provide insights into, on the one hand, why desegregation efforts may fail and, on the other hand, how their full potential may be realized.

To provide evidence for the phenomenon of resegregation, we studied seating patterns among 16- to 18-year-old students in a high-school cafeteria. At the time of the study there were 2,333 students enrolled in the school (59 percent White; 35 percent Asian,[2] mainly of Pakistani or Bangladeshi heritage; and 6 percent of other ethnicity).

Figure 11.1 shows the four areas of the cafeteria and the exact location of the tables and chairs. We made observations during 30-minute periods over two days by having trained observers systematically note the ethnicity of each individual seated in occupied chairs. Our trained observers also recorded "social units" (determined by the presence or absence of conversation between students,

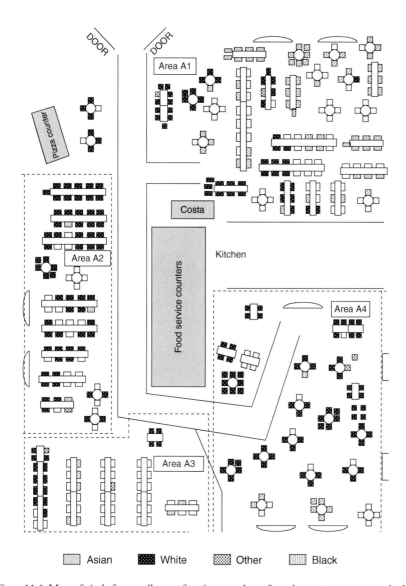

Figure 11.1 Map of sixth-form college cafeteria: snapshot of seating patterns at a particular time interval—on day 2, 12.00–12.25pm.

and the orientation of a student's head or body towards some students and away from others; see McCauley *et al.*, 2001). Using this methodology, we could define social units as either ethnically "mixed" or "homogeneous" (see Figure 11.2 for an example of a table with a mixed social unit).

We then calculated aggregation indices based on side-by-side (see Campbell *et al.*, 1966), and face-to-face (adapted from Campbell *et al.*, 1966) cross-ethnic

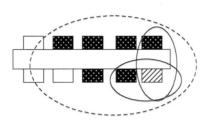

Figure 11.2 An example of a table taken from the above cafeteria snapshot, depicting White-Asian side-by-side and face-to-face adjacencies (solid), and the social unit (dashed).

seating adjacencies. These indices detail the extent to which students choose to sit in close proximity to ethnically similar or dissimilar others in each section of the cafeteria, thus providing a picture of the degree of ethnic resegregation in the cafeteria. The scores are based on the difference between the actual frequency with which White and Asian students sat opposite (beside) each other, and the expected frequency (see Al Ramiah *et al.*, 2014, for details). We found that both face-to-face and side-by-side indices were negative for each of the areas on both days, thus demonstrating more ethnic resegregation than would be expected under conditions of randomness.

Moving beyond mere proximity in seating, we looked at mixing at the level of social units in the cafeteria, where people were engaged in meaningful interaction. Across all coding intervals, and out of 775 social units involving White and/or Asian students, only 41 were mixed, i.e., roughly 5 percent of all possible social units involved cross-group interactions (with one or more out-group members), despite high levels of students from both groups in the cafeteria (although this varied through the day). Comparatively, there was little evidence of segregation on the basis of gender.

We then assessed the distribution of individuals from different ethnic groups across the four main areas of the cafeteria. We calculated an adapted segregation index of dissimilarity, *D* (Clack *et al.*, 2005), which measures segregation as a function of the "evenness" of the distribution of individuals from different ethnic groups across the social space. Analyses showed that students did not choose where to sit in a random manner. Rather, ethnicity seemed to have played a role in their decision-making (for the vast majority of the 30-minute intervals coded, the *D* value was higher than what one would expect under conditions of random mixing).

Finally, we investigated whether students from the two ethnic groups favored sitting in particular areas of the cafeteria. We found that Asian students chose significantly to cluster in area A1 more than in any other area, whereas White students predominated in the other three areas of the cafeteria (the differences in the proportion of Asian to White students between area A1 and all other areas were all highly significant).

Having thus documented resegregation in this context, we conducted a second study to investigate *why* it might occur. As Clack *et al.* (2005) suggested, resegregation is likely to be shaped by individuals' intergroup perceptions. But when interpreting pronounced segregation in any ecology it is important to consider that such effects may not necessarily be the result of extreme attitudes towards, or desire to remain apart from, the out-group. In his theory of agent-based modelling (ABM), Schelling (1971) posited that minor preferences for in-group proximity can result in segregation over time, even if one's tolerance threshold for the proportion of out-group members is only occasionally violated. Such segregation, which can result from intergroup perceptions and practices, can shape the way future entrants into the ecological space order their own preferences and behaviors. In our second study we sought to explain why resegregation occurs and whether it is, as the Schelling model suggests, the outcome of factors other than extreme attitudes towards the out-group.

In this next study we were especially interested in the role that intergroup attributions play in promoting, or impeding, cafeteria contact (actual or hypothetical). Intergroup attributions refer to the explanations that individuals make for the behaviors of members of their own and other social groups. We were guided in this research by Shelton and Richeson's (2005) prior work. Drawing upon the pluralistic ignorance framework, in which people privately reject a norm or belief, but incorrectly believe that others support it (see Vorauer and Ratner, 1996), Shelton and Richeson argued that attributions, and particularly attributional biases, play a central role in the avoidance of contact. In other words, individuals make divergent explanations for their own versus out-group members' identical intergroup behaviors, which might prohibit mixing.

Shelton and Richeson (2005) argued that individuals differ in the degree to which they believe their in-group and the out-group 1) fear rejection on the basis of ethnicity, and 2) are uninterested in the out-group/in-group. They found that both Black and White American college students attributed their own unwillingness to sit with out-group members (in a hypothetical cafeteria scenario) to their *fear of being rejected* by the out-group, while they attributed the out-group's unwillingness to sit with the respondent to *lack of interest* in the respondent's in-group.

In our second study (Al Ramiah *et al.*, 2014, Study 2), we attempted a conceptual replication of Shelton and Richeson's work, using a sample of British high-school students (sampled from the same school in which Study 1 was conducted). We assessed whether attributions differed when explaining own versus the out-group's behavior, and whether such attributions were moderated by participant group membership. We first assessed the ethnic group membership of the students with whom participants reported that they sat in the cafeteria. We collected data from 313 male and female students (aged 16 to 18 years; M_{age} = 16.85; 60 percent White, 40 percent Asian) using a web-based questionnaire.

We first asked participants to report on the ethnic group membership of the students they usually sit with in the college cafeteria. We then analyzed responses only from those students who reported that they did *not* have cafeteria contact with out-group members, so that we would be able to understand the factors that drove habitual self-reported contact avoidance in a meaningful way. As the vast majority of students reported sitting only with in-group students (94 percent of

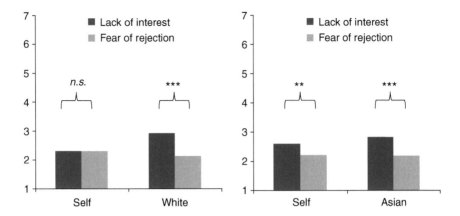

Figure 11.3 Causal attributions of in-group and out-group avoidance behavior to "lack of interest" and "fear of rejection" from Study 2 (left panel: Asian students; right panel: White students).

White respondents and 90 percent of Asian respondents), we filtered only these self-segregating participants to respond to four questions, adapted from Shelton and Richeson (2005): two gauging *fear of rejection* (their own fear of rejection by the out-group, and the out-group's perceived fear of rejection by the in-group), and two gauging *lack of interest* in intergroup contact (their own apathy about getting to know the out-group, and the out-group's perceived indifference about getting to know them).[3]

The results are shown separately for white and Asian participants in Figure 11.3. For white participants own lack of interest was greater than own fear of rejection. In addition, they perceived Asians' lack of interest in getting to know them to be higher than Asians' fear of rejection. Thus, there was a correspondence in attributing both own and out-group's failure to mix more to lack of interest than to fear of rejection; however, the attribution of lack of interest was more likely to be made about the out-group than the self, while the attribution of fear of rejection was similar for the self and the out-group. For Asian participants, no significant difference emerged between their own lack of interest and own fear of rejection. However, they similarly perceived whites' lack of interest to be higher than whites' fear of rejection.

To summarize, these results do not indicate stark attributional bias, with one explanation for "us" (e.g., "we're afraid of being rejected"), and a different explanation for "them" ("they're not interested in getting to know us"). Rather, white participants showed a *correspondence* between attributions for own and the out-group's failure to mix; in both cases, they attributed their mutual inaction more to lack of interest than to fear of rejection. Asian students did, however, give somewhat different attributions for the same behavior by the self and the out-group: they attributed the out-group's unwillingness to mix more to lack of interest, while there was no clear attributional preference for their own unwillingness to mix.[4]

We next sought to conceptually replicate our attributional findings, and moreover to assess, longitudinally, possible predictors of the likelihood of engaging in cafeteria contact (Al Ramiah *et al.*, 2014, Study 3). Beyond participants' own explanations, or justifications, for their avoidance of cafeteria contact, Shelton and Richeson tested the extent to which these attributions predicted contact. They conducted a longitudinal study using only white participants, in which these attributions, measured at the start of the semester were treated as predictors of change in contact with blacks over the course of the semester. They found that white students' pluralistic ignorance (attributing own inaction to fear of rejection *more* than they attributed the out-group's inaction to fear of rejection) predicted a decline in contact with blacks over the semester.

Our third study also investigated the role of injunctive *norms*—shared beliefs about the appropriate conduct for group members (Jetten *et al.*, 1996). Norms have long been central to the social psychology of prejudice and have been shown to be powerful predictors of behavior (Aboud and Sankar, 2007; Deutsch and Collins, 1951; Sims and Patrick, 1936). In less abstract terms, it matters whether a prejudiced stance, or the opposite, is the norm in a given context. The amount of prejudice people express is strongly predicted (Patchen, 1982; Pettigrew, 1958) and even causally affected by (Stangor *et al.*, 2001) the (perceived) level of prejudice of others in that context. This influence can come from others who are in-group members (see self-categorization theory; Hogg and Turner, 1987; Turner, 1982) but also from out-group members (Shelton and Richeson, 2005; Tropp and Bianchi, 2006).

We longitudinally assessed the extent to which both intergroup attributions and in-group and out-group norms explained the likelihood of contact in the cafeteria, while also taking into account other relevant explanatory variables such as own diversity beliefs, out-group attitudes, intergroup anxiety (feelings of discomfort and nervousness that arise in intergroup encounters; Stephan and Stephan, 1985), number of out-group friends, and percentage of out-group members in each school. We focused especially on intergroup attributions and norms, and treated the other variables as variables that should be controlled for.[5]

First, we again investigated intergroup attributions, using a larger and different student sample, and a vignette involving likelihood of contact in an imagined cafeteria scenario. We collected data from students (aged 11–12) at nine secondary schools in the same city where Studies 1 and 2 were conducted. In comparison to Studies 1 and 2, the students were younger and were in their first year of secondary school (the equivalent of Grade 7 in the US); this allowed us to assess whether cafeteria preferences and explanations for them are already evident from the start of secondary schooling. Data was collected at two time points separated by seven months. The final sample, based on participants who took part at a single time point or both, was 2,013 (76 percent white; 24 percent Asian). We collected the data using a web-based questionnaire. The independent variables were asked at Time 1, while the dependent variable, participants' self-rated likelihood of their choosing to sit with out-group members in the cafeteria, was asked at both time points.

We first examined the attributional data, and found that in this data set the pattern of results did not differ between White and Asian participants. The results revealed that both White and Asian participants attributed their own inaction more to lack of interest in the out-group than fear of being rejected by them. Similarly, both groups attributed the out-group's inaction more to lack of interest than fear of rejection. However, both sets of participants also explained inaction differently for the in-group compared with the out-group; they attributed inaction less to fear of rejection, and more to lack of interest, for the out-group.

We then conducted multiple-group path analyses for the White and Asian samples to identify longitudinal predictors of seating choice. We regressed the likelihood of choosing to sit with out-group members in the cafeteria scenario at Time 2 on all other variables measured at Time 1. For both the White and Asian samples, the likelihood of choosing to sit with the out-group at Time 2 was marginally negatively predicted by lack of interest in getting to know the out-group at Time 1, and was positively predicted by both number of out-group friends at Time 1, and perceived positive in-group norms towards intergroup contact with the out-group at Time 1. In addition, for the Asian sample only, perceived positive out-group norms at Time 1 positively predicted likelihood of choosing to sit with the out-group at Time 2.

Thus Study 3 identified some of the variables that might drive cafeteria resegregation. Lack of interest in the out-group among White and Asian participants (marginally) inhibited likelihood of cafeteria contact in the scenario, while having out-group friends promoted it. In-group norms predicted likely cafeteria contact for both majority and minority group participants. Consistent with past research (Tropp and Bianchi, 2006), out-group norms seemed to matter only for minority but not for majority participants.

If we consider these first three studies together, the strong evidence for resegregation is consistent with people's well-established preference for sticking with others who are like them (MacKinnon *et al.*, 2011; McPherson *et al.*, 2001). Thus, it is not surprising that ethnicity should be a highly salient and powerful organizing feature in mixed settings (Miller and Prentice, 1999). It is, however, possible that cafeteria contact is different from some other forms of contact, for at least two reasons. First, a person is likely to be observed by in-group and out-group members in a cafeteria setting and, if the existing norms are for different ethnic groups to sit apart, then, given that we are studying visible ethnic groups, one's own choice to mix will be clearly and visibly counternormative. Second, cafeteria contact potentially requires a high degree of deliberation and motivation. Other research has shown that interracial interactions can temporarily deplete executive attentional resources (Richeson *et al.*, 2003), particularly in those who have high levels of racial bias. Interracial interactions may be exhausting over time, and since mixing is a part of the normal school day, students may opt for self-segregation when they get the opportunity. These considerations notwithstanding, we made progress in better understanding some of the factors driving the phenomenon, namely attributions and norms. We turn now to other forms of contact and consider their impact on out-group attitudes.

Research in ethnically mixed and homogeneous schools

Although our research on resegregation reports a relative failure to take up opportunities for contact in the cafeterias of mixed schools, this is not to say that intergroup contact avoidance is the rule, nor that contact fails to impact out-group attitudes. We now turn to our ongoing program of research in ethnically mixed and homogeneous schools located in the same city as our earlier studies, in which we had access to students in all the city's state-run secondary schools. Of special interest to us, these schools ranged from almost completely homogeneous Asian or White schools, to mixed schools. Our research has studied the impact of mixing on out-group attitudes in both cross-sectional and longitudinal studies, and among ethnic majority and minority students.[6]

Using data from all 11 schools, we compared homogeneous, low percentage-Asian, and high percentage-Asian schools, looking at the results for the White and Asian students separately. We first compared mean levels of contact and other key variables across school types on the four above-mentioned types of intergroup contact: quantity, positive quality, negative contact, and out-group friends.

For White pupils, we found, as expected, that a greater proportion of Asian students in the school led to more intergroup contact and more out-group friends. Interestingly, while the positive quality of contact was slightly higher in more mixed schools, and much higher than negative contact, the level of negative contact was also higher in more mixed schools. We think this adds an important note of realism to our work, and to the field. It is, of course, statistically likely that *both* positive and negative contact should be higher the more mixed a social environment is. The importance of negative, as well as positive, contact has only recently been acknowledged, however, and there is evidence that negative contact, while much lower in frequency, has stronger effects (Barlow *et al.*, 2012). Intergroup anxiety was also lower in more mixed schools, and both norms and out-group attitudes were more positive the more mixed the school. Results for Asian students were quite similar. Quantity of contact with White students, its positive quality, and number of out-group friends were all highest in low percentage-Asian schools (where Asian students had the greatest opportunity for contact with White students). Both norms and out-group attitudes were also most positive where opportunities for mixing were highest; but there was no difference between school types for intergroup anxiety.

These results, of course, are only based on overall means, and are provided merely to give some background. Intergroup contact theory makes predictions at the individual level, with those students who have more and better quality contact expected to have more positive out-group attitudes. Contact theory also argues that contact will predict attitudes over time when longitudinal data is available.[7]

To test the predictions set forth by contact theory, we conducted a 2-wave longitudinal survey of White (n = 160) and Asian (n = 102) students' (aged 16–18 years) contact and attitudes over the course of a year in one school. Our results also support the predictions of contact theory. For both ethnic groups of students, contact was a significant predictor of out-group attitudes over time. Asian students had significantly more positive out-group attitudes than White students, but, for both groups, contact at Time 1 was significantly associated with out-group attitudes at Time 2 (quality of contact positively, and negative contact negatively) controlling for Time 1 out-group attitudes. Such longitudinal data increases our confidence in the causal effect of contact on attitudes, but still falls short of demonstrating a causal effect (Cliff, 1983).

Experimental data would, of course, provide the most convincing evidence of causal effects but this is extremely difficult to obtain in a school setting. In the next section we consider data from a "natural experiment" that provided such evidence.

Prospective study of a merger between two ethnically different schools

We were fortunate enough to be studying all the schools in a city where three planned mergers of schools were taking place, each involving a move to a new location. These mergers were planned for a variety of reasons, including the desire to integrate largely separate schools for each community, following serious ethnic disturbances in 2001. In the most dramatic case, a White school (93 percent) and an Asian school (86 percent) were to be merged, and we were able to profit from the opportunity to assess contact and attitudes pre- and post-merger in a pencil-and-paper survey (n = 107 White and n = 97 Asian students of Pakistani heritage; age range 11–13 years). We were also able to collect data in two other mergers, which will help us isolate the impact of specific merging procedures, and we can consider the effects of this merger against the background of the general trends in contact and attitudes across all the schools in the city, for which we have data. We summarize here the most important results to date; later analyses will consider more precisely the effects of the mergers across all the schools. Among other measures, we assessed quantity and quality of intergroup contact, and out-group attitudes, and found evidence of the causal effect of contact on attitudes for both ethnic groups. For White students, contact quality at Time 1 positively predicted attitudes approximately six months later (i.e., post-merger), controlling for Time 1 attitudes (there was no effect of contact quantity). For Asian students, however, it was contact quantity at Time 1 that positively predicted Time 2 attitudes, again controlling for Time 1 attitudes (there was no effect of contact quality).

We continue to follow up on these students, and plan to do so through their secondary school education. For example, a second merger involves two ostensibly Roman Catholic schools, one of which is almost exclusively White, whereas the other is 55 percent Asian-Muslim.[8] This school allows us to study the impact of an ethnic merger within a school with a religious ethos, and in which ethnic mixing will be new to some of the students, but not to others. Finally, the third merged school brings together two predominantly White schools (86 percent and 93 percent), but in a new area of the city that has led to a significant intake of Asian students. Thus our future research will be able to compare the impact of diversity from different starting points and at different rates over time.

Secondary-transfer effects of intergroup contact

The potential of contact would be even greater *if* it could be shown that contact effects generalize from experience with a "primary" out-group to attitudes towards other *"secondary"* out-groups (e.g., positive contact between White and Asian students generalizes to positive attitudes towards other ethnic minorities). There is, in fact, growing evidence that this is the case (for a review, see Lolliot *et al.*, 2013). Tausch *et al.* (2010) reported the most extensive, including longitudinal, evidence to date, for three phenomena: 1) that secondary-transfer effects occur via a process of attitude generalization (i.e., from attitude towards primary out-group to attitude towards secondary out-group); 2) that they occur while controlling for direct contact with the secondary out-groups; and 3) that they cannot be explained in terms of socially desirable responding.

Although Tausch *et al.* reported strongest evidence for attitude generalization as the main process mediating secondary-transfer effects of contact, they also reported some evidence for mediation via deprovincialization (Pettigrew, 2009; Verkuyten *et al.*, 2010; see also Schmid *et al.*, Chapter 8, this volume), whereby getting to know individuals from different backgrounds leads to a less ethnocentric perception of out-groups as well as one's own group. The deprovincialization hypothesis thus proposes that intergroup contact, especially close contact with out-group members, leads in-group members to reappraise in-group norms and customs, and see that they are neither the only ones, nor superior to other norms and customs (Pettigrew, 1997, 1998).

We sought further evidence for this intervening process in a large cross-sectional study of segregated and mixed schools in Northern Ireland (here segregation/mixing refers to Catholic and Protestant religious groups, rather than to racial groups). We asked more than 3,000 students (68 percent Catholics, 32 percent Protestants; aged 11–15 years) to complete measures of both contact with and attitude to the ethno-religious out-group (the primary group) and to three other groups (racial minorities, travelers, and the disabled; the secondary out-groups). As a measure of deprovincialization, we also asked them to complete a short multiculturalism scale (asking whether out-groups should be allowed to maintain own traditions and culture; whether the in-group should respect out-group cultures; and whether the in-groups should learn about the traditions and culture of different groups). While controlling for contact with the secondary out-groups, we found support for a path model whereby primary out-group contact (friendships with the ethno-religious out-group) impacted secondary out-group attitudes via attitudes towards the primary out-group and supportive views of multiculturalism. This survey is the first wave of a planned series of five annual surveys, and we now hope to confirm this model using longitudinal data.

Wider effects of intergroup contact: beyond interpersonal contact

Notwithstanding this consistent support for the positive consequences of intergroup contact, most of this research has taken an interpersonal or dyadic approach to the issue of whether contact reduces prejudice; in the next section, however, we show that contact has a wider impact, operating both at the contextual level (i.e., school level) and via social networks.

The impact of intergroup contact is not limited to the effect of direct contact, as assessed in the research we have reviewed thus far. "Extended" contact, i.e., knowing that another in-group member has positive out-group contact, can also reduce out-group prejudice (Wright *et al.*, 1997; for a review see Dovidio *et al.*, 2011). However, even this notion of extended contact may be limited by its focus on interpersonal aspects of contact. Could prejudice be a function of not only whom you know, but also where you live? And could contact have effects beyond the dyadic level, via people's social networks? We consider these questions in this section.

We tested Putnam's (2007) claim—that ethnic diversity negatively affects intergroup relations—not in neighborhoods, but in schools, varying in diversity (see also Chapters 9 and 10, this volume; and prior studies by Dinesen, 2011; Keating and Benton, 2013; Janmaat, 2012; Tolsma *et al.*, 2013). We did this using part of a large data set yielded by the Children of Immigrants Longitudinal Survey in Four European Countries (CILS4EU) project. This dataset included a sample of 20,000 students (aged 14 years at wave 1) from more than 400 schools, at four levels of ethnic density, across four countries (Germany, the Netherlands, Sweden, and the UK), over three waves.[9] In each country students completed a pencil-and-paper questionnaire about many aspects of family, school, and social life, including measures of out-group contact and attitudes. The out-groups varied across countries, depending on the major ethnic minorities/immigrants in each (e.g., Germany: Turks, Poles, Russians, and Italians; the Netherlands: Moroccans, Surinamese/Antilleans, and Turks; Sweden: Turks, Poles, Russians, and Italians; UK: Asians, blacks). Thus far we have only completed the analysis for the majority group respondents in the UK, at wave 1. Using multilevel modeling, we tested the impact of diversity and contact on attitudes (measured for each of the two ethnic out-groups, Blacks and Asians, considered as joint dependent variables in the same model). At the between-schools-level, using ethnic mix of the school as the measure of diversity, we found that the direct effect of diversity on attitudes to each out-group was negative, but non-significant. However, diversity had a positive impact on school contact with each out-group, and contact was significantly positively associated with attitudes towards Asians (the effect was positive, but non-significant for Blacks). At the within-schools-level, school contact with each out-group was significantly positively associated with attitudes towards that out-group (for similar findings of contact counteracting negative effects of diversity in diverse neighborhoods, see Schmid *et al.*, 2014; Schmid *et al.*, Chapter 8, this volume). We are currently extending this analysis to use the other three countries, and the longitudinal data covering three waves (one year apart).

The above analysis shows that, across schools, a higher school level of intergroup contact is associated with less prejudice. We have also tested the *contextual effect* of contact (Blalock, 1984; Christ *et al.*, 2014), that is, the difference between the effect of intergroup contact between schools (the *between-level effect*) and the effect of individual-level contact within schools (the *within-level effect*; see Raudenbush and Bryk,

2002) on prejudice. Evidence for this contextual effect of positive contact would indicate that studying in a school in which other in-group members interact positively with members of the out-group should reduce prejudice, beyond one's own contact experiences and irrespective of whether one knows personally the other in-group members experiencing intergroup contact. Thus a student in a school which has a higher mean level of positive intergroup contact is likely to be less prejudiced than a person with the same level of direct positive contact, but studying in a school with a lower mean level of intergroup contact. Evidence, especially longitudinal data, for this contextual effect of contact would demonstrate that intergroup contact at the social context level has greatest consequences for individuals' attitudes (and behaviors), and that the processes involved cannot be reduced to characteristics of individuals or specific situations in which intergroup contact occurs (Oishi and Graham, 2010) or selection bias (for such evidence, see Christ *et al.*, 2014).

Using our own large data set of 51 Northern Irish schools, and by means of multilevel modeling, we showed that at the between-level, school differences in intergroup contact negatively predicted prejudice on the school level; similarly, at the within-level, contact was negatively associated with prejudice. Going one step further, using a measure of positive social norms based on diversity beliefs (Tropp and Bianchi, 2006; e.g., believing that the mix of different groups in school enriched social life), we tested the hypothesis that perceived in-group norms in schools with higher levels of positive out-group contact were more tolerant, supporting positive interactions with out-group members. We could, indeed, show that studying in a school in which students have, on average, more positive contact is associated with more tolerant social norms within these contexts, and these norms were associated with more tolerant out-group attitudes, over and above the effect of individual contact experiences. Thus positive social norms mediated the school-level impact of contact on prejudice.

As a final, complementary demonstration of the wider impact of contact, we turn to recent data on students' social networks, collected as part of the CILS4EU project introduced above (Wölfer and Hewstone, 2014; see also Kalter and Kruse, Chapter 10, this volume).[10] To date the potential value of studying intergroup contact using a social network approach has been relatively ignored (for an exception see Munniksma *et al.*, 2013). Here we note, briefly, at least two advantages that we have sought to exploit in our research. First, this approach does justice to the quantity and quality of social ties in a person's social network (e.g., a classroom) in a way that highlights reciprocal friendship links. For example, it is easy for someone to claim in a self-report survey item that they have out-group friends, because this cannot be verified; using social networks, we can test A's claim that s/he and out-group member B are friends, by seeing whether B reciprocates A's friendship. Second, social networks can also verify and use more precise measures of extended contact, without relying exclusively on self-reports. A potential weakness of self-reports to assess extended contact is that respondents may lack information about the friends of their friends, or may give biased estimates of this information.

Utilizing a multimethod approach, we broke down the complex two-step process of assessing the friends of one's friends by taking the first step with social network analyses (objective identification of a person's reciprocal connection within the network) and taking the second step with self-reports (considering the amount of out-group contact reported in responses to the survey of contact in and out of school, completed separately from the network). More specifically, we elicited social networks via students' nominations of their five best friends in a class setting, and assessed the ethnic status of students (categorized into majority and minority group) as well as the diversity of schools (four levels of ethnic density). We then identified each student's reciprocal connections (i.e., direct in-group and out-group friends) from the network data, selected the respective *in-group* friends, and averaged their self-reported out-group contact. Thus, we can investigate the impact on out-group attitudes of the level of contact of respondents' in-group friends. This revised extended contact information was translated into multilevel analyses (within-level: students; between-level: classes), separately for majority and minority students, in order to predict out-group attitudes, while controlling for direct contact, number of in-group friends, density, and reciprocity in network data.

We found significant positive effects of direct contact on out-group attitudes for both majority and minority students. Beyond that, we revealed significant extended contact effects for both the majority and minority. Finally, there was no interaction between direct and extended contact, but a status-specific interaction between contact and diversity: while direct contact effects increased with increasing diversity for the majority, extended contact effects increased with increasing diversity for the minority. These preliminary results reveal significant effects of extended contact, enriched via social network analysis, and underscore the value of this approach for contact research. Findings also highlighted the moderating role of diversity, and pointed to an equally important effect of contact for both the minority and majority, especially in diverse settings. This last finding is interesting, because prior research has reported that contact may be less effective for minority than majority members (e.g., Binder *et al.*, 2009; Tropp and Pettigrew, 2005). Using a precise multimethodological approach of self-reports and network data, we could not confirm this claim, and suggest that the comparison of contact effects between minorities and majorities merits future research, in a wide range of settings.

All three pieces of work reviewed in this section testify to the impact of contact beyond dyadic, interpersonal encounters. In doing so, they make a theoretical contribution to better understanding the consequences of diversity, and a practical contribution to underlining the policy potential of contact as a social intervention to improve intergroup relations on a wider level (Hewstone, 2009; Pettigrew and Tropp, 2011).

Conclusion

After following this broad overview of our research, we hope that the reader will share our conviction that studying intergroup contact in schools is an important research topic. Using a variety of techniques, and studying intergroup relations in many different settings, we have found unequivocal evidence that positive contact is associated with more positive out-group attitudes. It therefore holds great potential for using schools to promote tolerance and defeat prejudice.

This does not mean that the impact of diversity in schools is a simple matter. First, contact must actually take place, and not be avoided. Our evidence of resegregation, and our pursuit of its causes, indicates that it is a real and important phenomenon. While some readers may feel that students should be allowed to indulge their preferences for where, and with whom, they sit at lunchtime, we believe that a failure to intervene risks failing to capitalize on the opportunities provided by desegregated settings, and may model separation as the norm for new students entering such settings. Having highlighted the importance of intergroup attributions and norms, we would like to see future social interventions designed with the aim of changing assumptions, for example, that "they are not interested in meeting us," and promoting norms that support the value of integration, not segregation. Second, we have provided consistent evidence for the positive impact of contact, generalizing across out-groups, and operating beyond interpersonal settings in social networks and at the contextual level. We also noted that in mixed settings positive contact may take place alongside negative contact, and future research should study the interactive effects of these different forms of contact.

Methodologically, we have conducted cross-sectional, longitudinal, and quasi-experimental research; we have recently begun to exploit the potential of research using social networks; and we have begun to explore contextual influences on individual attitudes by way of multilevel modeling. Much of this work is still ongoing, and there remains a need for much more longitudinal research, preferably over multiple waves, and less future reliance on cross-sectional studies. Experimental studies in field settings, such as our own research on school mergers (see also Chapters 4 and 9, this volume), are likely to provide the strongest evidence for the causal impact of contact. Theoretically, we have sought to separate the effects of diversity and intergroup contact, and to investigate with a wide range of measures just how wide the impact of contact can be. This has included, importantly, a shift from a traditional, narrow focus on interpersonal encounters to a broader analysis of social networks and contextual effects of contact. These lines of research show that positive contact can reduce prejudice on a macro-level, whereby people are influenced by the norms, attitudes, beliefs, and behavior of others in their social context, not merely on a micro-scale, via individuals' direct experience of positive contact with out-group members. These findings reinforce the view that contact has a significant role to play in prejudice reduction, and has great policy potential as a means to improve intergroup relations, because it can simultaneously impact large numbers of people.

Although our research program is ongoing, and far from finished, we believe that the results so far already constitute incontrovertible evidence for the impact of contact in educational settings. Mixing at a young age in school can easily fulfill the conditions that Allport (1954) highlighted as likely to be associated with contact reducing prejudice: the groups involved are given equal status, they work

Table 11.1 Overview of studies presented in this chapter.

	Context	Mechanism investigated	Effect found
Study 1	Northwest England	Resegregation at the level of seating adjacencies; social units; and larger cafeteria area	Significantly less cross-ethnic mixing at all three levels than expected by random mixing
Study 2	Northwest England	Self-report attributions of in-group and out-group mixing behavior	Correspondence of attributions for in-group/out-group in white participants
Study 3	Northwest England	Longitudinal effects of intergroup attributions and norms on contact likelihood	T1 out-group friends and positive in-group contact norms positively predict T2 contact; T1 lack of interest in out-group contact negatively predicts T2 contact
Study 4	Northwest England	Effects of diversity of school on self-reported out-group attitudes	Out-group friends increase with the proportion of out-group members in the school
Study 5	Northwest England	Effects of diversity of school on longitudinal effects of contact on out-group attitudes	T1 quality of contact significantly predicts out-group attitudes at T2
Study 6	Northwest England: merger school	Causal effects of contact on attitudes	White participants' T1 quality of contact positively predicts T2 out-group attitudes; Asian participants' T1 quantity of contact positively predicts T2 out-group attitudes
Study 7	Northern Ireland	Role of deprovincialization in the secondary transfer effect of out-group attitudes	Contact has an effect on secondary out-group attitudes via positive change in support for multiculturalism
Study 8	England	Effects of diversity on out-group contact and attitudes	In the UK, diversity of school is positively related to levels of out-group contact and attitudes
Study 9	Northern Ireland	Contextual effects of contact on attitudes	School-level intergroup contact and positive social norms are positively related to individual out-group attitudes
Study 10	Germany, the Netherlands, Sweden	Social network analysis of the effects of contact on out-group attitudes	Significant positive effect of direct and extended contact on out-group attitudes; interaction between contact type and diversity

collaboratively towards common goals, the contact has institutional support, and perceptions of common group interests and identity are encouraged. Although we now understand these conditions as being "facilitating" rather than "essential" (Pettigrew, 1998), they are likely to serve as good guides for what to do in such mixed settings. But perhaps the clearest message of our work is that desegregated settings should not be confused with integrated settings. Merely having students from different groups attend the same school appears unlikely to suffice, especially if they fail to mix, and then resegregate. If we are serious about using educational settings as places in which to *transform* attitudes, then we need to intervene more actively, encourage and engineer contact, and work actively to promote supportive norms. Anything less is not good enough.

Notes

1 We think of segregated contexts as those within which people have no *opportunities* to mix with ethnically dissimilar others, as opposed to desegregated contexts in which they do. We use the terminology of resegregation, because we have studied desegregated contexts in which people choose to segregate themselves into ethnically homogenous groupings.

2 In Britain, the term "Asian" typically refers to people who are of South Asian (primarily Indian, Pakistani, or Bangladeshi) heritage.

3 For exact wording of the questions, see Al Ramiah *et al.* (2014). While it is of course interesting to know why people do engage in contact, the sample sizes for those who reported having intergroup cafeteria contact were too small to allow a meaningful analysis in this dataset, which is why we focused only on those (the majority) who had no contact.

4 We do not focus here on differences between our own results and those of Shelton and Richeson (2005), but we note in passing that their respondents were whites and blacks at elite universities in the US (for discussion of this issue, see Al Ramiah *et al.*, 2014).

5 In order to isolate the impact of attributions and norms in promoting intergroup contact, it was necessary to control for prior attitudes (due to possible self-selection; Pettigrew and Tropp, 2006, 2011), intergroup anxiety (related to contact avoidance; Plant, 2004; Plant and Devine, 2003), number of out-group friends (a particularly powerful form of intergroup contact for reducing prejudice; Davies *et al.*, 2011) and percentage of out-group members in school (a measure of opportunity for such contact).

6 Reports of this research have not yet been written up for publication, but interested readers may consult the first author for papers as soon as they are ready.

7 Research has also sometimes found evidence of reverse paths from attitudes-to-contact, as well as contact-to-attitudes (e.g., Binder *et al.*, 2009). This reverse path indicates some degree of self-selection (i.e., those with positive attitudes seek out contact, and/or those with negative attitudes avoid it). However, our view is that provided that the path from contact to attitudes is significant, this confirms that contact is an influential agent in changing attitudes, and that contact can be used in social interventions to reduce prejudice.

8 Readers may be surprised to find that a Roman Catholic school has substantial numbers of Muslim students. This is, in fact, not rare. Religious schools are typically committed to providing education within a religious ethos; as demographics have changed, so have the school's students. There is simply provision for each student's religion within the school.

9 For more information on the project see www.mzes.uni-mannheim.de/d7/en/projects/children-of-immigrants-longitudinal-survey-in-four-european-countries-cils4eu.

10 To date, data from the UK for social networks has not yet been finalized, so this preliminary report focuses on only three countries.

References

Aboud, F. E. and Sankar, J. (2007) Friendship and identity in a language-integrated school. *International Journal of Behavioural Development*, 31: 445–453.

Allport, G. W. (1954) *The Nature of Prejudice*. Reading, MA: Addison-Wesley.

Al Ramiah, A., Schmid, K., Hewstone, M. and Floe, C. (2014) Why are all the white (Asian) kids sitting together in the cafeteria? Resegregation and the role of intergroup attributions and norms. *British Journal of Social Psychology*, advance online publication.

Barlow, F. K., Paolini, S., Pedersen, A., Hornsey, M. J., Radke, H. R., Harwood, J., Rubin, M., and Sibley, C. G. (2012) The contact caveat negative contact predicts increased prejudice more than positive contact predicts reduced prejudice. *Personality and Social Psychology Bulletin*, 38(12): 1629–1643.

Binder, J., Zagefka, H., Brown, R., Funke, F., Kessler, T., Mummendey, A., Maquil, A., Demoulin, S., and Leyens, J-P. (2009) Does contact reduce prejudice or does prejudice reduce contact? A longitudinal test of the contact hypothesis in three European countries. *Journal of Personality and Social Psychology*, 96: 843–856.

Blalock, H. M. (1984) Contextual-effects models: theoretical and methodological issues. *Annual Review of Sociology*, 10: 353–372.

Brown, R. J. and Hewstone, M. (2005) An integrative theory of intergroup contact. In M. Zanna (ed.) *Advances in Experimental Social Psychology*, Vol. 37. San Diego, CA: Academic Press, pp. 255–331.

Campbell, D. T., Kruskal, W. H., and Wallace, W. P. (1966) Seating aggregation as an index of attitude. *Sociometry*, 29: 1–15.

Christ, O., Schmid, K., Lolliot, S., Swart, H., Stolle, D., Tausch, N., Al Ramiah, A., Wagner, U., Vertovec, S., and Hewstone, M. (2014) Contextual effect of positive intergroup contact on out-group prejudice. *Proceedings of the National Academy of Sciences*, 111: 3996–4000.

Clack, B. Dixon, J. A., Tredoux, C. (2005) Eating together apart: patterns of segregation in a multiethnic cafeteria. *Journal of Community and Applied Social Psychology*, 14: 1–16.

Cliff, N. (1983) Some cautions concerning the application of causal modeling methods. *Multivariate Behavioral Research*, 18: 115–126.

Davies, K., Tropp, L. R., Aron, A., Pettigrew, T. F., and Wright, S. C. (2011) Cross group friendships and intergroup attitudes a meta-analytic review. *Personality and Social Psychology Review*, 15: 332–351.

Deutsch, M., and Collins, M. E. (1951) *Interracial Housing: A Psychological Evaluation of a Social Experiment*. Minneapolis, MN: University of Minnesota Press.

Dinesen, P. T. (2011) Me and Jasmina down by the schoolyard: an analysis of the impact of ethnic diversity in school on the trust of schoolchildren. *Social Science Research*, 40: 572–585.

Dovidio, J. F., Eller, A., and Hewstone, M. (2011) Improving intergroup relations through direct, extended and other forms of indirect contact. *Group Processes and Intergroup Relations*, 14: 147–160.

Hewstone, M. (2009) Living apart, living together? The role of intergroup contact in social integration. *Proceedings of the British Academy*, 162: 243–300.

Hogg, M. A. and Turner, J. C. (1987) Social identity and conformity: a theory of referent information influence. In W. Doise and S. Moscovici (eds) *Current Issues in European Social Psychology*. Cambridge: Cambridge University Press, pp. 139–182.

Janmaat, J. G. (2012) The effect of classroom diversity on tolerance and participation in England, Sweden and Germany. *Journal of Ethnic and Migration Studies*, 38: 21–39.

Jetten, J., Spears, R., and Manstead, A. S. (1996) Intergroup norms and intergroup discrimination: distinctive self-categorization and social identity effects. *Journal of Personality and Social Psychology*, 71: 1222–1233.

Keating, A. and Benton, T. (2013) Creating cohesive citizens in England? Exploring the role of diversity, deprivation and democratic climate at school. *Education, Citizenship and Social Justice*, 8(2): 165–184.

Lolliot, S., Schmid, K., Hewstone, M., Al Ramiah, A., Tausch, N., and Swart, H. (2013) Generalized effects of intergroup contact: the secondary transfer effect. In G. Hodson and M. Hewstone (eds) *Advances in Intergroup Contact*. London: Psychology Press, pp. 81–112.

MacKinnon, S. P., Jordan, C. H., and Wilson, A. E. (2011) Birds of a feather sit together: physical similarity predicts seating choice. *Personality and Social Psychology Bulletin*, 37: 879–892.

McCauley, C., Plummer, M., Moskalenko, S., and Mordkoff, J. T. (2001) The exposure index: a measure of intergroup contact. *Peace and Conflict: Journal of Peace Psychology*, 7: 321–336.

McPherson, M., Smith-Lovin, L., and Cook, J. M. (2001) Birds of a feather: homophily in social networks. *Annual Review of Sociology*, 27: 415–444.

Miller, D. and Prentice, D. (1999) Some consequences of a belief in a group essence: the category divide hypothesis. In D. Prentice and D. Miller (eds) *Cultural Divides: Understanding and Overcoming Group Conflict*. New York: Russell Sage Foundation, pp. 213–238.

Munniksma, A., Stark, T. H., Verkuyten, M., Flache, A., and Veenstra, R. (2013) Extended intergroup friendships within social settings: the moderating role of initial out-group attitudes. *Group Processes & Intergroup Relations*, 16: 752–770.

Oishi, S. and Graham, J. (2010) Social ecology lost and found in psychological science. *Perspectives on Psychological Science*, 5: 356–377.

Orr, R., McKeown, S., Cairns, E., and Stringer, M. (2012) Examining non-racial segregation: a micro-ecological approach. *British Journal of Social Psychology*, 51: 717–723.

Patchen, M. (1982) *Black-White Contact in Schools: Its Social and Academic Effects*. West Lafayette, IN: Purdue University Press.

Pettigrew, T. F. (1958) Personality and sociocultural factors in intergroup attitudes: a cross-national comparison. *Journal of Conflict Resolution*, 2: 29–42.

—— (1997) Generalized intergroup contact effects on prejudice. *Personality and Social Psychology Bulletin*, 23: 173–185.

—— (1998) Intergroup contact theory. *Annual Review of Psychology*, 49: 65–85.

—— (2009) Secondary transfer effect of contact. *Social Psychology*, 40: 55–65.

Pettigrew, T. F. and Tropp, L. R. (2006) A meta-analytic test of intergroup contact theory. *Journal of Personality and Social Psychology*, 90: 751–783.

—— (2011) *When Groups Meet: The Dynamics of Intergroup Contact*. New York: Psychology Press.

Plant, E. A. (2004) Responses to interracial interactions over time. *Personality and Social Psychology Bulletin*, 30: 1458–1471.

Plant, E. A. and Devine, P. G. (2003) The antecedents and implications of interracial anxiety. *Personality and Social Psychology Bulletin*, 29: 790–801.

Putnam, R. (2007) *E pluribus unum*: diversity and community in the twenty-first century. *Scandinavian Political Studies*, 30(2): 137–174.

Raudenbush, S. W. and Bryk, A. S. (2002) *Hierarchical Linear Models: Applications and Data Analysis Methods*. California: Sage Publications.

Richeson, J. A., Baird, A. A., Gordon, H. L., Heatherton, T. F., and Wyland, C. L. (2003) An fMRI investigation of the impact of interracial contact on executive function. *Nature Neuroscience*, 6: 1323–1328.

Schelling, T. C. (1971) Dynamic models of segregation. *Journal of Mathematical Sociology*, 1: 143–186.

Schmid, K., Al Ramiah, A., and Hewstone, M. (2014) Neighborhood ethnic diversity and trust: the role of intergroup contact and perceived threat. *Psychological Science*, 25(3): 665–674.

Schofield, J. W. (1997) Resegregation. In C. A. Grant and G. Ladson Billings (eds) *Dictionary of Multicultural Education*. Phoenix, AZ: Oryx Press, pp. 234–235.

Schofield, J. W. and Eurich-Fulcer, R. (2001) When and how school desegregation improves intergroup relations. In R. Brown and S. L. Gaertner (eds) *Blackwell Handbook of Social Psychology: Intergroup Processes*. Oxford: Blackwell, pp. 475–494.

Shelton, J. N. and Richeson, J. A. (2005) Intergroup contact and pluralistic ignorance. *Journal of Personality and Social Psychology*, 88: 91–107.

Sims, V. M. and Patrick, J. R. (1936) Attitude toward the Negro of northern and southern college students. *Journal of Social Psychology*, 7: 192–204.

Stangor, C., Sechrist, G. B., and Jost, J. T. (2001) Changing racial beliefs by providing consensus information. *Personality and Social Psychology Bulletin*, 27: 486–496.

Stephan, W. G. and Stephan, C. (1985) Intergroup anxiety. *Journal of Social Issues*, 41: 57–176.

Tatum, B. D. (2003) *Why Are All the Black Kids Sitting Together in the Cafeteria?: A Psychologist Explains the Development of Racial Identity*. New York: Basic Books.

Tausch, N., Hewstone, M., Kenworthy, J. B., Psaltis, C., Schmid, K., Popan, J. R., Cairns, E., and Hughes, J. (2010) Secondary transfer effects of intergroup contact: Alternative accounts and underlying processes. *Journal of Personality and Social Psychology*, 99: 282.

Taylor, D. M. and Moghaddam, F. M. (1994) *Theories of Intergroup Relations: International Social Psychological Perspectives* (2nd edition). London: Praeger.

Tolsma, J., van Deurzen, I., Stark, T. H., and Veenstra, R. (2013) Who is bullying whom in ethnically diverse primary schools? Exploring links between bullying, ethnicity, and ethnic diversity in Dutch primary schools. *Social Networks*, 35: 51–61.

Tropp, L. R. and Bianchi, R. A. (2006) Valuing diversity and intergroup contact. *Journal of Social Issues*, 62: 533–551.

Tropp, L. R. and Pettigrew, T. F. (2005) Relationships between intergroup contact and prejudice among minority and majority status groups. *Psychological Science*, 16(12): 951–957.

Turner, J. C. (1982) Towards a cognitive redefinition of the social group. In H. Tajfel (ed.) *Social Identity and Intergroup Relations*. Cambridge: Cambridge University Press, pp. 15–40.

Verkuyten, M., Thijs, J., and Bekhuis, H. (2010) Intergroup contact and in-group reappraisal examining the deprovincialization thesis. *Social Psychology Quarterly*, 73: 398–416.

Vorauer, J. and Ratner, R. (1996) Who's going to make the first move? Pluralistic ignorance as an impediment to relationship formation. *Journal of Social and Personal Relationships*, 13: 483–503.

Wölfer, R., Hewstone, M. (2014) Effects of intergroup contact: network analytic enrichment of traditional measures. In K. Phalet (Chair) *School diversity: Bridging Minority and Majority Group Perspectives*. Symposium conducted at the meeting of the European Association of Social Psychology, Amsterdam, Netherlands.

Wright, S. C., Aron, A., McLaughlin, T., and Ropp, S. A. (1997) The extended contact effect: knowledge of cross-group friendships and prejudice. *Journal of Personality and Social Psychology*, 73: 73–90.

Index

Printed in Poland
by Amazon Fulfillment
Poland Sp. z o.o., Wrocław

92556207R00148